Phantasmagoria Presents

DAVID BRILLIANCE'S
MIDNIGHT TREASURY

Edited by
Trevor Kennedy

Artwork by
Randy Broecker
Dave Carson
Allen Koszowski
Johnny Mains
and Jim Pitts

Border artwork by Dave Carson

This book is dedicated to my marvellous, much-missed mother who endured many a late night staying up with me as a kid watching horror films on TV, back in the days of the 1970s B.C. (Before Covid).
—**David Brilliance**

Artwork by Allen Koszowski

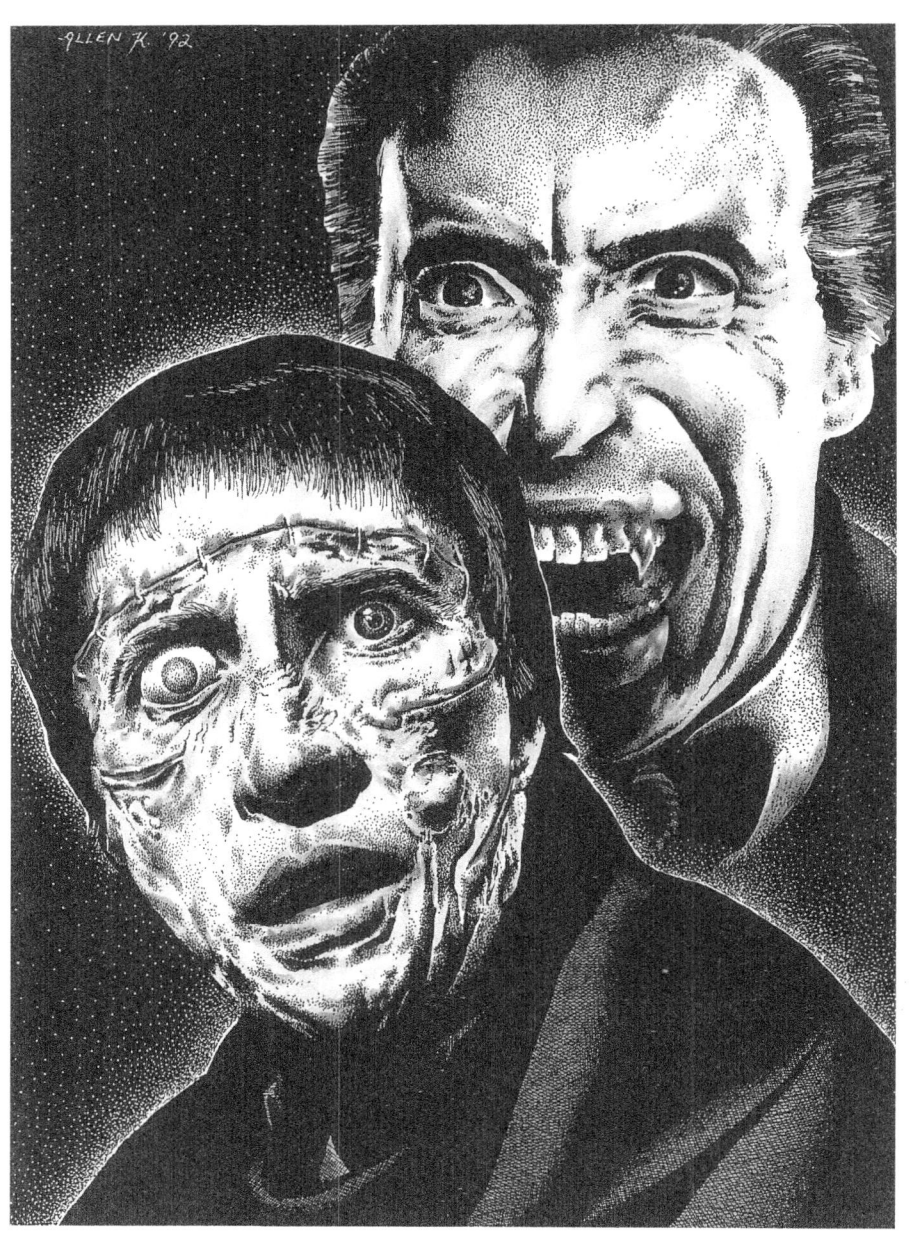

Artwork by Allen Koszowski

COPYRIGHT INFORMATION

Text copyright © David Brilliance and
TK Pulp/Trevor Kennedy 2021

Artworks copyright © Randy Broecker, Dave Carson,
Allen Koszowski, Johnny Mains and Jim Pitts 2021

Cover design and *Phantasmagoria* logo
copyright © Adrian Baldwin 2021, www.adrianbaldwin.info

Cover image: Production designer Albin Grau's cover illustration for the German production book for Prana-Films' *Nosferatu, eine Symphonie des Grauens* (Dir: F. W. Murnau, 1922), an unauthorized adaptation of Bram Stoker's *Dracula*.

No portion of *David Brilliance's Midnight Treasury* may be reproduced in any form without express permission
from the authors and artists

The authors and artists are, and remain, the sole copyright owners of their individual works and as such, they retain all rights to them at all times

All rights reserved

Published in 2021 by TK Pulp through KDP

"FROM THE INTRODUCTION TO THE DIVERSITY OF THE STORIES TO THE NECROLOGY AT THE END, THE WHOLE CONTENT IS OUTSTANDING."

—HELEN SCOTT, PHANTASMAGORIA #12 HALLOWEEN SPECIAL, 2019

"THE ENDURING POPULARITY OF THE JONES 'BEST OF' EMPIRE ACROSS THREE DECADES SHOWS THAT READERS OF QUALITY HORROR ARE AN INTELLECTUALLY SOPHISTICATED AUDIENCE."

—CLARE RHODEN, AUREALIS #134, 2020

NOW AVAILABLE FOR PRE-ORDER.

IF YOU PRE-ORDER THE DELUXE EDITION HOUSED IN AN ILLUSTRATED SLIPCASE AND LIMITED TO 100 SIGNED COPIES FOR £60.00, YOU WILL RECIEVE A FREE TRADE PAPERBACK.

OR, PRE-ORDER A TRADE PAPERBACK EDITION FOR £14.99.

WWW.PSPUBLISHING.CO.UK

With special thanks to master of the macabre
Stephen Jones *for his invaluable support and advice*

"Stephen Jones" by Allen Koszowski

CONTENTS

Page 1: **Foreword by Trevor Kennedy**

Page 5: **Introduction by David Brilliance**

Page 9: *Chapter 1*: **The Phantom of the Opera (1925)**

Page 13: *Chapter 2*: **Dracula (1931) and Son of Dracula (1943)**

Page 19: *Chapter 3*: **Frankenstein (1931), Bride of Frankenstein (1935), Son of Frankenstein (1939) and The Ghost of Frankenstein (1942)**

Page 29: *Chapter 4*: **Dr. Jekyll and Mr. Hyde (1931)**

Page 35: *Chapter 5*: **Freaks (1932)**

Page 39: *Chapter 6*: **The Mummy (1932), The Mummy's Hand (1940), The Mummy's Tomb (1942), The Mummy's Ghost (1944) and The Mummy's Curse (1944)**

Page 47: *Chapter 7*: **The Black Cat (1934) and The Raven (1935)**

Page 53: *Chapter 8*: **The Wolf Man (1941) and Frankenstein Meets the Wolf Man (1943)**

Page 59: *Chapter 9*: **House of Frankenstein (1944) and House of Dracula (1945)**

Page 65: *Chapter 10*: **The Body Snatcher (1945)**

Page 69: *Chapter 11*: **Dead of Night (1945)**

Page 75: *Chapter 12*: **Creature from the Black Lagoon (1954) and Revenge of the Creature (1955) and The Creature Walks Among Us (1956)**

Page 81: *Chapter 13*: **Devil Girl from Mars (1954)**

Page 85: *Chapter 14*: **Bride of the Monster (1955)**

Page 89: *Chapter 15*: **The Curse of Frankenstein (1957), The Revenge of Frankenstein (1958), The Evil of Frankenstein (1964), Frankenstein Created Woman (1967), Frankenstein Must be Destroyed (1969), The Horror of Frankenstein (1970)** and **Frankenstein and the Monster from Hell (1974)**

Page 99: *Chapter 16*: **Night of the Demon (1957)**

Page 105: *Chapter 17*: **Dracula (1958), Dracula: Prince of Darkness (1966), Dracula Has Risen from the Grave (1968), Taste the Blood of Dracula (1970), Scars of Dracula (1970), Dracula A.D. 1972 (1972)** and **The Satanic Rites of Dracula (1973)**

Page 119: *Chapter 18*: **The Alligator People (1959)**

Page 125: *Chapter 19*: **The Curse of the Werewolf (1961)**

Page 129: *Chapter 20*: **The Phantom of the Opera (1962)**

Page 133: *Chapter 21*: **Tales of Terror (1962)**

Page 137: *Chapter 22*: **The Birds (1963)**

Page 141: *Chapter 23*: **X: The Man with the X-Ray Eyes (1963)**

Page 147: *Chapter 24*: **At Midnight I'll Take Your Soul (1964)** and **This Night I Will Possess Your Corpse (1967)**

Page 153: *Chapter 25*: **The Skull (1965)**

Page 159: *Chapter 26*: **The Reptile (1966)**

Page 163: *Chapter 27*: **Munster, Go Home! (1966)**

Page 167: *Chapter 28*: **The Mummy's Shroud (1967)**

Page 171: *Chapter 29*: **Quatermass and the Pit (1967)**

Page 175: *Chapter 30*: **The Devil Rides Out (1968)**

Page 179: *Chapter 31*: **Night of the Living Dead (1968)**

Page 183: *Chapter 32*: **Curse of the Crimson Altar (1968)**

Page 187: *Chapter 33*: **The Vampire Lovers (1970), Lust for a Vampire (1971) and Twins of Evil (1971)**

Page 195: *Chapter 34*: **Mumsy, Nanny, Sonny & Girly (1970)**

Page 201: *Chapter 35*: **The House That Dripped Blood (1971)**

Page 209: *Chapter 36*: **The Blood on Satan's Claw (1971)**

Page 215: *Chapter 37*: **The Abominable Dr. Phibes (1971), Dr. Phibes Rises Again (1972), Count Yorga, Vampire (1970), The Return of Count Yorga (1971), Blacula (1972) and Scream Blacula Scream (1973)**

Page 227: *Chapter 38*: **The Corpse (1971)**

Page 233: *Chapter 39*: **Tales from the Crypt (1972)**

Page 241: *Chapter 40*: **The Crazies (1973)**

Page 247: *Chapter 41*: **Theatre of Blood (1973)**

Page 251: *Chapter 42*: **Don't Be Afraid of the Dark (1973)**

Page 255: *Chapter 43*: **The Wicker Man (1973)**

Page 261: *Chapter 44*: **The Exorcist (1973)**

Page 277: *Chapter 45*: **From Beyond the Grave (1974)**

Page 283: *Chapter 46*: **The Texas Chain Saw Massacre (1974)**

Page 287: *Chapter 47*: **Night Train Murders (1975)**

Page 291: *Chapter 48*: **Race with the Devil (1975)**

Page 295: *Chapter 49:* **Suspiria (1977)**

Page 301: *Chapter 50:* **Eraserhead (1977)**

Page 305: *Chapter 51:* **I Spit on Your Grave (1978)**

Page 309: *Chapter 52:* **The Amityville Horror (1979)**

Page 315: *Chapter 53*: **The Monster Club (1981)**

Page 321: *Chapter 54*: **The Woman in Black (1989 and 2012 versions)**

Page 327: *Chapter 55*: **The Silence of the Lambs (1991)**

Page 331: *Chapter 56*: **The Blair Witch Project (1999)**

Page 337: *Chapter 57*: **Eden Lake (2008)**

Page 341: *Chapter 58*: **Drag Me to Hell (2009)**

Page 345: *Chapter 59*: **You're Next (2011)**

Page 349: *Chapter 60*: **V/H/S (2012)**

Page 355: *Chapter 61*: **The Conjuring (2013)**

Page 359: *Chapter 62*: **Oculus (2013)**

Page 363: *Chapter 63*: **It Follows (2014)**

Page 367: *Chapter 64*: **The Witch (2015)**

Page 371: *Chapter 65*: **A Ghost Story (2017)**

Page 373: *Chapter 66*: **Just When You Think It's All Over…**

Page 389: **Biographies**

Page 393: **Acknowledgements**

Phantasmagoria Magazine

SPECIAL COLLECTOR'S EDITIONS

OUT NOW on AMAZON

and FORBIDDEN PLANET INTERNATIONAL (Belfast)

Artwork by Dave Carson

FOREWORD

Trevor Kennedy

LET'S TALK ABOUT horror films, past and present. Or at very least, let's discuss the author of this book's favourite genre classics from the last almost a century.

Phantasmagoria's resident historian of all things strange and startling, David Brilliance, has now selected what he considers to be the best (and in a lot of the cases the most important and influential) horror movies of all time. There's one hundred in total (although technically there may be one hundred and one, not to mention the dozens of others that are given honourable mentions!).

If I was to pick my own "Top 100" horror flicks (and I may well do so one day), whilst there would indeed be some similarities, there would naturally be quite a few differences as well (*The Conjuring*,

David – seriously??). For example, mine would include titles such as Benjamin Christensen's *Häxan* (1922), F.W. Murnau's *Nosferatu* (1922), Hitchcock's *Psycho* (1960), Romero's *Dawn of the Dead* (1978), Landis's *An American Werewolf in London* (1981), Raimi's *The Evil Dead* (1981), Barker's *Hellraiser* (1987), and from more recent years Ari Aster's *Hereditary* (2018) and Robert Egger's *The Lighthouse* (2019).

"Nosferatu" by Johnny Mains

Carpenter's *The Thing* (1982), Blatty's grossly underrated *Exorcist III* (1990) and Adrian Lyne's *Jacob's Ladder* (1990) would be in there too, along with several of the works of David Lynch, most definitely *Twin Peaks: Fire Walk With Me* (1992) and *Lost Highway* (1996). I might even be tempted to throw in the 2013 version of *Evil Dead* with Cronenberg's 1986 take on *The Fly*, as rare cases of remakes done well.

To name but a few of my own top picks.

Then, of course, I would have to decide what exactly defines a horror film. Should non-supernatural thrillers and dramas that deal with the much more terrifying horrors of the real world count – Scorsese's *Taxi Driver* from 1976 is an example which is classified as a horror film in some quarters, although I disagree with this take. Or how about Alan Clarke's bleak British borstal drama *Scum* from 1979, or even Shane Meadows' revenge masterpiece from 2004, *Dead Man's Shoes*? Robin Hardy's *The Wicker Man* from 1973 (featured on David's list here and would also certainly be on my own) contains no supernatural elements whatsoever and could even be argued to be a musical! Additionally, I consider the original *Terminator* from 1984 to be more of a slasher/horror film than a sci-fi and will happily argue that point with anyone.

On top of this, I'd have to consider the inclusion of titles based mainly on cultural significance. I don't particularly rate the Lugosi *Dracula* from 1931 in terms of quality (*Frankenstein* from the same year is a much better film overall) but the impact it has made cannot be ignored.

But alas, dissecting and debating our most favoured (and disliked) films is all part of the fun and something I really do enjoy immensely. And, of course, to each their own, as we all bring our individual tastes, experiences and reasons as to why we choose the ones we do.

I'm sure you'll enjoy this brand new book of David's, even (or perhaps especially?) if you don't agree with all of his choices. He really is a walking, talking encyclopedia of horror movie lore, all self-taught, so much of it learnt through that Friday night film slot on the UK regional television channel Tyne Tees that he references regularly within the following pages.

Midnight Treasury is the first in what we hope will be a series of spin-off books from *Phantasmagoria*, with David in the hot seat and yours truly on editorial duties.

Before I hand you over to David, our "host with the most", I'd like to give a word of thanks to everyone who has made this book possible in such a polished manner: Stephen Jones, for his continued and treasured advice and support, my mother Doreen for her infinite encouragement and help, Adrian Baldwin for his usual top drawer cover and logo design, and the wonderful artists Randy Broecker, Dave Carson, Allen Koszowski, Johnny Mains and Jim Pitts, whose sublime work is on display here too.

So, enough of my waxing lyrical. Go pour yourself a nice drink, sit back and relax in a comfy chair, and allow David Brilliance to enthral you with his *Midnight Treasury*...

—**Trevor Kennedy,
Belfast, Northern Ireland,
March, 2021**

A MASSIVE COLLECTION OF WORK
BY MULTIPLE AWARD WINNING ARTIST
DAVE CARSON

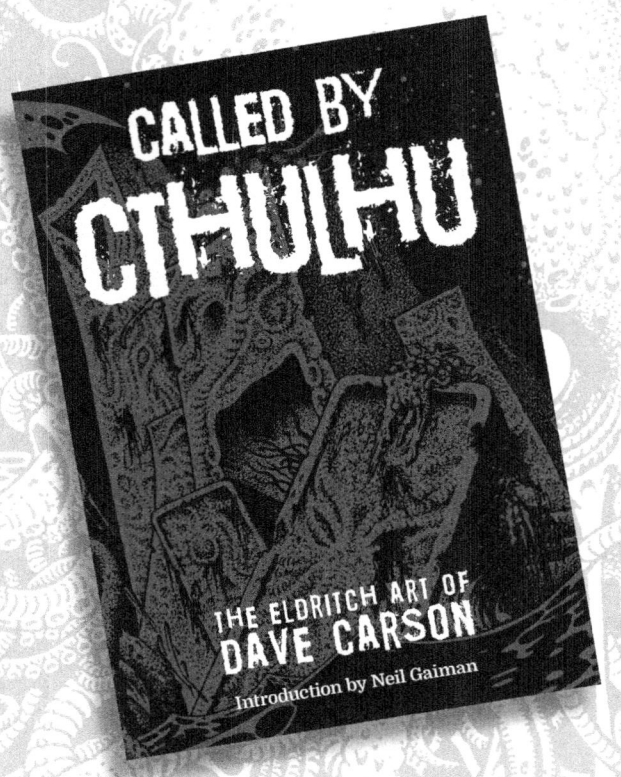

AVAILABLE ON AMAZON NOW

INTRODUCTION

David Brilliance

I'VE LOVED THE genre of the fantastique since I was born (or shortly afterwards anyway). Whilst my friends and schoolmates were turned on by the sight of a load of men running around a field kicking a ball, I was turned on by the delights of books like Alan Frank's *Horror Movies* and magazines like *House of Hammer* and *Movie Monsters*. As I grew older, I came to realise that the kids who had enjoyed seeing those aforementioned ball-kicking men had grown up and become rather narrow-minded adults who had a weird tendency to accuse anyone who wasn't into the sight of men chasing each other round a grass field of being "strange" or "not normal". Pot. Kettle. Black. I'll say no more.

So what's this book all about then? Well, it's a very personal lot of chat about my favourite horror films basically. It's not meant to be a definitive guide to the very best the horror genre has to offer, nor is it intended to be particularly informative as I'm guessing that the readers who might be moved to pick up a copy (no standing reading it next to the shelf mind – get to that counter and buy it!) will know their onions when it comes to this type of film anyway. It is, however, intended to be fairly entertaining, as I work my way through one hundred films that, in my opinion, are representative of the horror genre as a whole, and which, rather than necessarily being the best, are my favourites. So, they're my subjective best.

If you're looking for pretentious, in-depth analysis of these films, you'll be disappointed too: while there are some genre films that have hidden subtext with more to say than what we see on screen, the majority are basically "what you see is what you get" – trying to find clever, long-winded, with pseudo-intellectual meanings, connections and highbrow relevancies in these films is like trying to analyse a sardine sandwich: you might see all sorts of things in it, but it's basically just sardines, butter and bread!

Usually in intros, the writer of a book gets to thank a long list of people. Not here. I have one person mainly to thank for this book resting in your hands now, and that's Editor Trevor Kennedy who has managed what nobody else has ever managed to do, and gotten me to get off my lazy backside and get this thing actually written! So, thank you Trevor, the artists involved also, and thank you to the people who've bought the book (I know you're out there, I can hear your breathing). Hopefully, there'll be others following this at some point and, virus permitting, bookshops will be open to allow people to buy it too.

Happy reading!

—David Brilliance
County Durham, England,
March, 2021

Artwork by Jim Pitts

CHAPTER 1

THE PHANTOM OF THE OPERA (1925)

Lon Chaney as the title character in
The Phantom of the Opera (1925)

Directed by: Rupert Julian, Lon Chaney (uncredited), Ernst Laemmle (uncredited) and Edward Sedgwick (uncredited).

Written by: Gaston Leroux (from the 1910 celebrated novel by), Walter Anthony (uncredited), Elliott J. Clawson (uncredited), Bernard McConville (uncredited), Frank M. McCormack (uncredited), Tom Reed (uncredited), Raymond L. Schrock (uncredited), Richard Wallace (uncredited) and Jaspar Spearing (uncredited).

Starring: Lon Chaney, Mary Philbin, Norman Kerry, Arthur Edmund Carewe, Gibson Gowland, John St. Polis and more.

Studio: Universal Pictures.

ORGAN GRINDER

BACK IN THE early 1980s, my cousin told me that he and his dad had watched a silent horror film once that had them in hysterics. Apparently, it was impossible to follow, with all its endless action scenes of characters falling down holes, running down dark passages, being chased and locked in rooms etc, thus leading to the hilarity. I'm not 100 per cent certain, but I'm sure the film my cousin was referring to was this one. The timing would be right, as *Phantom...* was shown one evening on BBC2 in early 1982, on a Friday. This was a season of silents that included Buster Keaton and Tom Mix films, as well as *Dr. Jekyll and Mr. Hyde* (the John Barrymore version, where a giant ghostly tarantula crawls into Jekyll's bedroom and climbs onto his sleeping body on his four-poster bed, and the good Doctor wakes up as a human spider!).

I'm not a huge fan of silent films of any sort, but this is where the horror film more-or-less began and where better to start than at the (almost) beginning? There are a handful of silent-era gems – *Haxan*, *Nosferatu*, *Waxworks*, *The Cabinet of Dr. Caligari* – but Universal's 1925 production of *The Phantom of the Opera* is my favourite. It's a great movie and there's a lot more to it than just the falling through trapdoors aspect mentioned earlier.

The star of the film is Lon Chaney, whose expertise with make-up had resulted in *The Hunchback of Notre Dame* two years earlier and would result in the famously-lost *London After Midnight* two years later. And, more-or-less two years after that, Chaney was dead from throat cancer in 1930.

But back to this film and happier times. It's based on the story by Gaston Leroux and has Chaney playing the part of Erik, a horribly deformed character who has escaped from Devil's Island and set up shop, so to speak, in the cellars underneath the Opera House in Paris.

The production of the film is certainly sumptuous, with the most amazing sets and, like all other Universal horrors to come in the '30s and '40s, it's amazing to think this was all filmed in a studio in hot and sticky Los Angeles, California. The interiors are large and colourful even in black and white, and equalled by the stunning outside sets as the Phantom is pursued by the mob and rushes past Notre Dame Cathedral, before he goes into the Seine (the mob catches up with him by the river, he pretends he has a bomb, then foolishly reveals he hasn't, gets clubbed to death, then chucked in the river)!

There are two highlights in the film. First, of course, is the unmasking scene where Christine tentatively reaches out and eventually yanks off Erik's mask to reveal the skull-like visage beneath. The other is a scene set during the Bal Masqué where "all Paris mingled, forgetful of caste" dressed in fancy costumes and having a great time – until the Phantom pops up in his costume, that of the 'Red Death' from Poe. This scene would be effective anyway but seeing it in a primitive form of colour makes it stand out all the more. The film is tinted in various colours, with the whole screen being either red, blue or green but this doesn't detract from the experience, in fact, in a funny sort of way it enriches it.

I haven't, at the time of typing, seen any other Chaney silent films but I might seek out a few others – *The Unholy Three* and *The Hunchback of Notre Dame* are probably worth a look, though it's a shame that *London After Midnight* is lost as it's probably the best of the rest.

In this case anyway, silence is indeed golden.

The Phantom of the Opera *(1925)*

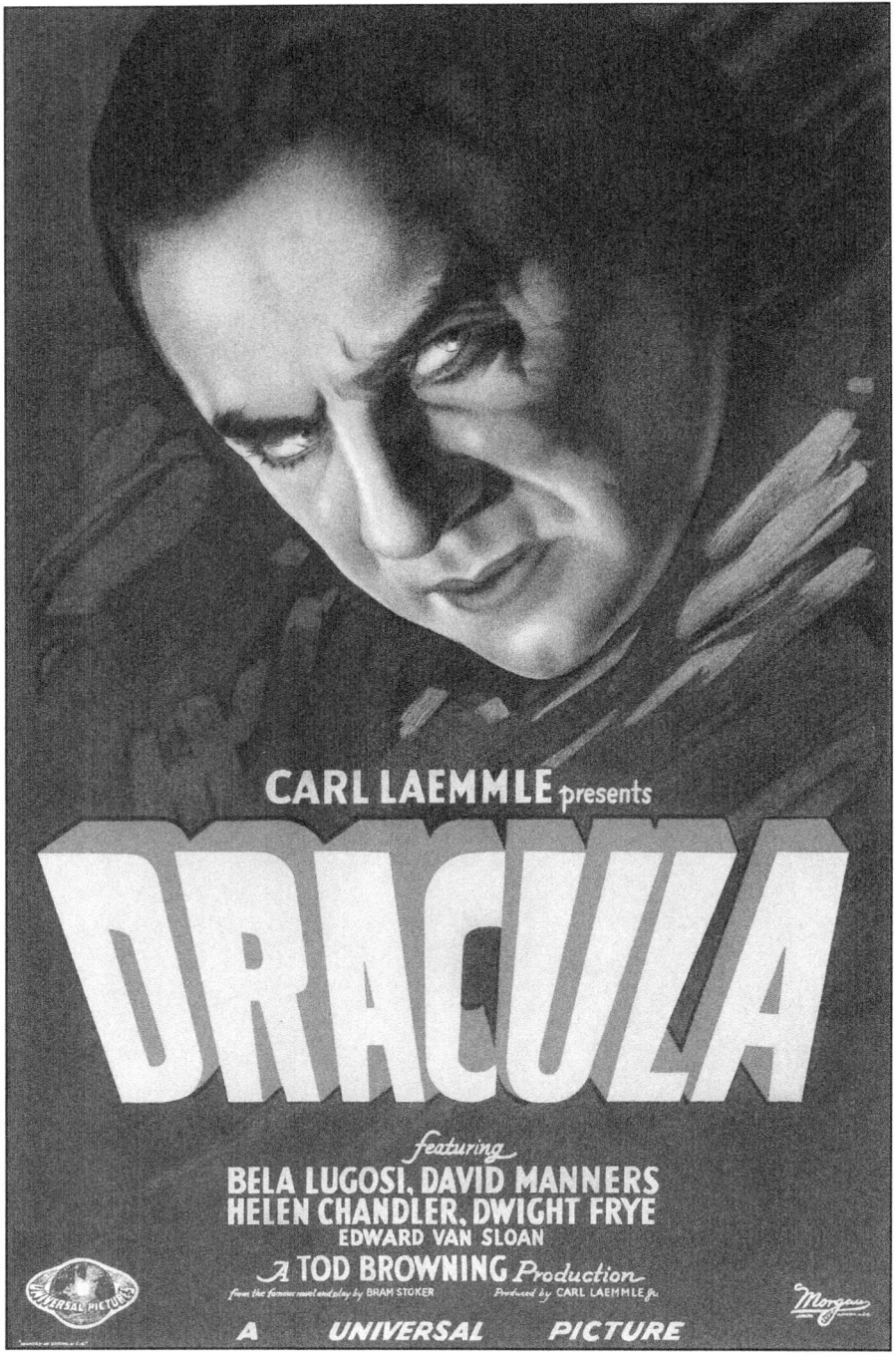

CHAPTER 2

DRACULA (1931)
and
SON OF DRACULA (1943)

Bela Lugosi plays the title role in Dracula *(1931)*

DRACULA (1931):

Directed by: Tod Browning and Karl Freund (uncredited).

Written by: Bram Stoker (by), Hamilton Deane (from the play adapted by), John L. Balderston (from the play adapted by), Garrett Fort (play), Louis Bromfield (uncredited), Tod Browning (uncredited), Max Cohen (uncredited), Dudley Murphy (uncredited), Frederick Stephani (uncredited) and Louis Stevens (uncredited).

Starring: Bela Lugosi, Helen Chandler, David Manners, Dwight Frye, Edward Van Sloan, Herbert Bunston and more.

Studio: Universal Pictures.

SON OF DRACULA (1943):

Directed by: Robert Siodmack.

Written by: Eric Taylor (screenplay) and Curtis Siodmack (original story).

Starring: Lon Chaney Jr., Robert Paige, Louise Allbriton, Evelyn Ankers, Frank Craven, J. Edward Bromberg, Samuel S. Hinds and more.

Studio: Universal Pictures.

DRACULA AND SON

THE GENERAL CONSENSUS among horror film fans is that director Tod Browning's 1931 film *Dracula* starts off well then loses its way and becomes a mere shadow of what it could have been – and those horror film fans are right. Having said that, the original novel by Bram Stoker isn't that great either: it has some fantastic ideas (in both senses of the word) but dumps them into a leaden and badly-written book, in which the whole story is related as a series of letters and journal extracts. I tried to get through the whole book several times and failed, and it seems I wasn't alone as the whole novel was rewritten in the 1990s to get the great ideas across to a modern readership, freed from Stoker's dreary prose.

Dracula is still a great film, of course, just not quite as great as it could have been – it's definitely not as good as *Frankenstein* but it still packs a punch and can be regarded as the beginning of the sound era of horror films. The film begins with Renfield (Dwight Frye) travelling to Transylvania and Castle Dracula, stopping off briefly at a small village where the innkeeper and his wife try to get him to change his mind. Good thing they don't succeed or this would have been a rather short film. The beginning of the film is stunning, with location shots on the Universal backlot combining with a marvellous glass matte painting to depict the towering mountains and treacherous roads that Renfield's coach is rattling along on its way to the castle. This ride is made all the more unsettling for the occupant of the coach, as the driver has mysteriously vanished and the horses are being rallied along by a flapping bat!

Once at the castle, the film shifts into higher gear – the first appearance of Dracula is iconic and I wonder how many horror-mad kids like myself in the 1970s were quoting the film's lines along with the characters when they first saw this one on telly. The massive set depicting Dracula's ruined hole of a castle, the "children of the night" line, the giant cobweb, the "spider spinning its web for the unwary fly...", all classic moments. The film sometimes, for a more modern audience, edges dangerously close to funny with Lugosi's hammy staring when his guest pricks his finger and draws blood, and his subsequent pantomime flinching when he spies Renfield's crucifix, being memorably laughable. One thing I could never understand is why Renfield suddenly collapses when a bat appears outside the open window – is he such a wimp that the sight of a flying mouse causes him to faint? Whatever, he soon ends up under Dracula's spell and gives quite a creepy performance, especially when he emerges from below decks when the ship he and his new master have travelled to England on reaches Whitby Harbour.

The film slowly grinds to a virtual standstill once the 'action' switches to England – Professor Van Helsing (Edward Van Sloan) investigates the deaths of several people and discovers that a vampire was behind them, while Dracula moves into Carfax Abbey and makes the acquaintance of several people on a nocturnal trip to the theatre, including one Doctor Seward (Herbert Bunston), his daughter Mina (Helen Chandler), her boyfriend John Harker (David Manners) and a gloomy lass called Lucy (Frances Dade) who takes a macabre shine to the Count and vice versa – just look at the creepy lingering look Lugosi gives her as the scene fades to black!

Some fun is to be had with the character of Renfield, who ends up in Seward's sanitorium eating flies and spiders, while the confrontation between Dracula and Van Helsing which ends up with a smashed cigarette case mirror and the battle lines clearly drawn shakes the viewer out of their lethargy for a brief spell, but it doesn't last and before long we're back in gently dozing territory again.

The film ends not with a bang, but a whimper, as Dracula is staked through the heart off-screen and done in so casual and off-hand a manner that I didn't at first realise what had actually happened the first time I saw the film all the way through. Despite the film being a bit of a let down, it still deserves its place here: not just because it's a landmark movie – the proper beginning of the sound horror film – but for the great entertainment of at least twenty-five minutes of its seventy-two minute running time. And the film is an utter masterpiece compared to the bloody awful Spanish language version which was filmed at night on the same sets. I'd like to see the original wrap-up to the film though, as Edward Van Sloan appeared in front of the curtains to give a chilly warning to audiences – "there are such things!"

Son of Dracula (1943) is my personal favourite of the Dracula films from Universal and features the new(ish) horror star on the Universal payroll, Lon Chaney Jr.. Chaney Jr. had already played the Frankenstein Monster and the Mummy, as well as creating the character of the Wolf Man, and here he plays Count Dracula, or rather, his son. The film has Dracula Jr. arriving in America rather than England and, for the only time in a Universal film, we see him change to mist (in the slow-as-hell Spanish version, we see the mist change to Dracula). The Dracula-into-a-bat effect is shown for the first time (as opposed to off-screen in the 1931 film) and is also quite effective and though critics and horror fans have often criticised Chaney's casting, he does well in the role even though there's definitely a touch of Oliver Hardy in his performance in the scenes where he's being charming with women! The film has a vaguely silly plot but, like the other Universal horrors of the 1940s, the film as a whole, with such incongruous scenes as Dracula being driven along in an automobile, works because it's all treated deadly seriously.

Title card for Son of Dracula *(1943)*

The plot involves Dracula (or Count Alucard as he calls himself here) arriving in the grounds of Dark Oaks, a creepy bayou-bound house and the home of his latest conquest, one Katherine Caldwell

(Louise Allbritton), a gloomy lass who has met and fallen in love with the Count, and vice versa. Katherine's boyfriend, Frank (Robert Paige) is understandably miffed about this, especially after he accidentally shoots his former lover when the bullets pass through Dracula's body and kill her. It's not long before creepy Katherine returns as a vampire, seducing Frank in his jail cell with promises of immortality and telling him of Dracula's hiding place. Frank escapes and sets fire to the Count's coffin, though it's not long before the Count catches up with him.

I love the ending of this film which is both frightening and funny – watch Dracula frantically trying to put out the flames licking around his coffin and resist thinking, that that's what happens when you smoke in bed! Chaney pulls some quite frightening faces here before he expires – nice effect, as his arm becomes a bony skeleton when he's exposed to the rays of the sun – though the film runs five minutes more after Dracula's demise, to wrap everything up in time for the inappropriately jolly music accompanying the end credits.

Lon Chaney Jr. in Son of Dracula *(1943)*

CHAPTER 3

FRANKENSTEIN (1931)
and
BRIDE OF FRANKENSTEIN (1935)
SON OF FRANKENSTEIN (1939)
THE GHOST OF FRANKENSTEIN (1942)

Frankenstein *artwork by Allen Koszowski*

FRANKENSTEIN (1931):

Directed by: James Whale.

Written by: John L. Balderston (based upon the composition by), Mary Shelley (as Mrs. Percy B. Shelley, from the novel by), Peggy Webling (adapted from the play by), Garrett Fort (screenplay), Francis Edwards Faragoh (screenplay), Richard Schayer (scenario editor), Robert Florey (uncredited) and John Russell (uncredited).

Starring: Colin Clive, Mae Clarke, John Boles, Boris Karloff, Edward Van Sloan, Frederick Kerr and more.

Studio: Universal Pictures.

BRIDE OF FRANKENSTEIN (1935):

Directed by: James Whale.

Written by: Mary Wollstonecraft Shelley (suggested by: the original story written in 1816 by), William Hurlbut (adapted by), John L. Balderston (adapted by), Josef Berne (uncredited), Lawrence G. Blochman (uncredited), Robert Florey (uncredited), Philip MacDonald (uncredited), Tom Reed (uncredited), R.C. Sherriff (uncredited), Edmund Pearson (uncredited) and Morton Covan (uncredited).

Starring: Boris Karloff, Colin Clive, Valerie Hobson, Ernest Thesiger, Elsa Lanchester, Gavin Gordon and more.

Studio: Universal Pictures.

SON OF FRANKENSTEIN (1939):

Directed by: Rowland V. Lee.

Written by: Mary Wollstonecraft Shelley (suggested by the story written in 1816) and Wyllis Cooper.

Starring: Basil Rathbone, Boris Karloff, Bela Lugosi, Lionel Atwill, Josephine Hutchinson, Donnie Dunagan and more.

Studio: Universal Pictures.

THE GHOST OF FRANKENSTEIN (1942):

Directed by: Erle C. Kenton.

Written by: Scott Darling (screenplay) and Eric Taylor (original story).

Starring: Lon Chaney Jr., Cedric Hardwicke, Ralph Bellamy, Lionel Atwill, Bela Lugosi, Evelyn Ankers and more.

Studio: Universal Pictures.

OPERATING FABLE

FRANKENSTEIN (1931) IS A landmark horror film and is much more successful than the slower and stagier *Dracula* from the same year. Based on the famous 19th century horror yarn by Mary Wollstonecraft Shelley, the 1931 Universal film made a star of William Henry Pratt aka Boris Karloff, and put poor old Bela Lugosi and Dracula right in the shade (perhaps a good thing though for a vampire!).

Frankenstein is a film it took me many years to see – I completely missed its BBC2 showing in 1977, finally catching up with it in 1983, and wasn't disappointed. Boris Karloff earned his place in horror film star history with just his first scene alone – the newly 'born' monster backs into the room (illogical, but technically necessary for the scene's impact), turns slowly to camera and the camera cuts in close with a series of rapid zooms. The effect is thoroughly successful.

I'm assuming that the people reading this book – I know there are some as I can hear them breathing – know the ins and outs of the storyline: Dr. Frankenstein and his hunchback assistant Fritz create a man from parts of corpses and the brain of a nutter. The resulting monster is by turns dangerous and placid, killing Fritz by hanging, strangling Doctor Waldman – mind, he was in the process of dissecting the monster at the time! – and beating his creator around the head with a flaming torch, while in other moments, he befriends a little girl by a lake (shortly before throwing her in and drowning her, but hey ho...), and reaches out in appeal, wanting people to be kind and to be his friend.

Ultimately though, the Monster's overtures of friendship and kindness are lost on the general masses – as is often the case in real life – and the creature is hunted down and finally killed. Or so the audience and characters in the film, think...

Frankenstein *(1931)*

Bride of Frankenstein from 1935 is definitely the best Universal horror film of the 1930s and ranks very well in the genre as a whole. Getting off to a nice start with Mary Shelley being pressed by Lord Byron and Percy Shelley for further details of what happened after the end of Frankenstein, we go straight into the brilliant blend of horror and black comedy that this seminal film does so well – Una O'Connor is a delight as Minnie, an old crone, in equal parts scary and funny, who sees the Monster (which has survived the burning windmill it was trapped in at the end of the first film by tumbling into an underground lake) and simply freaks out. The film is filled with such bizarre characters, but the most memorable of them all is Doctor Pretorius.

Pretorius is the creepy, slightly effeminate scientist who blackmails Frankenstein into creating a female monster, and Ernest Thesiger gives a career-best performance. Whether toasting a pile of bones and a skull in a crypt, while settling down to a mild repast, or proudly and ghoulishly showing off his own weird little miniaturised creations, Pretorius is always interesting and deserved a film of his own. The effects in the 'little people' scenes are stunningly good and if anyone ever criticises 'old' films as being technically shoddy, show 'em this. The bit where Pretorius uses some tweezers to grab the little King who has climbed out of his jar and is rushing towards the diminutive Queen in her jar, before plopping him back on his throne is a brilliant moment: part comedy, part bizarre horror and technically amazing, especially for the time.

Bride of Frankenstein *artwork by Allen Koszowski*

When the Bride finally appears, she's no disappointment, even with the relatively short time she's on screen. The make-up and performance are so iconic, that the Bride is immediately recognisable to horror film buffs and the average man on the street even today. Nice idea to hear a peal of wedding bells on the soundtrack too, and to have Elsa Lanchester play the Bride, having already appeared in the film's prologue as Mary – creator and creation.

The film ends with an explosion, initiated by the monster, in which the Baron can clearly be seen standing against the wall of the laboratory. That's because the ending was re-filmed, to allow Frankenstein and his bride to get away, while his creation and his bride apparently perish.

Son of Frankenstein marked a new golden age for Universal horror in 1939, bringing the genre back after a few years of dormancy. Unlike the first two films, which took place in the early 20th century, this one is contemporary and has a very 1930s Wolf Frankenstein (Basil Rathbone – a great actor who should have been a horror star but wasn't), his wife and kid travelling to the town of Frankenstein to claim his inheritance, i.e. the castle and everything in it.

Bela Lugosi and Boris Karloff in Son of Frankenstein *(1939)*

Funnily enough, when the Frankenstein family arrive at the train station, a whole load of the townsfolk have turned out – purely to snub Wolf and co.! Lionel Atwill is on hand to play a police inspector with a wooden arm who sort of befriends Wolf but gets suspicious when things get stranger later on.

The film basically has Wolf encountering the Monster, and being convinced by Ygor (Bela Lugosi), a werewolf-like shepherd with a broken neck who is the Monster's only friend, to reactivate it. This is the first of the films to utilise the idea that the Monster is basically knackered and needs to be given a large influx of electricity to get it back to full strength and power, an idea that would be used in the rest of the series to varying degrees of success (in *Frankenstein Meets the Wolf Man* for example, the revitalised Monster is no different from before).

Though Karloff rightly gets a lot of credit for the success of the Monster, he's actually my least favourite in the role – he gave a brilliant performance and imbues the Monster with a few qualities that the other actors who played the part didn't bother with, such as pity, kindness and a yearning for friendship, not to mention the enjoyment of a fine cigar and glass of wine. But it's the sympathetic qualities he brings to the part that make him the least frightening.

The Ghost of Frankenstein (1942) illustrates the above statement perfectly, with ex-Lennie (*Of Mice and Men*) Lon Chaney Jr. playing the part and being so damn good and scary, that it's a pity he wasn't in every scene!

For some reason, the Monster turns out to be a bit of a backstabber here, throwing Ygor about like a rag doll and reacting angrily to the suggestion that the hairy shepherd should have his brain in the Monster's head – the little girl who it befriends earlier being the Monster's preferred choice. Why the Monster turns against its best and only friend is a mystery, as is the fact that Ygor sticks with it – if I'd been him, I would have stuffed my horn in my sack and got the hell out of it!

The Monster's more violent and murderous tendencies are shown early on: upon gaining entrance to Ludwig Frankenstein/ Ghost of Henry Frankenstein's house/surgery, the Monster casually strides up to the kindly Dr. Kettering and kills him for no reason.

The film is a bit gorier too, with close-ups of disembodied brains being wheeled into view on surgical trolleys, and the Monster's face being horribly blistered in the final fire.

Ultimately, the film is regarded as being the poor relation of the Frankenstein series, after the highs of the first three, but it's more accurate to describe it as a very slightly lesser piece of the same standard of excellence.

Frankenstein *artwork by Jim Pitts*

"Bride of Frankenstein" by Jim Pitts

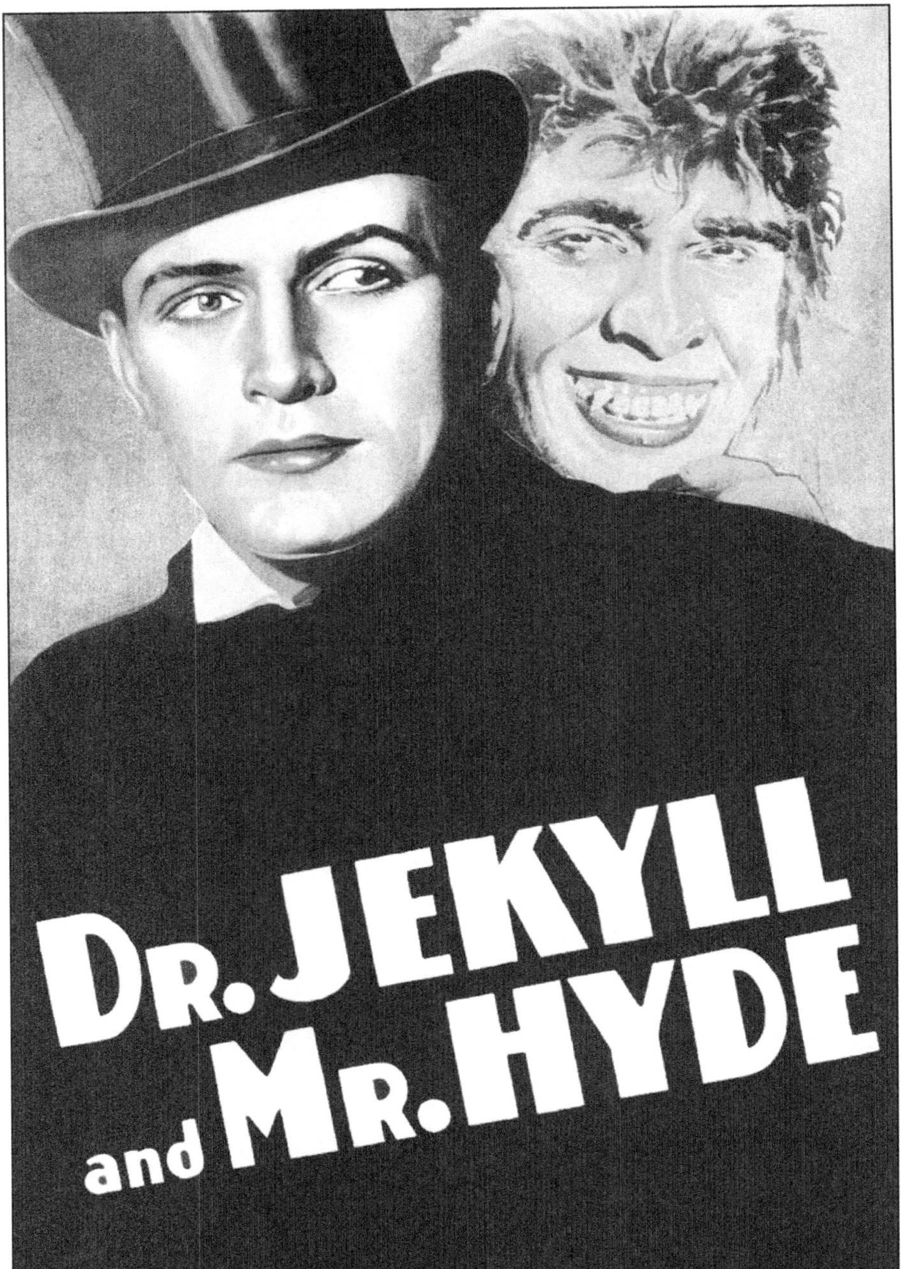
DR. JEKYLL
and MR. HYDE

CHAPTER 4

DR. JEKYLL AND MR. HYDE (1931)

Fredric March in Dr. Jekyll and Mr. Hyde *(1931)*

Directed by: Rouben Mamoulian.

Written by: Samuel Hoffenstein (screenplay), Percy Heath (screenplay) and Robert Louis Stevenson (based on the novel by).

Starring: Fredric March, Miriam Hopkins, Rose Hobart, Holmes Herbert, Halliwell Hobbes, Edgar Norton and more.

Studio: Paramount Pictures.

HYDE AND SHRIEK

TO BEGIN WITH, I must admit I'm not the greatest fan of horror novels, or at least, ones from the 19th century. I *quite* like some of them, but I'm not an ardent admirer – attempting to read Bram Stoker's *Dracula* put me off (for those who haven't yet had the 'pleasure', the novel is written as a series of letters, diary entries etc and it's like wading through jam – no wonder the novel had to be re-written in the 1990s to make it more appealing to a modern audience). Robert Louis Stevenson wrote *Strange Case of Dr Jekyll and Mr Hyde* in 1886, and the novella became a huge success. Dealing with a scientist's experiments into the dual nature of Man, the novel had a philosophical bent as well as scary thrills involving a sort-of monster. The book became a film several times over but the only really 'classic' retelling of it is this 1930s version for Paramount, directed by Rouben Mamoulian.

As I've mentioned elsewhere, I used to miss a lot of great old films on TV back in the 1970s – *Dr. Jekyll and Mr. Hyde* was one of them. Shown in August 1976, as one of the first offerings in BBC2's *Masters of Terror*, this 1931 classic formed the back half of the first week's double bill (with 1925's *The Phantom of the Opera*) and I fell asleep after an eventful evening and missed them both. It would be almost ten years before I got the chance to see the film again, in another BBC horror film season, this time on BBC1.

Dr. Jekyll and Mr. Hyde is one of the best horror films of the 1930s, ranking above even most of the Universal offerings – though it doesn't beat the three 1930s Frankensteins, it's certainly 'hyde' and shoulders above the likes of *Dracula*, *Dracula's Daughter*, *The Mummy* and *The Old Dark House*. In the BBC2 season mentioned above, I wondered briefly as a kid why the film was included – surely, Fredric March wasn't a "Master of Terror", to be spoken of in the same breath as Christopher Lee, Boris Karloff and Peter Cushing?? Though he wasn't/isn't a famous horror film star, March was most definitely eligible for inclusion by virtue of the fact his performances in this film won him an Oscar for Best Actor.

The film begins with a nice burst of classical music – the same music used at the start of Amicus' splendid *Tales From the Crypt* (1972) and after that, we see 19th century London through the eyes of Henry Jekyll, a scientist who is interested in exploring the different facets of humanity, good and evil, which we all carry within us.

When I first saw the film, I was impressed with the unusual idea of showing the first few minutes of the film through the eyes of the central character, and after a while, I began to wonder if the whole film was going to be shot that way, at least until we saw the transformation. March gives a solid performance but is almost edged out by Miriam Hopkins, who plays a chirpy bar singer called Ivy, whose sexy flirting strikes a chord with the medical man – to show how she lingers in his mind, we see her swinging leg on screen for several seconds after the scene has ended. The film has a strong sexual tone, this being the pre-Production Code days when anything went (even bestiality, as in *Island of Lost Souls* in 1933) and there's lots of salaciously kinky stuff involving the cruel Hyde's mistreatment of the clinging Ivy...

Dr. Jekyll and Mr. Hyde *(1931)*

Ah yes... Hyde! The first transformation scene is fascinating, as the change is totally different (and more convincing) than what we would later see in the Wolf Man films from Universal. Coloured make-up was applied to March which was invisible in black and white, but became visible to the viewer when coloured filters were added to the camera. This has the effect of making Jekyll's face change instantly, with no noticeable 'jump' or cut. The first appearance of Hyde has the character appearing more ape-like, and with a more mischievous manner, stretching out in ecstasy and relishing the feel of the rainwater cascading on his head. With each successive transformation though, the make-up is modified to make Hyde progressively more hideous, and a nice reflection of how evil the character is becoming – by the end of the film, Hyde really has become quite grotesque and it makes one wonder how the character's appearance would have altered still further had he not been shot by the coppers in the lively finale. One person who didn't approve of the make-up was Cinematographer Karl Struss, who felt the literal transformation of Jekyll was too unsubtle and looked foolish. It may have been unsubtle, but it looks anything but foolish, and a huge part of the success of the film is down to the fascination with the appearance of the evil and hirsute Hyde.

Fredric March in Dr. Jekyll and Mr. Hyde *(1931)*

Hyde becomes fascinated with Ivy, remembering his earlier sexually-charged encounter with her as Jekyll. We have some entertaining scenes with Hyde visiting the pub/music hall where Ivy works and getting the waiter to ask her to visit him at his table. Just watch how her expression and manner change as she catches sight of the brutish lout! This all leads to Ivy's sexual abuse and psychological cruelty at Hyde's hands, as the ape-man offers to pay for her board in return for certain "favours".

Some stunning acting goes on in the scenes between Hyde and Ivy – during one visit, Hyde says that he's going to be going away for a while. Ivy can't hide her joy from her tormentor and Hyde cruelly dashes her hopes and announces that he's staying after all. It all ends badly for Ivy, who ends up dead at Hyde's hands. The central character(s) also end up dead by the end of the film, in contrast to the novel in which Hyde lives on. The story lived on too, with over 120 film versions of greater and lesser quality, plus a stage show, radio plays, comic adaptations... even a Bugs Bunny cartoon!

To better illustrate how successful this version of the story is, one need only cast a glance at the rather dire 1941 version starring Spencer Tracey. It's bloody awful, to put it mildly, being a virtual remake of the earlier film but without any of its fine qualities – Tracey's make-up as Hyde is dreadful, making him look like he's hungover – more well-oiled than werewolf-ish, and the only really good bit in the film is the famous dream sequence where Jekyll imagines the two women in his life (played by Lana Turner and Ingrid Bergman) as symbolic horses being whipped by him. Apart from that brief bit, the film is eminently worth missing.

Fredric March in Dr. Jekyll and Mr. Hyde *(1931)*

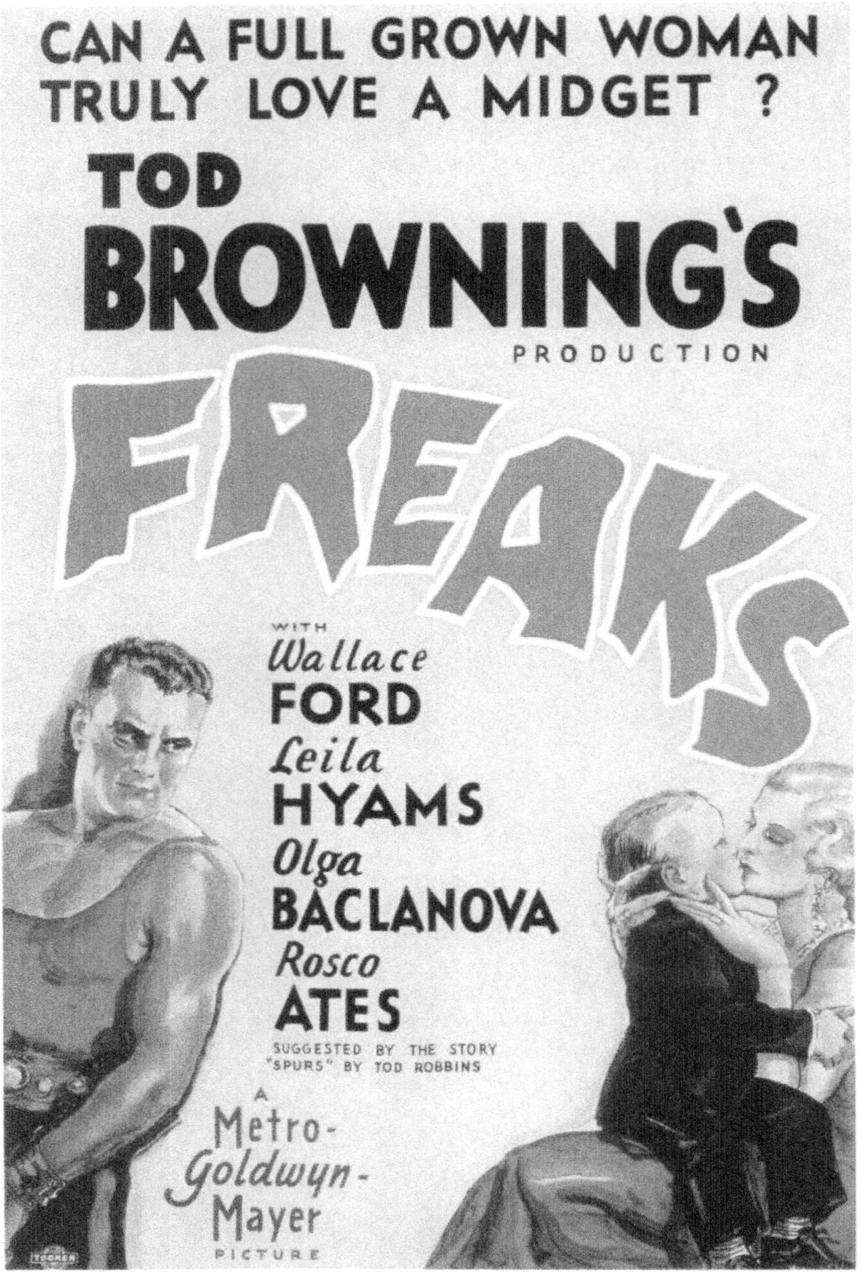
CAN A FULL GROWN WOMAN
TRULY LOVE A MIDGET ?
TOD
BROWNING'S
PRODUCTION
FREAKS
WITH
Wallace
FORD
Leila
HYAMS
Olga
BACLANOVA
Rosco
ATES
SUGGESTED BY THE STORY
"SPURS" BY TOD ROBBINS
A
Metro-
Goldwyn-
Mayer
PICTURE

CHAPTER 5

FREAKS (1932)

Harry Earles and Daisy Earles in Freaks *(1932)*

Directed by: Tod Browning.

Written by: Clarence Aaron "Tod" Robbins (suggested by story "Spurs", Willis Goldbeck (screenplay), Leon Gordon (screenplay), Al Boasberg (uncredited), Charles MacArthur (uncredited) and Edgar Allan Woolf (uncredited).

Starring: Wallace Ford, Leila Hyams, Olga Baclanova, Roscoe Ates, Henry Victor, Harry Earles and more.

Studio: Metro-Goldwyn-Mayer (MGM).

MIDGET GEM

I FIRST HEARD/read about this classic 1932 film from *Dracula* director Tod Browning when I was perusing Alan Frank's great *Horror Films* book, sometime in the early 1980s. That book has long since gone to the great pulping factory in the sky, so my memory of what Mr. Frank actually had to say about the film is somewhat non-existent. However, it was a photo from the film that really caught my attention, intriguing and disturbing me in equal measure. It showed a gaggle of the freaks gathered round what appeared to be a bearded lady on a bed, and one of them looked bloody horrible – a bald character, I couldn't tell if it was male or female, but the image haunted me for many years.

It might have been Alan Frank's write-up or it might have been another write-up elsewhere, but I discovered the film had been banned in the UK for many years, and I assumed that meant no appearances on late-night telly either. However, the film did turn up on late-night telly, on Channel 4 in the summer of 1983. I was ensconced in my first job after leaving school a few months earlier – a carpet factory – and I remember trying to get one of my workmates interested in the film that was showing that (Friday) night but he didn't seem keen, his attention more focussed on a discarded piece of machinery that somebody had written "fucked" on in felt tip.

The film was on at about 11.30pm or thereabouts and I fell asleep and missed the first twenty or so minutes. Upon awaking, I quickly gathered my wits and settled back on the comfortable pouf that was my usual resting place to watch TV.

Freaks is a real revelation for those who might think 1930s horror films are tame – this is possibly one of the most unsavoury and disgusting films ever made. After a short written intro explaining the nature of freaks and deformed individuals and how society has reacted to them, we see the freaks for the first time playing by a river. No special effects here folks, when we see a 'human-worm' or a man with only half a body (the top half), it's the real deal. You can't help but feel a bit sorry for these people, and they definitely are people – the film pulls no punches in showing them in all their glory, but also shows them as the real individuals they are, with all their attendant quirks, fears and hopes.

Some of the freaks aren't too bad – the bearded lady just needs a shave to become 'normal', the hermaphrodite who is part muscle man, part ballet dancer is bizarre but won't make you lose your lunch, and the attractive Siamese twins who are physically joined, each one feeling everything the other does, are similarly odd but otherwise fairly fanciable. The aforementioned 'human worm' is weird, as we see him light a cigarette without the benefit of any arms and legs, and Johnny Eck, the man with only half a body, might not be as palatable if we were to find ourselves next to him in the flesh (how did he go to the toilet??). The baldy character who so unnerved me in the Frank book photo was a guy by the name of Schlitzie, who appeared in a few other films but was primarily a constant presence in various sideshows over the years.

The film was originally 90 minutes but was reduced to 64, after a test screening had the audience allegedly screaming and tearing out their hair. Unfortunately, the lost footage no longer exists, so the chances of a fancy deluxe Blu-ray set filled with extras are smaller than the central character. Pity. The film's story was apparently suggested by that central character, one of the 'freaks' themselves, midget Harry Earles, who was a friend of director Browning. It involves midget Hans (Earles) falling for circus trapeze artist Cleopatra (Olga Baclanova) who in turn is having a 'Pharaoh' time with the strongman Hercules (Henry Victor)! When Cleo finds out Hans is loaded (and not with the cold), she plots to woo and wed him, planning to kill him by poison and make off with the moolah. Unfortunately for her, the freaks get wise and in a bizarre, nightmarish ending, the strongman gets sorted (or, should that be 'shorted') out (I'm sure I read somewhere as a kid that he gets his balls burnt off on a hot stove!) and the hapless Cleo literally turns chicken, as the freaks transform her into a bird woman! This ending plays out during a thunderstorm and the scenes of the freaks crawling inexorably towards Cleopatra through the rain and mud illustrates exactly why the film caused cinema patrons to shriek, scream and faint (and that was just the men!) back in the '30s.

The film ends as it began, the story being told in flashback. Definitely a milestone in cinema history, this is the sort of thing that in later years would become par for the course on late night Channels 4 and 5 in the UK, but I wonder how many unsuspecting viewers back then rolled in from the chippy via the pub and wondered what the heck they were watching.

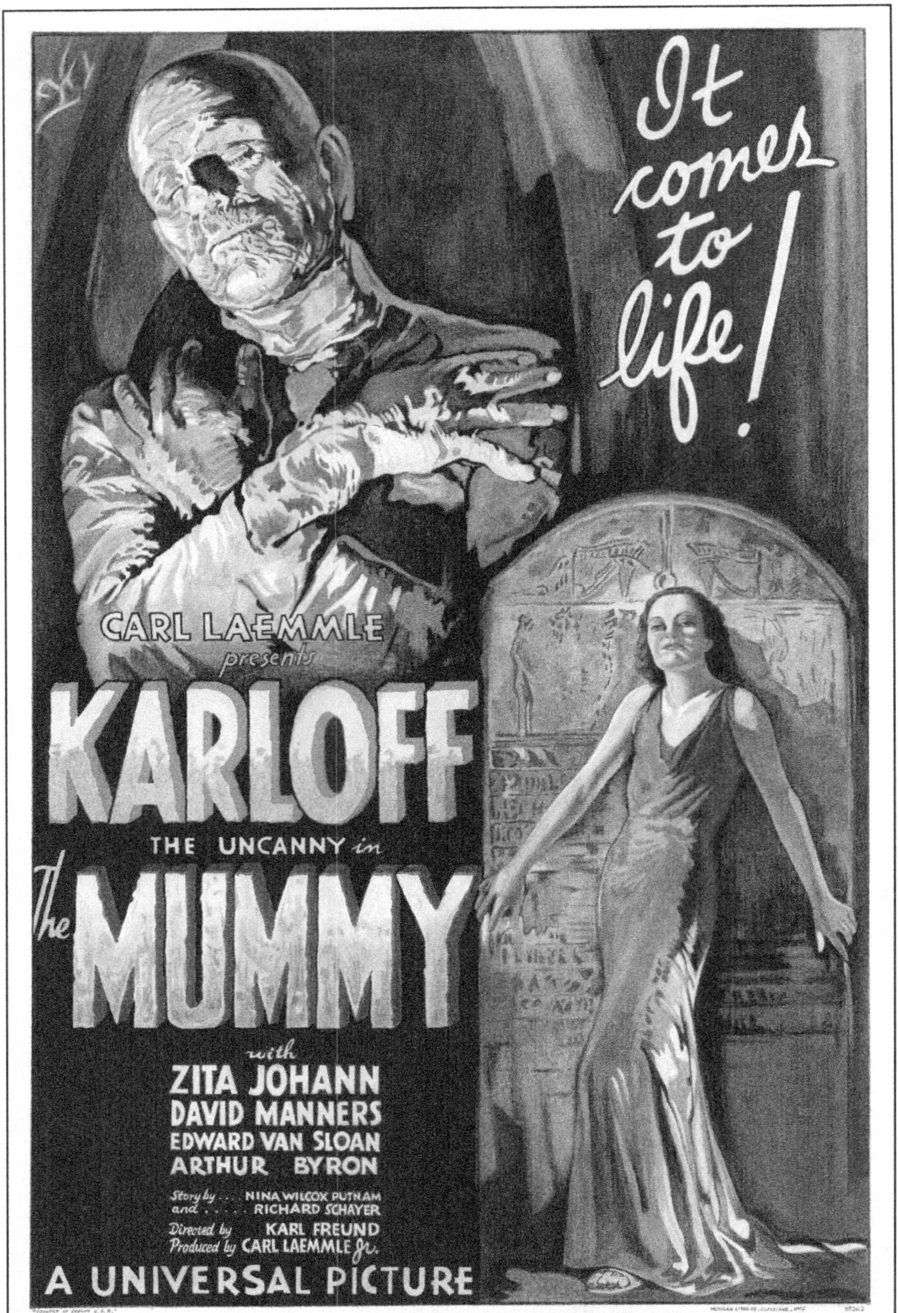
It comes to life!
CARL LAEMMLE presents
KARLOFF
THE UNCANNY in
The MUMMY
with
ZITA JOHANN
DAVID MANNERS
EDWARD VAN SLOAN
ARTHUR BYRON
Story by . . . NINA WILCOX PUTNAM
and . . . . RICHARD SCHAYER
Directed by KARL FREUND
Produced by CARL LAEMMLE Jr.
A UNIVERSAL PICTURE

CHAPTER 6

THE MUMMY (1932)
and
THE MUMMY'S HAND (1940)
THE MUMMY'S TOMB (1942)
THE MUMMY'S GHOST (1944)
THE MUMMY'S CURSE (1944)

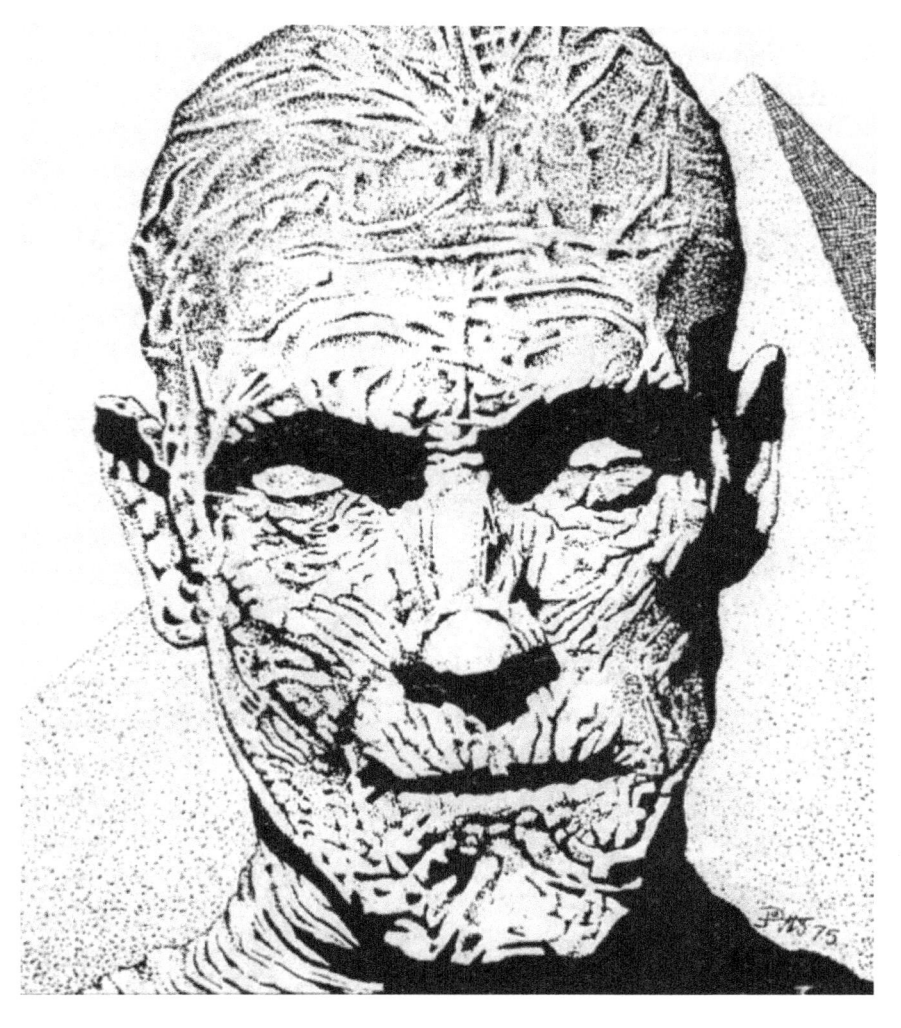

The Mummy *artwork by Jim Pitts*

THE MUMMY (1932):

Directed by: Karl Freund.

Written by: Nina Wilcox Putnam (from a story by), Richard Schayer (from a story by) and John L. Balderston (screenplay).

Starring: Boris Karloff, Zita Johann, David Manners, Arthur Byron, Edward Van Sloan, Bramwell Fletcher and more.

Studio: Universal Pictures.

THE MUMMY'S HAND (1940):

Directed by: Christy Cabanne.

Written by: Griffin Jay (story and screenplay), Maxwell Shane (screenplay), John L. Balderston (uncredited), Ben Pivar (uncredited), Nina Wilcox Putnam (uncredited) and Richard Schayer (uncredited).

Starring: Dick Foran, Peggy Moran, Wallace Ford, Eduardo Ciannelli, George Zucco, Cecil Kellaway and more.

Studio: Universal Pictures.

THE MUMMY'S TOMB (1942):

Directed by: Harold Young.

Written by: Griffin Jay (screenplay), Henry Sucher (screenplay) and Neil P. Varnick (original story).

Starring: Lon Chaney Jr., Dick Foran, John Hubbard, Elyse Knox, George Zucco, Wallace Ford and more.

Studio: Universal Pictures.

THE MUMMY'S GHOST (1944):

Directed by: Reginald Le Borg.

Written by: Griffin Jay (story and screenplay), Henry Sucher (story and screenplay) and Brenda Weisberg (screenplay).

Starring: John Carradine, Robert Lowery, Ramsay Ames, Barton MacLane, George Zucco, Frank Reicher and more.

Studio: Universal Pictures.

THE MUMMY'S CURSE (1944):

Directed by: Leslie Goodwins.

Written by: Bernard Schubert (screenplay), Leon Abrams (original story and adaptation), Dwight V. Babcock (original story and adaptation), Oliver Drake (uncredited) and Ted Richmond (uncredited).

Starring: Lon Chaney Jr., Peter Coe, Virginia Christine, Kay Harding, Dennis Moore, Martin Kosleck and more.

Studio: Universal Pictures.

IT'S A WRAP

THE MUMMY (1932) IS a Universal film in which the film poster spotlighted "Karloff the Uncanny!" who was so famous by this point, that only his surname was necessary to pull in the crowds. Unfortunately, the film is a bit boring, it has to be said. In fact, it reminds me of the 1931 *Dracula* – both films have the most memorable and best bits at the start, and then slowly grind to the proverbial slow crawl with their turgid telling of a supernatural love story.

The Mummy has a very effective beginning, when archaeologists find the tomb of an Egyptian mummy, Imhotep (Boris Karloff), and accidentally bring him to life by reading the words from a sacred scroll. You don't see much of the Mummy here – the scene concentrates on his hands and feet, as he comes slowly to life and reaches out for the scroll, then disappears off into the night while the poor feller who witnesses this (played by Bramwell Fletcher) goes mad. After this the tepid 'Tep' turns up a few years later, now bereft of the bandages and wearing a fetching fez, to guide another group of explorers to the tomb of the Princess Ankh su namun.

It turns out that Imhotep, or Ardath Bey (as he now calls himself), was actually a High Priest who was smitten with the Princess and tried to use the forbidden Scroll of Thoth to bring her back to life but was caught mid-recitation and turned into a mummy. Now, all these years later, Bey finds that his crush still hasn't worn off and he wants to be re-united with her – her soul is in the body of a young woman named Helen (Zita Johann), and Bey intends to sacrifice her, and be with the Princess. But it all goes wrong... and so does the film really. By this point, most viewers will be stifling yawns waiting for some action. It seems Universal Studios – and maybe the cinema-going public themselves – weren't thrilled with this one, as it was eight years before the Mummy returned.

Boris Karloff as Imhotep in The Mummy *(1932)*

When the Mummy did return, it was a new character – Kharis, another priest of ancient Egypt who couldn't keep it in his Shendyt and seeks to bring his love back to life – this time it's the Princess Ananka. *The Mummy's Hand* (1940) has a couple of likeable characters, Steve Banning and Babe Jenson (played by Dick Foran and Wallace Ford), putting together an expedition to the Hill of the Seven Jackals – I only counted four! – to find Ananka's tomb and instead finding her mummified guardian Kharis. The other main expedition members include a comical stage magician (played by Cecil Kellaway) and his very attractive daughter Marta (Peggy Moran). A nice addition to the Mummy mythos is the introduction of tana leaves here, the juice from three being enough to keep Kharis alive and the juice from six giving him the power to move and kill! The juice from nine tana leaves would result in Kharis becoming an unstoppable monster, the like of which the world has never seen!

Once Kharis has been juiced up, he starts to murder the expedition members, beginning with a kindly professor who is feeling for a pulse just as the Mummy flickers into life and grabs his wrist. One effective touch here is that the Mummy's eyes are blacked out which adds a creepy frisson.

Peggy Moran who plays Marta is, in my opinion, the best of the Universal horror heroines and it's a pity she only appeared in two such films (*Horror Island* being the other) as she is quite a bombshell and gives the great Evelyn Ankers a run for her money. It's nice that she survives the events of this film but a pity she didn't return for the sequel, though the Steve Banning character mentions her. The film has a strange tone to it, and if it wasn't for the various murders, it could almost be a slightly screwball comedy – Dick Foran is Bud Abbott to Wallace Ford's Costello, with Peggy Moran as the sexy bombshell caught in the middle.

Kharis ultimately runs out of juice and is set afire by Steve, while Babe dishes out a round of bullets to the sinister High Priest Andoheb (George Zucco), and everyone goes home happy. Apart from the poor sods who have met death at the literal hand of the Mummy who has a penchant for slowly dragging himself up to his victims and strangling them one-handedly.

The Mummy's Tomb (1942) is next and it's a film I have a soft spot for. It never turned up on telly in the 1970s and I had to finally catch up with it on Channel 4 in 1986, as part of their Saturday night *Monster Horrors* season. It introduced Lon Chaney Jr. to the role of Kharis, a part he reportedly hated – "There wasn't a thing you could do with the Mummy", he once complained. I'd argue that there wasn't all that much you could do with the Wolf Man (Chaney Jr.'s 'baby') either!

The chronology of these films is odd – *The Mummy's Hand* takes place in the then-present day of 1940, but *The Mummy's Tomb* must take place at least thirty years later, as the two youthful heroes of the previous film are now white-haired old men (unless their terrifying experiences made them age prematurely!), so we'll say it's set in 1970 – but everything is recognisable in the 1940s! Basically, a new High Priest (played by Turhan Bey) is shipped over from Egypt with a handy 'to do' list: Find and return Kharis, find the Mummy of Ananka and return with it, and kill the survivors from the previous film. Well, three out of five isn't bad – Bey doesn't manage to return to Egypt with the Mummies (in fact, he doesn't return anywhere as another gun-load of bullets settles his hash!) but he does find them, and Steve and Babe from the previous movie are indeed despatched, which seems quite shocking that the two likeable heroes from 1940 are finally caught and done in.

The Mummy's Ghost (1944) takes place about a year later, and has John Carradine as yet another High Priest called Bey shipped from Egypt with the same bucket list as his unfortunate predecessor. Carradine fares no better here, in fact he gets a worse deal as he is murdered by Kharis (Lon Chaney Jr. again) when the latter overhears Carradine foolishly gloating to himself about how he intends to forsake his vows and cop off with the young lovely (Ramsay Ames) who is Ananka's reincarnation! After sorting out Carradine, the Mummy picks up Ames and strides off into a swamp – end of film. Though it doesn't really offer anything new from the established formula, I like *The Mummy's Ghost* a lot despite, once again, being set in a strange alternate future where it's always the 1940s. The makers of these films obviously couldn't take a peek into the future to see how the world changed by the 1990s (though they clearly expected World War II to last for another thirty years at least!) but it's a good thing they didn't attempt to set the films in an imagined future of moving pavements, hover cars and ray guns!

For *The Mummy's Curse* (also 1944), the time period in which it is set doesn't matter as it all takes place in Bayou Country – all swamps, trees, quicksand and derelict old buildings.

This film is set twenty-five years after the end of ...*Ghost* and is therefore, as mentioned earlier, in the late '90s. Virginia Christine is even sexier than Peggy Moran, and plays a revived Ananka, getting out of the swamp she ended up in at the end of the previous film. The film follows the usual formula – High Priest sent from Egypt to find the Mummy and his Princess (tick), victims edging into a corner and the Mummy slowly creeping up and killing them with a one-handed strangle-hold (tick) and the tana leaves (tick). The ending though, brings the curtain down on the Mummy series, and a ruined building's roof on Kharis himself, as he bashes down a door to get at his last victim but brings down the roof instead.

Somewhere in an alternate universe, there's another film in the series, in which Kharis was battered but not killed by the collapsing roof and yet another High Priest is sent over to find him and bring him home.

The Mummy *artwork by Allen Koszowski*

CARL LAEMMLE presents
KARLOFF and
BELA LUGOSI in
"The EDGAR ALLAN POE'S
BLACK CAT"
with
DAVID MANNERS ◇ JACQUELINE WELLS ◇
LUCILLE LUND ◇ EGON BRECHER ◇ HARRY CORDING
HENRY ARMETTA ◇ ALBERT CONTI ◇ LOUIS ALBERNI
SCREEN PLAY BY PETER RURIC
DIRECTED BY EDGAR G. ULMER
PRODUCED BY CARL LAEMMLE JR.
A UNIVERSAL PICTURE

CHAPTER 7

THE BLACK CAT (1934)
and
THE RAVEN (1935)

Bela Lugosi and Boris Karloff in The Black Cat *(1934)*

THE BLACK CAT (1934):

Directed by: Edgar G. Ulmer.

Written by: Edgar Allan Poe (suggested by a story by), Peter Ruric (story and screenplay), Edgar G. Ulmer (story) and Tom Kilpatrick (uncredited).

Starring: Boris Karloff, Bela Lugosi, David Manners, Julie Bishop, Egon Brecher, Harry Cording and more.

Studio: Universal Pictures.

THE RAVEN (1935):

Directed by: Lew Landers (as Louis Friedlander).

Written by: Edgar Allan Poe (poem), David Boehm (screenplay), Guy Endore (uncredited), Florence Enright (uncredited), John Lynch (uncredited), Clarence Marks (uncredited), Dore Schary (uncredited), Michael L. Simmons (uncredited) and Jim Tully (uncredited).

Starring: Boris Karloff, Bela Lugosi, Lester Matthews, Irene Ware, Samuel S. Hinds, Spencer Charters and more.

Studio: Universal Pictures.

THE BLACK RAVEN

THE BLACK CAT from 1934 was a landmark moment in horror films. For the first time, two recognised stars of the genre appeared together in the same film: Bela Lugosi and Boris Karloff had both been a great hit in *Dracula* and *Frankenstein* respectively and had both appeared in other horrors since – *White Zombie*, *Murders in the Rue Morgue* for the former and *The Mummy* and *The Old Dark House* as examples for the latter. But here they were together! Audiences at the time must have been very excited at the prospect and probably wondered how the hammy Hungarian and the lisping Limey would hit it off together, both on screen and off it. Well, I don't know about off screen, but on, they do very well and the electricity between them just sparkles, especially in the former film.

The Black Cat, directed by Edgar G. Ulmer, purports to be based on the Edgar Allan Poe story, or rather 'suggested'. The actual story is okay, involving a man killing his wife but also walling up her beloved cat with her and it's screeching alerts the police. Not exactly a masterpiece, this and the other Poe stories tend to be overrated by people who have never actually read them or know what they are about – it's called "The Black Cat" (spooky title!) and is written by Poe, so it must be good! Anyway, this film owes more to the life of Aleister Crowley than anything written by Poe.

Crowley was a notorious, real-life Satanist who dabbled in the black arts and generally took part in various unholy ceremonies, that left their mark on his sanity. Karloff's character in this film has a touch of Crowley about him, and the central thrust is the clash between Werdegast (Lugosi) and Poelzig (Karloff), with the other characters being basically irrelevant onlookers. Set in the then-present day, Lugosi and the rest end up at Karloff's ultra-modern castle after the taxi taking them from the train station crashes during a thunderstorm – Werdegast was on his way there anyway, the others are excess baggage.

David Manners and Jacqueline Wells play the young couple here, Mr. and Mrs. Alison, who end up at Castle Poelzig and quite out of their depth, as actors and as characters. Manners and Wells seem as if they have strayed in from a light romantic comedy and indeed the few moments of 'humour' in the film come from these two – for example, the scene where they are discussing their creepy host, and generally taking the P out of Poelzig.

Lugosi gives a good performance, in his usual enjoyably hammy style, a highlight of which is when he throws a knife at an intruding cat (Werdegast suffers from a fear of cats, which just about justifies the title), killing it! Karloff is also effective as Poelzig, but then he never really gave a bad performance in any film. I love the weird way he rises from his bed, when his servant announces the arrival of his unexpected guests though!

The game of cat and mouse continues throughout the film, as it transpires that not only did Poelzig betray Werdegast's people during the War but subsequently married Werdegast's wife and killed her (her body is preserved in a glass case in the dungeon), and is now married to his hated enemy's grown-up daughter! The final reckoning has the aghast Werdegast skinning Poelzig alive – some nice direction here, as we don't really see much, only Poelzig's hands writhing in agony – shortly before the inept Manners shoots him, and the place blows up.

A good film anyway, one of the best of the non-Monster Universal horrors. Whereas both stars were of equal importance here, in 1935's *The Raven*, Lugosi is clearly the star and Karloff is relegated to a supporting role.

In *The Raven*, Lugosi plays Dr. Richard Vollin, a brain surgeon who should have operated on himself, as he is clearly not working with a full set of scalpels. Having saved the life of a young woman and accepted the gratitude of her family, he then proceeds to become smitten with her, inviting her and her family, including her fiancée, to spend the night at his mansion. Vollin is obsessed with the works of Poe and has a working pendulum in his basement. However, his guests aren't really impressed, and even less so when Vollin's disfigured servant Bateman (Karloff) pops up – Bateman is a killer and has come to Vollin wanting the deranged doctor to change his face. However, Vollin makes him look fairly ghastly and promises only to restore his looks if Bateman helps him in his vendetta against the family.

Bela Lugosi and Boris Karloff in The Raven *(1935)*

The make-up on Karloff is quite substandard – the disfigurement is basically just a false eyepiece, which looks like a bit of cloth stuck on, and the scene where Karloff sees his reflection post-surgery has, contrary to what I said earlier, a daft bit of acting from him as he shakes his fist at the laughing Lugosi and does a growling impression of the Frankenstein Monster!

A good cast again, with Irene Ware as the hapless object of Lugosi's twisted affections and Samuel S. Hinds as her father, Judge Thatcher, who complains later that "It's dangerous to be under this man's roof!". Too late, Judge. The Judge ends up being found guilty and is stretched out on a rack as the razor-sharp pendulum swings towards him. Needless to say, it all ends well – except for Bateman who gets shot, and Vollin ends up stuck in a room where the walls close in and his crush on Ware leads to him being crushed himself. There's even time for a spot of light comedy, with the sleepy antics of two of Lugosi's guests who sleep through the nocturnal disturbances and wake up after it's all over.

The film is very entertaining but in 1935 it was a flop, particularly in England where the audience's distaste for the film and its themes led to a ban on horror films that lasted several years and was further reinforced by a change in management at Universal, with the new owners being idiots who had no interest in the macabre – fortunately, the genre was reignited in 1939, with the great success of *Son of Frankenstein* with the American public.

Boris Karloff as Edmond Bateman in The Raven *(1935)*

The
WOLF MAN
with
CLAUDE RAINS
WARREN WILLIAM
RALPH BELLAMY
PATRIC KNOWLES
BELA LUGOSI
MARIA OUSPENSKAYA
EVELYN ANKERS
and
LON CHANEY
as "The Wolf Man"
Directed by GEORGE WAGGNER
A UNIVERSAL PICTURE
Associate Producer GEORGE WAGGNER

CHAPTER 8

THE WOLF MAN (1941)
and
FRANKENSTEIN MEETS THE WOLF MAN (1943)

The Wolf Man *artwork by Allen Koszowski*

THE WOLF MAN (1941):

Directed by: George Waggner.

Written by: Curt Siodmack (original screenplay).

Starring: Claude Rains, Warren William, Ralph Bellamy, Patric Knowles, Bela Lugosi, Maria Ouspenskaya and more.

Studio: Universal Pictures.

FRANKENSTEIN MEETS THE WOLF MAN (1943):

Directed by Roy William Neill.

Written by: Curt Siodmack (original screenplay).

Starring: Lon Chaney Jr., Ilona Massey, Patric Knowles, Lionel Atwill, Bela Lugosi, Maria Ouspenskaya and more.

Studio: Universal Pictures.

PURE AT HEART, FURRY OF FACE

FRANKENSTEIN MEETS THE Wolf Man (1943) was the first horror film I ever saw, which makes me love this great film all the more. I had to wait about two years before I saw the film that led to it, *The Wolf Man* (1941) but, funnily enough, I wasn't impressed – we saw a lot of the Man all right but it seemed to take forever before we saw anything of the Wolf and back then, as a ten year old, I finally lost patience and went to bed.

Now however, I love the earlier film too. Apparently intended as a vehicle for Boris Karloff in 1932, it was rejected as being a bit too near the knuckle and so the original script was discarded. When the film was finally made, it had a new story by Curt Siodmak and starred Universal's new horror star Lon Chaney Jr. Chaney plays Lawrence Talbot, who returns to his family home in Llanwelly – it's assumed to be in Wales but nobody onscreen states that or speaks in a Welsh accent – to bury the hatchet with his estranged father (Claude Rains). After chatting up a sexy young woman called Gwen (Evelyn Ankers), Talbot invites her to accompany him to a gypsy camp outside the village. However, it all goes wrong when the girl acting as chaperone, Jenny, has her throat torn out by a wolf and Chaney Jr. is bitten by the same creature before killing it with his fancy silver wolf's head cane.

The wolf is actually a werewolf called Bela (Bela Lugosi) and Chaney Jr. is now regarded as a murderer. Worse is to come as he finds that, like Bela before him, he is now doomed to become a wolf man on nights of a full moon. Funny, that Bela was an actual wolf but Chaney becomes a wolf man. Equally strange is the fact that, no matter what Larry is wearing, when we see him as the wolf man, he's always wearing the same breast-pocketed shirt – I suppose he would have looked silly in a vest though.

The Wolf Man *(1941)*

Chaney Jr. and Evelyn Ankers (as Gwen) apparently didn't get on at all, as Chaney was quite rough and ready while she was all airs and graces, which is ironic as they appeared in a few Universal films together and though Chaney Jr. isn't exactly a dreamboat, the chemistry between Talbot and Gwen just flows from the screen!

The film takes it's time getting to the juicy transformation scene and when it comes, it concentrates on Larry's feet rather than his face! The atmospheric, foggy woodland sets work a treat and the final moments, as Talbot Snr. wrestles with his feral offspring then gets the upper hand and bashes Larry's hairy bonce in with his beloved cane, bring the film to an emotional, as well as action-packed, close. The music is excellent too, and several themes would recur from related film to film.

The sequel, *Frankenstein Meets the Wolf Man*, followed a few years later and by this time, Chaney Jr. had played Count Dracula and the Frankenstein Monster as well, with a stint as the Mummy to follow. The sequel gets off to a great start when two grave robbers break into the Talbot mausoleum at the local cemetery and aren't the slightest bit surprised to see Larry looking as fresh as a Daisy, and covered in blooming wolfbane! Once the full moon shines, Larry is up and about (scratch one grave robber) and obsessed with suicide. Why he can't just shoot himself in the head, or take an overdose or whatever is never explained. He decides that he needs the help of someone very clever to bring about an elaborate end to his cursed existence and Dr. Frankenstein in Vasaria fits the bill quite adequately...

The continuity of these films is very confused by this point – the last Frankenstein we saw was Ludwig, one of the original monster-making Baron's sons, and the Monster was trapped in a fire in his house. Here though, everybody is talking about Ludwig as if he was the original Monster-maker! Larry is accompanied by the gypsy woman Maleva (Maria Ouspenskaya) on his quest, she regarding him as a surrogate son, and the bit where Larry is riding along with her in a horse and cart, shortly before the full moon catches up with him and he runs off, was the point at which I first saw this film, back in 1975. It was the Friday night film slot on Tyne Tees, and I knew this film was on and wanted to stay up to watch it but 11.05pm seemed an eternity away to a seven-year-old and, as usual, I was deep in the arms of Morpheus by the time 10pm rolled around, never mind 11. For some reason, my family hadn't gone to bed though and when I was shaken gently awake and realised the time, I demanded the TV be put on – just in time to see the aforementioned scene!

In Wolf mode, Larry ends up at the castle, and discovers the frozen body of the Monster. Strangely, Larry has no fear of the brute at all and after thawing it out, he and the Monster become quite chummy. Unfortunately, although scenes of the Monster speaking in Lugosi's voice were filmed, they were cut out completely (along with all references to the Monster's blindness) as a preview audience burst out in gales of raucous laughter every time Lugosi opened his mouth! I've visualised the Monster speaking in Lugosi's voice and it doesn't seem remotely funny to me... creepy but not funny (nor indeed was it even slightly funny when the exact same thing happened at the end of *The Ghost of Frankenstein* a year earlier)!

It's often remarked that Bela Lugosi was miscast as the Monster and wasn't very good in the role but I beg to differ. He certainly looks a little odd, with his little mole/beauty spot and the strange gurning faces he pulls, but he's quite sinister, especially when he hisses and snarls and throws things out of his way. His groping is explained by the fact the monster was supposed to be blind, and it's inconsistent as the Monster seems able to see okay in some scenes.

The battle between the monsters comes at the end and is preceded by a magnificent shot of Lugosi, strapped on an operating table with electricity pouring into him, turning and looking at Patric Knowles (who appeared in *The Wolf Man* in a different role, here he plays a doctor who becomes obsessed with seeing the Monster at full strength) and giving the most horrible grin! When Chaney Jr. turns into the Wolf Man, he spends the next few minutes climbing on top of laboratory equipment in order to leap down at the Monster who is played by stuntman Eddie Parker for most of these shots – in years to come, Chaney Jr. would claim that he played the Monster in some scenes too, to ease the burden on Lugosi and the production schedule, but a very large slab of salt is needed with this I think.

When the surly local landlord blows up the dam, the raging river crushes the castle and the two battling monsters are swept away and presumably drowned like rats.

But it wouldn't be long before both these characters would be back on cinema screens.

Frankenstein Meets the Wolf Man *(1943)*

ALL TOGETHER..!
FRANKENSTEIN'S MONSTER!
WOLF MAN!
DRACULA!
HUNCHBACK!
MAD DOCTOR!
HOUSE OF FRANKENSTEIN
Starring
BORIS KARLOFF
LON CHANEY
with
JOHN CARRADINE
J. CARROL NAISH
ANNE GWYNNE PETER COE ELENA VERDUGO LIONEL ATWILL
Screen Play by Edward T. Lowe Based on a Story by Curt Siodmak
Directed by ERLE C. KENTON Produced by PAUL MALVERN A UNIVERSAL PICTURE

CHAPTER 9

HOUSE OF FRANKENSTEIN (1944)
and
HOUSE OF DRACULA (1945)

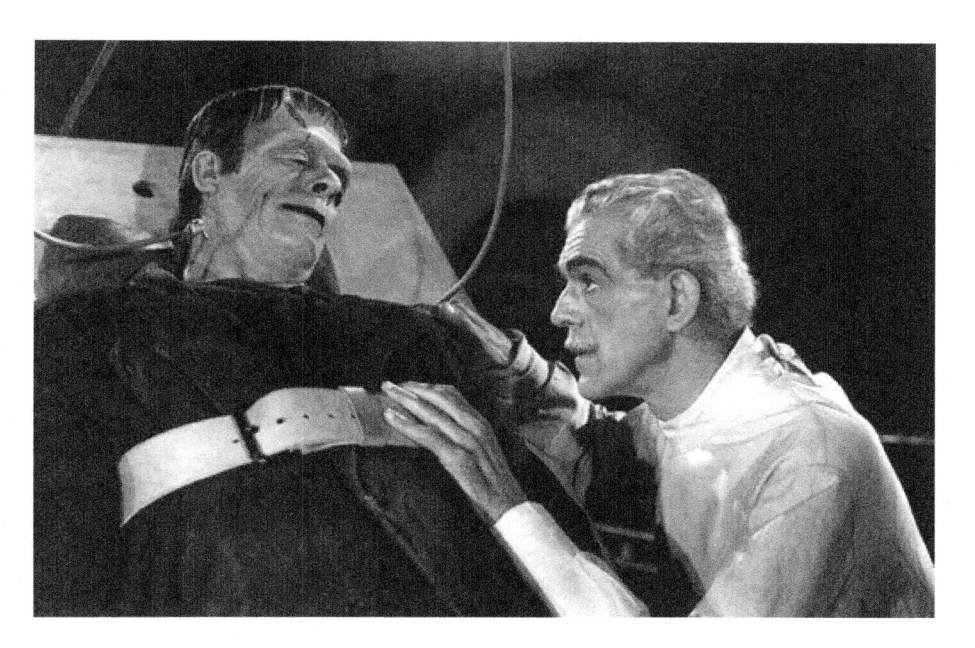

Glenn Strange and Boris Karloff in House of Frankenstein *(1944)*

HOUSE OF FRANKENSTEIN (1944):

Directed by: Erle C. Kenton.

Written by: Edward T. Lowe Jr. (screenplay) and Curt Siodmack (story).

Starring: Boris Karloff, Lon Chaney Jr., J. Carrol Naish, John Carradine, Anne Gwynne, Peter Coe and more.

Studio: Universal Pictures.

HOUSE OF DRACULA (1945):

Directed by: Erle C. Kenton.

Written by: Edward T. Lowe Jr. (original screenplay), Dwight V. Babcock (story, uncredited) and George Bricker (story, uncredited).

Starring: Lon Chaney Jr., John Carradine, Martha O'Driscoll, Lionel Atwill, Onslow Stevens, Jane Adams and more.

Studio: Universal Pictures.

THE DEVIL'S BROOD

FRANKENSTEIN MEETS THE Wolf Man had been such a success in 1943, that Universal decided to repeat the formula of having more than one monster in a movie but this time, with *House of Frankenstein* in 1944, they would add another to the mix, and throw in a mad scientist and a hunchback for good measure.

House of Frankenstein was described by film critic and writer William K. Everson as "the silliest and dullest" of the Frankenstein films. I disagree on two counts – firstly, it's not a Frankenstein film as such and secondly, it's certainly not dull. Silly? Well, the jury is still out on that one. The film is entertaining though and it's a joy to see Boris Karloff back again, this time playing Dr. Gustav Niemann, who is obsessed with his hero Frankenstein and as the film starts, is busily bigging up the infamous monster-maker to his hunchbacked assistant and fellow prisoner Daniel (J. Carroll Naish), telling him how Frankenstein transplanted the brain of a man into the head of a dog (never witnessed or referred to onscreen in any of the previous films).

A lucky accident occurs shortly after, which enables the pair to escape and before long, they've found transport in the form of one Professor Lampini (George Zucco) and his travelling chamber of horrors: it's not much of a chamber though as there seems to be only one exhibit – the skeletal remains of Count Dracula. Lampini is soon despatched, and Niemann's plan is to return to Vasaria to find the Monster and get revenge on the town council who had him thrown in prison. Along the way they encounter some gypsies, one of whom Ilonka (Elena Verdugo) joins them and Daniel becomes smitten – unfortunately, the shallow Ilonka proves to be a plonker and soon loses interest in Daniel when she spies his hump.

Dracula is played by the suave and dapper John Carradine, perhaps the least-threatening portrayal of the Count ever seen on screen. The bit where Niemann removes the stake and Dracula is resurrected is nice, as we see the veins and blood vessels form before the Count is up and about, though not for long – Dracula is despatched fairly quickly, though he manages to kill one of the townspeople responsible for the mad Niemann's imprisonment, Hussman (Sig Ruman), before being done in by the rays of the Sun. The chase which leads to Dracula's demise is well done and it's one of the rare scenes which makes it clear that these Universal classics, despite their great Gothic atmosphere, were actually made in sunny Los Angeles, California.

Once the bodies of Talbot (Lon Chaney Jr.) and the Frankenstein Monster (Glenn Strange) are found, the line-up is complete. Chaney Jr. is excellent as ever, though the Wolf Man is used sparingly (watch for the transformation scene where his hands remain normal). There's a nice subplot in which Ilonka falls for Larry's charms but they end up killing each other: as the Wolf Man he murders her but not before she manages to shoot him with a handy silver bullet. Take note too, that the rhyme which debuted in *The Wolf Man* in 1941 is re-used again and once again, it's a bit different. Originally, it was:

> *Even a man who is pure in heart,*
> *And says his prayers by night;*
> *May become a wolf when the wolfbane blooms,*
> *And the autumn moon is bright.*

But the rhyme varies with each film – the autumn moon becomes the *moon is full and bright* and our pure-hearted man says his prayers *at* night, rather than *by*.

The Daniel/Talbot/Ilonka triangle leads to one very amusing scene, where we see Daniel madly lashing the prone form of the Monster (Daniel hoped to have his brain transplanted into Talbot's head and thus get the girl, but the Monster's brain is to be used or something. The game of 'Musical Brains' used in this film sometimes gets confusing!). Talking of the Monster, Strange looks very creepy indeed but is sadly wasted and only gets to get up from the operating table in the last five minutes, dispensing with his tormentor Daniel and stomping off into the swamps with Niemann. The film ends abruptly, with both of their heads vanishing beneath quicksand.

Apart from a rather dull opening credit scene, the film has a lot to offer though it could have been better, of course; there's no interaction between Dracula and the other monsters and as mentioned before Strange is not used enough, but overall a great slice of 1940s Universal horror. And there was more to come...

House of Dracula from 1945 is a slightly better film: it has the same blend of ludicrous plotting made perfectly acceptable through the conviction of the cast and director and the same mix of monsters. The film has Dracula (John Carradine again but better here than in the previous film) flying as a bat into the castle/surgery/laboratory of Dr. Edlemann (Onslow Stevens) and asking the doctor to find a cure for his vampirism! The film ignores the fact that Dracula is a supernatural being – how do you *cure* someone who is undead?! – and puts his plight down as a medical condition! Needless to say, Edlemann accepts the case but soon wishes he hadn't, as Dracula's blood infects him and he becomes a cackling vampire/mad scientist.

John Carradine as Dracula in House of Dracula *(1945)*

The hunchback here is an otherwise attractive nurse called Nina (Jane Adams – pity they didn't get Evelyn Ankers for the role), and it's an absurd coincidence that Lawrence Talbot (Lon Chaney Jr., sporting a tash that makes him resemble Roger Moore in *The Man Who Haunted Himself* at times!) turns up, also wanting to be cured. *The Wolf Man* isn't seen much in this film, but it has a happy ending for the character, as Talbot is cured! Again, this ignores the supernatural nature of Talbot's 'affliction' and presents the transformation as the result of pressure on the brain! The Monster's body is discovered, along with the skeleton of Dr. Niemann in a nice touch of continuity, but once again, the Monster (Glenn Strange) gets a raw deal and remains comatose until the ending, which involves a fire.

Another great element of these Universal films are the scores, with some of the music being reused from film to film – the rousing music when we see the Wolf Man on his nocturnal prowlings, for example, is playing in our heads note-for-note as we recognise it from other films.

Apparently Universal had considered having even more monsters in these films – the Mummy, the Invisible Man and even the Mad Ghoul were slated at one point – but in retrospect, they couldn't make sufficient use of the ones they had so it's better that more didn't appear. Often dismissed as ignoble ends to the cycle of Universal horrors that began in 1931 with *Dracula*, these two films are corkers and it's a pity they couldn't have stretched to a third entry – "House of the Wolf Man", anyone? When the characters did return three years later, it was in the non-canonical company of a comedy double-act.

John Carradine and Martha O'Driscoll in House of Dracula *(1945)*

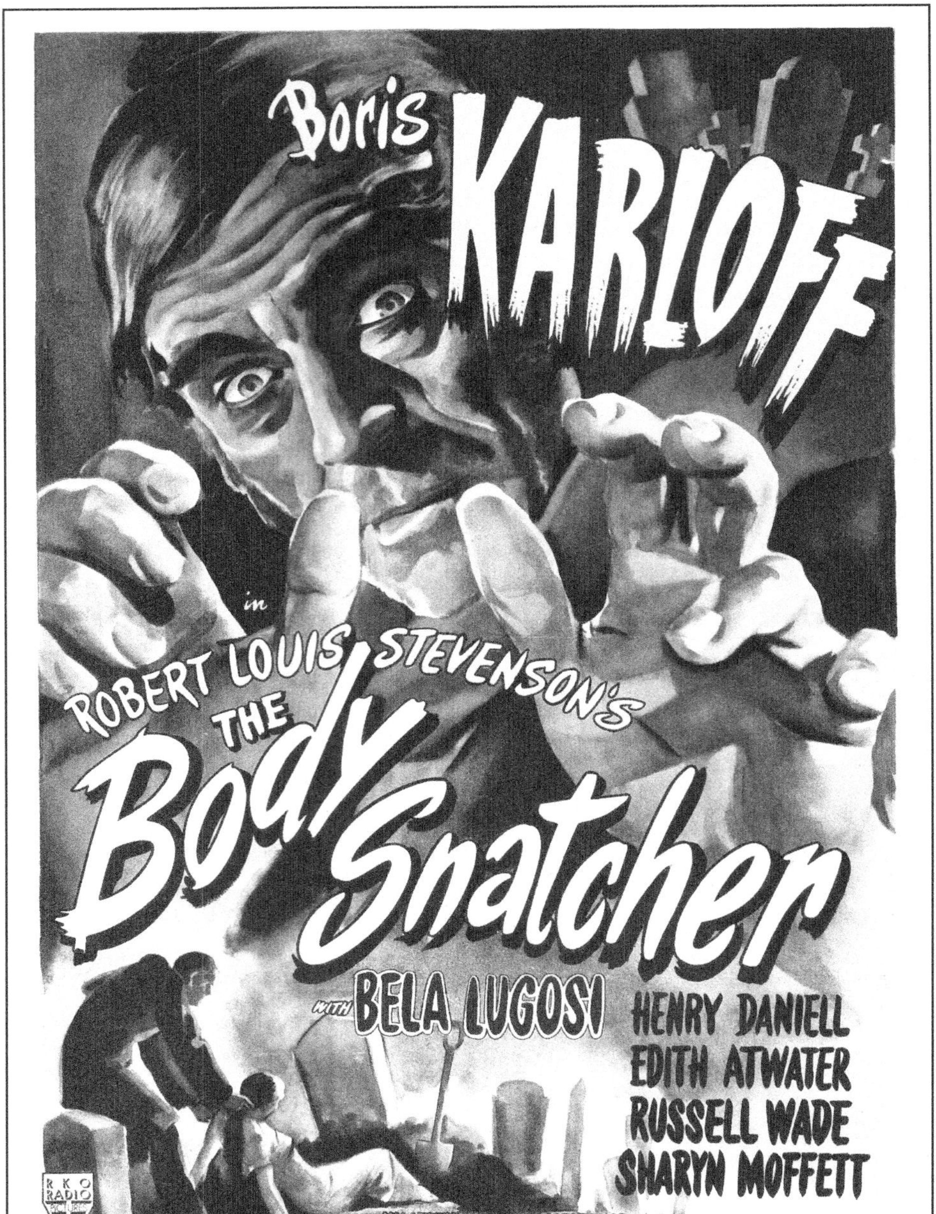
Boris KARLOFF
in
ROBERT LOUIS STEVENSON'S
THE Body Snatcher
WITH BELA LUGOSI
HENRY DANIELL
EDITH ATWATER
RUSSELL WADE
SHARYN MOFFETT
RKO RADIO PICTURES
PRODUCED BY VAL LEWTON · DIRECTED BY ROBERT WISE
WRITTEN FOR THE SCREEN BY PHILIP MacDONALD AND CARLOS KEITH
45/85

CHAPTER 10

THE BODY SNATCHER (1945)

Boris Karloff in The Body Snatcher *(1945)*

Directed by: Robert Wise.

Written by: Robert Louis Stevenson (short story), Philip MacDonald (screenplay) and Val Lewton (screenplay, as Carlos Keith).

Starring: Boris Karloff, Bela Lugosi, Henry Daniell, Edith Atwater, Russell Wade, Rita Corday and more.

Studio: RKO Radio Pictures.

NEVER GET RID OF ME...

I'M NOT THE world's greatest fan of the Val Lewton films, I must confess. *Cat People* (1942) works mainly because Simone Simon is so appealing, and it has a nice couple of scare scenes. *The Leopard Man* (1943) is very good but not really a horror film. The other Lewton films are fairly dreary – even the two with Boris Karloff in (not including *The Body Snatcher*)! – but if you're in the right mood, they are watchable and even enjoyable, although if you're expecting full-blown chills and thrills (not to mention monsters!), forget it.

Val Lewton, as with some fans of the genre, was a snob and his particular brand of snobbery included a disdainful approach to the output of Universal and their emphasis on monsters. Eschewing shadowy creatures of the night, Lewton tried to give his films an artistic feel and the scares were provided by suggestion for the most part. However, cinema goers would be left tapping their feet waiting for some action – subtle horror is okay to a point but taken too far, it can lead to boredom, disappointment and a 'I thought this was supposed to be a horror film' response. *The Body Snatcher*, like the other eight Lewton horrors, is too subtle for its own good. True, it's best not to be beaten over the head, so to speak, as the crappy gore-obsessed films of the 1980s and '90s did so tiresomely. But you need to have *something* in a horror film, to make you think you've not wasted your time and money, and been better off watching a romantic comedy or a musical instead. *The Body Snatcher* manages to overcome Lewton's staid approach, emerging as a very fine film, and the only one of his horror films I can heartily recommend.

Karloff gives one of his best performances here as the 19th century cab driver Gray, who moonlights as a grave robber and supplier of corpses to Dr. McFarlane (Henry Daniell). The film takes place in 19th century Edinburgh and the place and time are carefully evoked, minus the Scottish accents for most of the cast! Once-great horror star Bela Lugosi had fallen so far by this time, that he is reduced to a small, virtual cameo role, as a servant who tries to blackmail Gray and ends up murdered. Sherlock Holmes' housekeeper, Mary Gordon, also has a part in the film, and the most distressing line – "They killed his poor wee doggie!", in regard to her dead son whose corpse has been dug up by Karloff, and to add insult to injury, had his faithful dog (which kept a graveside vigil) killed too.

Gray is an evil swine of a man – he is a small individual in every respect, but because he has a position of power over Dr. McFarlane it makes him feel good about himself and, like many people in jobs who are suddenly given greater responsibilities and, because they are basically stupid, under-achieving morons, lead to them using their newfound 'authority' to insult and belittle others who are far superior to them in every respect. This is similar to Gray and his attitude to the doctor he is blackmailing, but it proves to be his undoing as MacFarlane ends up killing him.

The film takes an unexpected supernatural twist at the end, as Gray's ghost seems to return, endlessly repeating an earlier statement of his to the doctor ("You'll never get rid of me") as the latter panics and whips the horses pulling the carriage he's in to a frenzy before the whole thing crashes. *The Body Snatcher*, being a Val Lewton production, has its slower moments, with a lengthy sub-plot involving a crippled child, and the film ends with an on-screen quote which was also usual for these films. If you've seen other Lewton horrors and not been impressed by their languid pace and lack of monsters, give this one a try.

Henry Daniell and Boris Karloff in The Body Snatcher *(1945)*

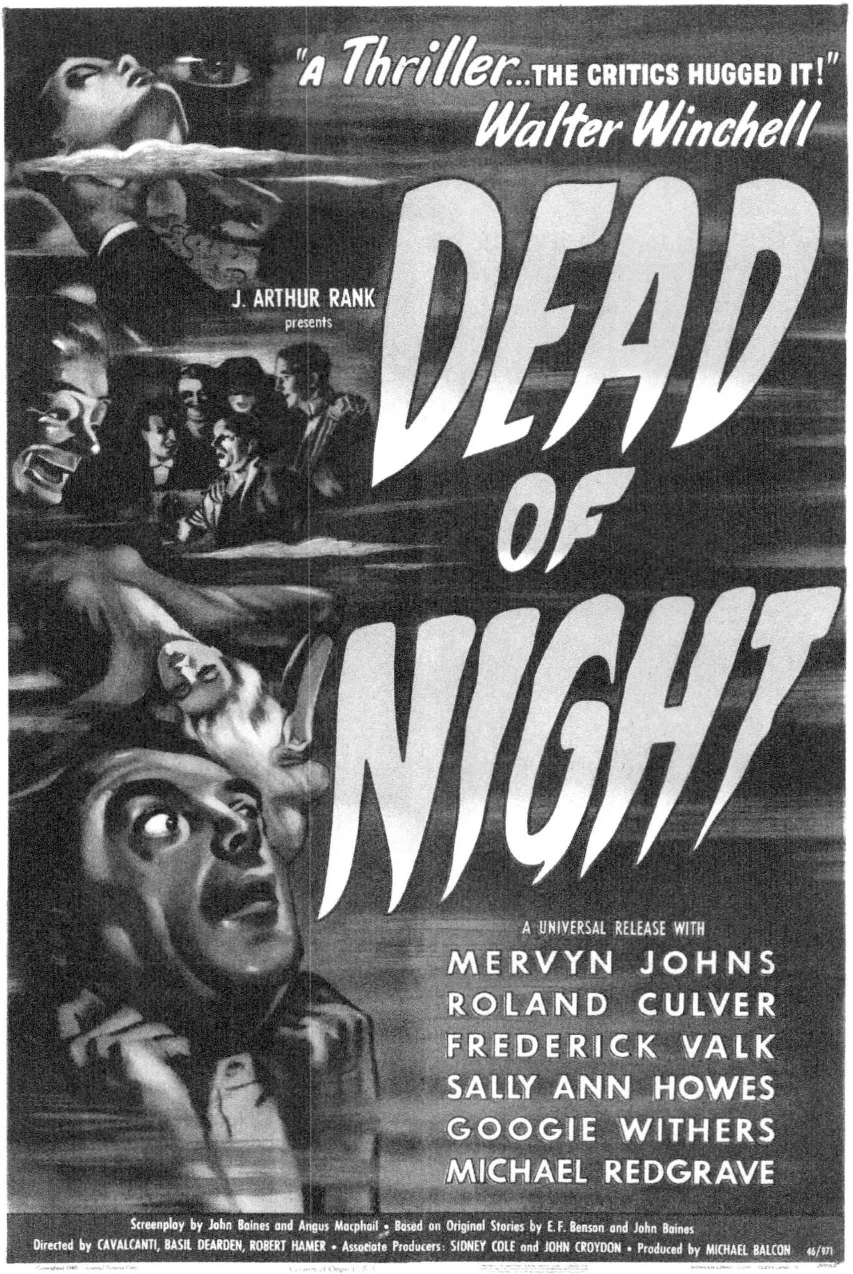
"A Thriller...THE CRITICS HUGGED IT!"
Walter Winchell
J. ARTHUR RANK
presents
DEAD OF NIGHT
A UNIVERSAL RELEASE WITH
MERVYN JOHNS
ROLAND CULVER
FREDERICK VALK
SALLY ANN HOWES
GOOGIE WITHERS
MICHAEL REDGRAVE
Screenplay by John Baines and Angus Macphail • Based on Original Stories by E. F. Benson and John Baines
Directed by CAVALCANTI, BASIL DEARDEN, ROBERT HAMER • Associate Producers: SIDNEY COLE and JOHN CROYDON • Produced by MICHAEL BALCON
46/971

CHAPTER 11

DEAD OF NIGHT (1945)

Michael Redgrave in Dead of Night *(1945)*

Directed by: Alberto Cavalcanti, Charles Crichton, Basil Dearden and Robert Hamer.

Written by: John Baines (screenplay and original story), Angus MacPhail (screenplay and original story), T.E.B. Clarke (additional dialogue), H.G. Wells (original story) and E.F. Benson (original story).

Starring: Mervyn Johns, Roland Culver, Frederick Valk, Sally Ann Howes, Googie Withers, Michael Redgrave and more.

Studio: Ealing Studios.

JUST ROOM FOR ONE MORE FILM INSIDE

I FIRST HEARD/read about this one in Alan Frank's superlative *Horror Films* tome in the late 1970s. It sounded very interesting indeed to a horror-obsessed ten-year-old: described by Frank as "an unrestrained assault" on susceptible wartime cinema audiences, the film is an anthology of eerie tales – and I loved anthologies, whether on TV (*Night Gallery*), comics (DC's great output in the '70s), or film (Amicus horrors such as *The House That Dripped Blood* and *Asylum* I'd seen at that point) so it was right up my dark alley!

I finally saw the film many years later, in 1985 on BBC2 late on a Saturday night. It wasn't quite the spine-chilling masterpiece Frank had led me to believe it was and it is definitely a film where the whole is more than the sum of its parts – but it works. I wouldn't say it was on a par with the Amicus anthologies but it ranks quite highly in 1940s horror and is light years ahead of similar staid and stuffy fare from the same period like *The Halfway House* and *Three Cases of Murder* (which has one great story and the rest a waste of time).

Dead of Night begins with architect Walter Craig (Mervyn Johns) visiting Pilgrim's Farm and meeting a bunch of people who he recognises. He soon realises they have all appeared in a recurring dream he has had for several weeks, and he can predict what each person is going to say and do before they say and do it...

The stories come as each guest relates their own tale of the supernatural. First up is the story of Hugh Grainger (Antony Baird), a racing driver who has a spooky experience of premonition when he gets up from his isolated hospital bed one evening to see it's suddenly daytime outside, and below is an old-fashioned hearse and driver (Miles Malleson) who looks up and says "Just room for one more inside, sir!". Upon leaving hospital, Grainger stops himself from boarding a bus where the conductor is the same man as the hearse driver, and is saying the same thing! Shortly after, the bus crashes...

This opening segment is short and to the point, and typical of the gentle "horror" of the film. More spooky than terrifying, the bit where Grainger's hospital radio suddenly stops playing 1940s music as he approaches his curtained window, and the camera closes in on the curtains, making the viewer think they are going to see something dreadful when those curtains are opened, is brilliantly eerie. Nice, but not overly convincing, model work during the bus crash sequence too.

The second story is the best, in my opinion, and has Sally Ann Howes as Sally O'Hara, a teenage girl who is attending a Christmas party for kids at a large country house. During a game of "Sardines" (basically "Hide and Seek" for posh people), Sally and a boy called Jimmy huddle up together and he relates the spine-chilling yarn of how the house was inhabited by an evil bitch who hated her younger brother, to the extent she ended up killing him.

Sally ends up in a secluded part of the large house, where she comforts a crying young boy – who turns out to the ghost of the aforementioned murder victim! Just writing this is sending the shivers up my spine, and director (Alberto) Cavalcanti never puts a foot wrong. A nice, scary little tale which doesn't outstay its welcome, this is probably the most underrated segment in any British anthology horror film.

Sally Ann Howes in Dead of Night *(1945)*

The third story is the weakest of the five. It's okay, but nothing special and a bit less subtlety would have worked better here. Ralph Michael and Googie Withers play a couple who buy a mirror which turns out to be haunted, and its ghostly unseen occupant ends up possessing Michael. Some nice moments where we see the reflection in the mirror shows a different room from a different time, but there are no real shocks or surprises and the haunted mirror idea would be done much better in Amicus' *From Beyond the Grave* (1974).

The fourth story is a weird deadpan comedy, but despite the fact it's nothing like the other stories it still fits in with the film as a whole. Basil Radford and Naunton Wayne play a couple of frankly odd golf enthusiasts called Parratt and Potter. They are both in love with the same girl, in a very understated English gentlemanly way, and decide to play a game of their favourite sport in order to decide who gets her. The caddish Parratt cheats and Potter drowns himself in a suitably genteel and English sort of way – but returns as a ghost. The humour in this one is actually funny (for example, the ghostly Potter giving the outraged Parratt an ultimatum to, not give up the girl, as we expect but to give up golf!) but the Americans didn't think so, and this and the spine-chilling "Christmas Party" story were cut out when the film was released over there.

Naunton Wayne, Peggy Bryan and Basil Radford in Dead of Night *(1945)*

The final segment is the most widely regarded and hyped-up. It's also the most overrated. The idea of a ventriloquist tormented and haunted by his evil dummy, which is somehow 'alive', is a good one but this story is too subtle. There are no scenes of the dummy moving or talking by itself – there's a fade-to-black scene where it looks as if the dummy may speak, but it doesn't – and as far as I'm concerned, this story is a chance that was thrown away. It's interesting and well-acted but it's a story about a ventriloquist who is mentally ill and has no real supernatural element.

Fortunately, *Dead of Night* ends on a high note. No sooner has Craig suddenly woken up and realised it was all a dream, than the opening of the film is replayed over the closing credits and we realise everything that has happened will happen again – unless it's all another dream? This ending is prefaced by a very effecting 'nightmare' sequence in which Craig is assaulted by characters, scenes and settings from the previous five stories, culminating in the poor sod trapped in a cell with Hugo, which does actually come to life here, advancing on the hapless architect and strangling him. This film, despite its success, didn't advance the cause for British horror films and that was largely it until Hammer horror in the 1950s.

Michael Redgrave in Dead of Night *(1945)*

CREATURE FROM THE BLACK LAGOON
Starring
RICHARD CARLSON · JULIA ADAMS
with RICHARD DENNING · ANTONIO MORENO · NESTOR PAIVA · WHIT BISSELL
DIRECTED BY JACK ARNOLD · SCREENPLAY BY HARRY ESSEX AND ARTHUR ROSS · PRODUCED BY WILLIAM ALLAND · A UNIVERSAL-INTERNATIONAL PICTURE
Universal International

CHAPTER 12

CREATURE FROM THE BLACK LAGOON (1954)
and
REVENGE OF THE CREATURE (1955)
THE CREATURE WALKS AMONG US (1956)

Creature from the Black Lagoon *artwork by Allen Koszowski*

CREATURE FROM THE BLACK LAGOON (1954):

Directed by: Jack Arnold.

Written by: Harry Essex (screenplay), Arthur A. Ross (screenplay), Maurice Zimm (story by) and William Alland (idea).

Starring: Richard Carlson, Julie Adams, Richard Denning, Antonio Moreno, Nestor Paiva, Whit Bissell and more.

Studio: Universal International Pictures (UI).

REVENGE OF THE CREATURE (1955):

Directed by: Jack Arnold.

Written by: William Alland (story) and Martin Berkeley (screenplay).

Starring: John Agar, Lori Nelson, John Bromfield, Nestor Paiva, Grandon Rhodes, Dave Willock and more.

Studio: Universal International Pictures (UI).

THE CREATURE WALKS AMONG US (1956):

Directed by: John Sherwood.

Written by: Arthur A. Ross (story and screenplay).

Starring: Jeff Morrow, Rex Reason, Leigh Snowden, Gregg Palmer, Maurice Manson, James Rawley and more.

Studio: Universal International Pictures (UI).

COME ON IN, THE WATER'S RED

I'VE ALWAYS HAD a soft spot for these films which signify the end of the run of the classic Universal Monsters, the Creature being in the same category as Dracula, the Frankenstein Monster, the Mummy, the Invisible Man and the Wolf Man. The Creature aka the Gill Man is a walking coelacanth, a relic from a bygone age who is still happily swimming about in a lagoon in the Amazon when the first film gets under way.

Creature from the Black Lagoon (1954) is a great film. I like the watery setting, which is odd as I think *Jaws* (1975) isn't all that great and off the top of my head, I can't think of any other horror/SF films with an aquatic theme that are very good – I might recollect some by the end of this article, but at the present time, it's only these three Creature films that really stand out when it comes to threats of the deep. The watery setting was a departure for director Jack Arnold, as he seemed to favour a desert setting in films like *It Came from Outer Space* (1953) and *Tarantula* (1955).

An expedition to the Amazon falls foul, not of late deliveries and unreasonable postage charges, but of a strange half-man/half-fish creature that stalks the party and their boat, remaining out of sight until it catches a fishy eyeful of the attractive young woman of the team Kay (Julia Adams). Naturally, the Creature is smitten and though other members of the team get mauled and sliced by the scaly Devonian, it makes off with Kay at the conclusion, carrying her off to his underwater grotto for unknown porpoises, before getting a bellyful of harpoons and sinking to his apparent death (the same shot of the dying Creature is reused at the end of the second film).

Other, perhaps more pretentious, film critics can find all sorts of hidden meanings and sub(ho-ho)texts lurking beneath the surface, but for me, it's just a straightforward 'monster on the loose in its native environment' film. It's a classic, and it made enough of a splash with receptive cinema goers to warrant two sequels, not to mention lots of associated merchandise (I have a little rubber Creature, bought from my local Post Office in 2007!).

Revenge of the Creature followed in 1955, also directed by Arnold. Like the first film, this was shot in 3D during the 3D boom of the 1950s and sees a slightly redesigned Creature (his eyes bulge noticeably here) being captured from his Amazon environment and taken to an Oceanarium park in Florida. Needless to say, it escapes before long and wreaks havoc in its pursuit of the obligatory sexy female scientist Helen (Lori Nelson).

This was the first of the Creature films I ever saw, back in the late '70s in the Friday night film slot, and I loved it. I spent the first half of the film waiting for the scene where the Creature overturns a car, which had become immortalized on one of the *You'll Die Laughing* bubblegum cards of the '70s which generally had stills from the Universal films accompanied by a jokey caption.

The location for the film's Oceanarium scenes was Marineland in Florida, the world's first such theme park, and the scenes where the Creature escapes and the crowds frantically try to get away have a feeling of reality absent from the other two entries which are set generally in the faraway Amazon and involve nobody but the relatively small casts. Once free, the Creature becomes obsessed with Helen, attacking her dog in Helen's own house and later, crashing into a restaurant and making off with the heroine, before being killed in a hail of bullets. Again, a very enjoyable entry. The scenes in the real-life Marineland give us an authentic taste of America at the time and the film has all the elements that made these '50s Universal SF/horrors so memorable, right down to the great score by Herman Stein which is playing in my head as I type this!

Revenge of the Creature *(1955)*

The Creature Walks Among Us (1956) is the last outing for the Gill Man and a sad and disturbing end it is too. It's also probably the best of the three films, though it wouldn't work as well if you hadn't seen the first two films beforehand. The Creature is captured again (despite having being killed at the end of the previous movie) and is badly burned as a result. This is partly its own stupid fault, as it picks up and pours a large can of gasoline over itself! This is a great invitation for one of the team to throw a lighted torch at it and they duly oblige.

Surviving the fire, the Creatures scales are burned off and its gills no longer function. Its eyes change too, becoming more human-like. The scenes where the Creature's bandages are removed from its face are genuinely disturbing and frightening – it now looks a bit more mammalian and less fish-like and it looks at the gaping scientists in a scene that equals the creepy visage of Bela Lugosi's Frankenstein's Monster grinning, at the conclusion of *Frankenstein Meets the Wolf Man* (1943)!

Headlining the cast here are Rex Reason and Jeff Morrow (who also appeared in Universal's SF opus *This Island Earth* a year earlier) and this film scores over the other two as the characters are more interesting. Morrow (try and recognise him without the oversized head he sported in the earlier SF film!) plays William Barton, the scientist who wants to capture the Creature and it soon becomes apparent he's not playing with a full set of flippers, especially when it comes to matters involving his wife Marcia (Leigh Snowden). Barton is insanely jealous and paranoid if anyone even looks at Marcia and it all ends in murder, with him intending to blame the Creature for the death of Jed (Gregg Palmer), whom he kills because of this jealousy involving his wife.

Once up and about, the transformed clothing-wearing Creature looks nothing like it did before and has put on a few stone in weight in the process. Shuffling about mindlessly in an outdoor pen and staring longingly at the ocean it can no longer survive in, the Creature is a tragic figure. Once enraged however, its colossal strength becomes clear and it kills Barton, demolishing a brick wall and an electrified fence, as well as most of Barton's house in the process! The final shots show the Creature overcome by its natural desire to be in its familiar environment and it shuffles off to certain death in the ocean...

I like to think though that maybe it survived. This is the world of cinema after all. However, no further sequels were forthcoming and it was (bar appearances in shows like *The Munsters, Buffy the Vampire Slayer* and, bizarrely, *The A-Team*!) the end for the aquatic horror and the classic run of Universal monster movies too.

Oh, and I've just recalled another horror/SF film with an aquatic theme that is good – *Piranha* (1978).

The FANTASTIC Night Of TERROR That Menaced The Fate Of The World!
INVASION FROM OUTER SPACE!... SIGHTS TOO WEIRD TO IMAGINE! DESTRUCTION TOO MONSTROUS TO ESCAPE!
"DEVIL GIRL FROM MARS"
starring Hugh McDermott · Hazel Court · Peter Reynolds · Adrienne Corri
Joseph Tomelty · Sophie Stewart · John Laurie · Patricia Laffan · Directed by David MacDonald
Produced by Edward J. Danziger & Harry Lee Danziger · A Spartan Release

CHAPTER 13
DEVIL GIRL FROM MARS (1954)

Patricia Laffan stars in Devil Girl from Mars *(1954)*

Directed by: David MacDonald.

Written by: John C. Mather (play) and James Eastwood (play and screenplay).

Starring: Hugh McDermott, Hazel Court, Peter Reynolds, Adrienne Corri, Joseph Tomelty, Patricia Laffan and more.

Studio: Danziger Productions Ltd.

DEVIL WITH A LEATHER DRESS ON

THIS IS A nice little British effort, directed by David MacDonald. It's set in and around a Scottish pub in the middle of nowhere, with a beleaguered bunch of characters who encounter a female from the red planet, who has come to Earth for that old standby of wanting to bring human males back to Mars for population purposes. The female in question is called Nyah (Patricia Laffan) and she has brought a destructive robot called Chani with her.

Nyah is a sexy-looking character – clad in a leather cape, with a leather mini-skirted dress, sheer black tights and boots, she's quite the Martian dominatrix and it's only the leather swimming cap she wears that lets her sartorial sexiness down. The robot is quite a nice design but it's used sparingly.

The film gathers together its bunch of characters in the pub The Bonnie Prince Charlie: we have a kid (Tommy [Anthony Richmond]), an escaped convict (Albert [Peter Reynolds]), the barmaid who is also the convict's girlfriend (Doris [Adrienne Corri]), the elderly couple who run the pub (Mr. and Mrs. Jamieson [John Laurie and Sophie Stewart]), a grumpy old Professor (Arnold [Joseph Tomelty]), a sexy woman (Ellen [Hazel Court]), and the hero (Michael [Hugh McDermott]). Oh, and the rather simple handyman David (James Edmond) who gets vaporised early on by Nyah.

The interactions between the assembled group as are you would expect – the attractive woman falls for the hero, reporter Michael Carter, and the convict briefly establishes a bond with the kid, and his former love the barmaid, before atoning for his crime and being the one who ends up sacrificing himself when he boards Nyah's ship to return with her to Mars, but blows it up! All that's missing is a sceptical priest.

The film has a reputation as a turkey but this is undeserved. Nice location, nice sets, a great spaceship, nice robot, decent effects, good cast and topping it all off, the uptight tights-wearing villain of the piece who despite her frosty demeanour must have been quietly looking forward to "experimenting" with an Earthman when back home! Once the ship has blown up, the surviving cast members all gather round the bar for a wee drink! A nice touch to end on.

One bit of interesting trivia: the Sound Editor on the film was a gentleman by the name of Gerry/Gerald Anderson. Maybe this film inspired him to create the SF television shows that would become hugely popular in the decades to come.

Patricia Laffan in Devil Girl from Mars *(1954)*

The screen's master of the WEIRD...
IN HIS NEWEST and MOST DARING
SHOCKER!
BELA LUGOSI
More horrifying than "DRACULA" "FRANKENSTEIN"
IT'LL MAKE YOUR SKIN CRAWL!
BRIDE OF THE MONSTER
TOR JOHNSON · TONY McCOY
LORETTA KING · HARVEY DUNN
EDWARD D. WOOD, Jr.
EDWARD D. WOOD, Jr. and ALEX GORDON
DONALD McCOY · TONY McCOY

CHAPTER 14

BRIDE OF THE MONSTER (1955)

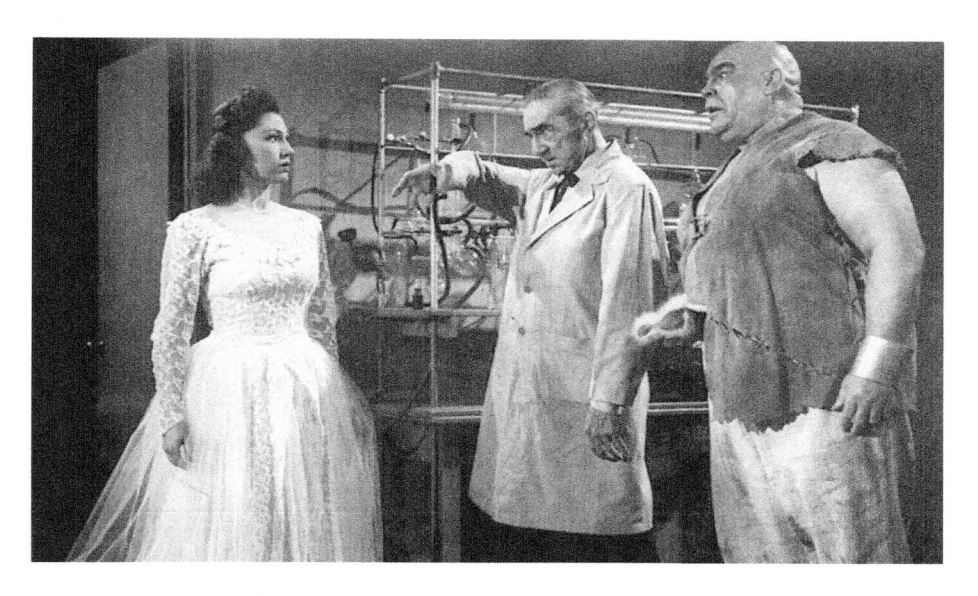

Loretta King, Bela Lugosi and Tor Johnson in
Bride of the Monster *(1955)*

Directed by: Edward D. Wood Jr.

Written by Edward D. Wood Jr. (original story and screenplay) and Alex Gordon (original story and screenplay).

Starring: Bela Lugosi, Tor Johnson, Tony McCoy, Loretta King, Harvey B. Dunn, George Becwar and more.

Studio: Rolling M. Productions.

ATOMIC DISASTER

WHO WOULD HAVE believed that the (in)famous *Plan 9 from Outer Space*, directed by the legendary Ed Wood, would turn out to be so bad? Regarded as an all-time 'golden turkey' (a film so bad, it's enjoyably good), the film is merely bad with hardly any enjoyment to be had – yes, the actors are bad but nothing particularly stands out; yes, the sets are shit but there has to be more to a film than just sets, fine or otherwise (hello, *Dracula* 1958!); yes, the dialogue is dire but not really juicy or particularly quotable. Basically, the film is a waste of time for all the wrong reasons (the reconstructions in 1994's *Ed Wood* were far better and funnier), unlike Wood's earlier *Bride of the Monster* which is a waste of time for all the right ones.

Edward D. Wood Jr. was a writer, producer, actor and director in Hollywood in the 1950s and was crap in all four capacities. Possessing an almost backward childish optimism and faith in his own abilities, he gathered together the naffest casts and crews of the time and sloppily 'directed' them to produce what in his eyes were masterpieces, but to anyone else was utter rubbish. I was able to watch about ten minutes of Wood's *Glen or Glenda* before being bored rigid (once you've seen the bits with Bela Lugosi, there's nothing else worthy viewing) and fast-forwarding through the rest. Other Wood efforts like *Plan 9...* and *Jail Bait* (1954) are similarly unrewarding. Films such as *Robot Monster* (directed by Phil Tucker and *not* Wood, incidentally) are far better to watch with some mates, for a merry night of laughter and drink. Which leads me to *Bride of the Monster*.

Bride of the Monster (1955) is watchable and FUN, unlike the lame *Plan 9...* Bela Lugosi plays Dr. Eric Vornoff, a mad scientist living in a creepy and isolated old house in the woods. Vornoff is obsessed with creating a race of atomic-powered supermen, and his only result to date is Lobo, played by Swedish wrestler Tor Johnson. Obviously with Lugosi well past his acting prime, the performances in the film aren't stellar and neither are the sets and effects (according to Alan Frank in his *Horror Films*, the machine Vornoff uses to carry out his experiments was a cheap photograph enlarger!). The stationary giant octopus, which Lugosi gleefully uses to dispose of snoopers is quite hilarious, as its victims have to manipulate the tentacles of the totally immobile prop around themselves, all the time screaming hammily for several minutes!

In one sequence Lugosi is called upon to deliver an impassioned speech, and some critics have speculated that the speech was a reference to Wood himself, left out in the cold in Hollywood and plotting his major comeback. This scene is a good example of Wood's jumbled attempts at writing dialogue, as Vornoff's rant comes to a limp end with the words, "Here, in this forsaken jungle hell, I have proved that I am... alright!" The rest of the acting is amateurish, but the film (again, unlike the dreary *Plan 9...*) is never boring and despite the fact it's clearly a low-rent turkey, it is quite an engaging little picture.

The film concludes with Vornoff being subjected to his own

machine, which has the effect of making him bigger and stronger than Lobo – crashing out of the house and into the swamps, Lugosi is knocked off his feet by a huge polystyrene boulder which sends him hurtling into the waiting tentacles of his beloved octopus! Not long after, there's an atomic explosion – which leaves the area noticeably undamaged! – and a clichéd wrap-up line about Lugosi tampering with stuff he shouldn't have done. The End.

Bride of the Monster incredibly took two years to complete, and was a sad end for the once-great Lugosi. Though he appeared in *Plan 9...* it was footage that had been filmed earlier, very brief and with no dialogue. So, *Bride...* was his filmic swan song.

Though definitely a poor film in all important respects, *Bride of the Monster* is, curiously, not really a bad one.

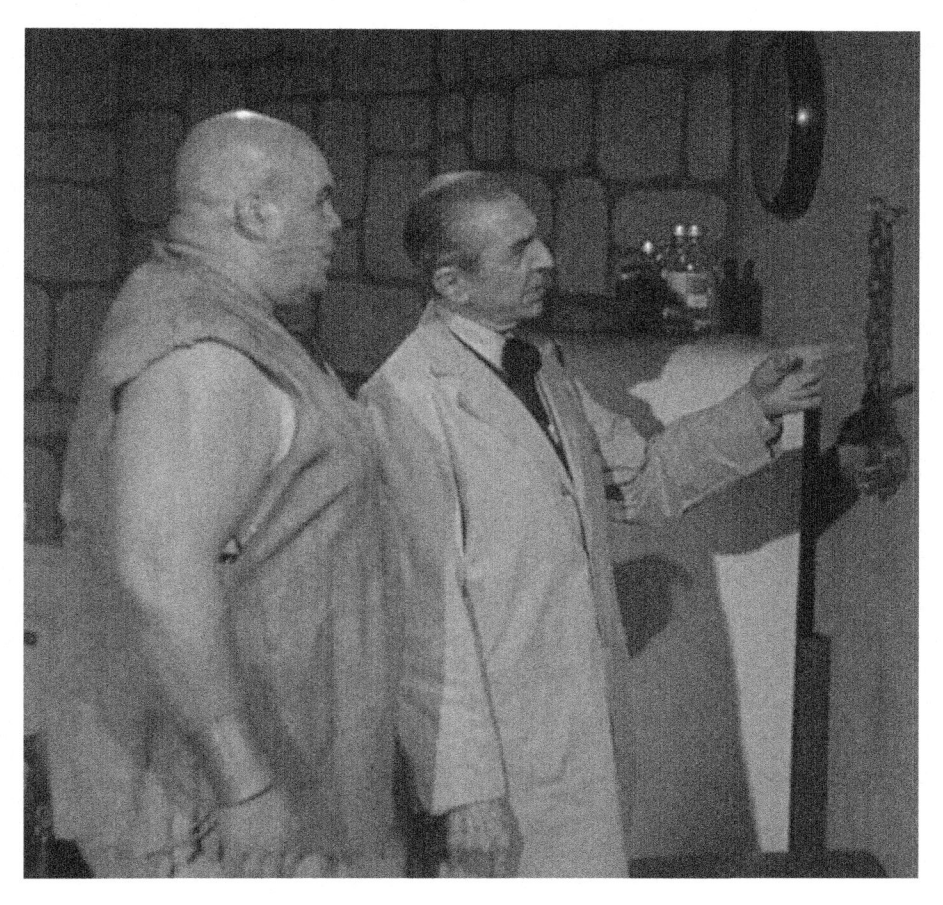

Tor Johnson and Bela Lugosi in Bride of the Monster *(1955)*

THE CREATURE CREATED BY MAN AND FORGOTTEN BY NATURE.
"THE CURSE OF FRANKENSTEIN"
will haunt you forever!
ALL NEW AND NEVER DARED BEFORE!
PLEASE TRY NOT TO FAINT. Not recommended for people of nervous disposition.
Presented in WARNERCOLOR by WARNER BROS.
PETER CUSHING · HAZEL COURT · ROBERT URQUHART AND CHRISTOPHER LEE
SCREEN PLAY BY JIMMY SAGSTER DIRECTED BY TERENCE FISHER EXECUTIVE PRODUCER MICHAEL CARRERAS

CHAPTER 15

THE CURSE OF FRANKENSTEIN (1957)
and
THE REVENGE OF FRANKENSTEIN (1958)
THE EVIL OF FRANKENSTEIN (1964)
FRANKENSTEIN CREATED WOMAN (1967)
FRANKENSTEIN MUST BE DESTROYED (1969)
THE HORROR OF FRANKENSTEIN (1970)
FRANKENSTEIN AND THE MONSTER FROM HELL (1974)

Christopher Lee as The Creature in
The Curse of Frankenstein *(1957)*

THE CURSE OF FRANKENSTEIN (1957):

Directed by: Terence Fisher.

Written by: Jimmy Sangster (screenplay) and Mary Shelley (based on the classic story by).

Starring: Peter Cushing, Hazel Court, Robert Urquhart, Christopher Lee, Melvyn Hayes, Valerie Gaunt and more.

Studio: Hammer Films.

THE REVENGE OF FRANKENSTEIN (1958):

Directed by: Terence Fisher.

Written by: Jimmy Sangster (screenplay), Hurford Janes (additional dialogue) and George Baxt (uncredited).

Starring: Peter Cushing, Francis Matthews, Eunice Gayson, Michael Gwynn, John Welsh, Lionel Jeffries and more.

Studio: Hammer Films.

THE EVIL OF FRANKENSTEIN (1964):

Directed by: Freddie Francis.

Written by: Anthony Hinds (screenplay, as John Elder).

Starring: Peter Cushing, Peter Woodthorpe, Duncan Lamont, Sandor Elès, Katy Wild, David Hutcheson and more.

Studio: Hammer Films.

FRANKENSTEIN CREATED WOMAN (1967):

Directed by: Terence Fisher.

Written by: Anthony Hinds (screenplay, as John Elder).

Starring: Peter Cushing, Susan Denberg, Thorley Walters, Robert Morris, Duncan Lamont, Peter Blythe and more.

Studio: Hammer Films.

FRANKENSTEIN MUST BE DESTROYED (1969):

Directed by: Terence Fisher.

Written by: Bert Batt (screenplay and from an original story by) and Anthony Nelson Keys (from an original story by).

Starring: Peter Cushing, Veronica Carlson, Freddie Jones, Simon Ward, Thorley Walters, Maxine Audley and more.

Studio: Hammer Films.

THE HORROR OF FRANKENSTEIN (1970):

Directed by: Jimmy Sangster.

Written by: Jeremy Burnham (screenplay), Jimmy Sangster (screenplay) and Mary Shelley (based on the characters created by).

Starring: Ralph Bates, Kate O'Mara, Veronica Carlson, Dennis Price, Jon Finch, Bernard Archard and more.

Studio: Hammer Films.

FRANKENSTEIN AND THE MONSTER FROM HELL (1974):

Directed by Terence Fisher.

Written by: Anthony Hinds (screenplay, as John Elder).

Starring: Peter Cushing, Shane Briant, Madeline Smith, David Prowse, John Stratton, Michael Ward and more.

Studio: Hammer Films.

THIS CHAPTER WILL HAUNT YOU FOREVER!

THE CURSE OF Frankenstein (1957) changed the face of horror cinema forever. Up until then, most cinematic horror films had been black and white, with an emphasis away from blood and gore. This film, which put Hammer films well and truly on the map, changed all that by concentrating on the blood (though not as much as critics made out at the time – the film is relatively bloodless, even without comparison to the gorier films of the '60s and '70s).

The film is told in flashback and recounts how Baron Victor Frankenstein (Peter Cushing), with his tutor Paul (Robert Urquhart) becomes obsessed with giving life to the dead and then, creating life. The film has a stately pace but it never becomes boring and the moment The Creature (Christopher Lee) is revealed in all its horrific glory is a real eye-opener – I first saw this film in 1979, at the age of 12, and I was prepared for what was to come as I was already a right little horror swot, with my collections of *House of Hammer* and *Quasimodo's Monster Magazine* and the Alan Frank *Horror Movies* and *Horror Films* books that I loved so much (so did the kids at school – I was always taking them there and showing them off). I also had a copy of Dennis Gifford's *A Pictorial History of Horror Movies* but I thought it was a bit rubbish even then – Mr. Gifford's jokey writing style was poor compared to Mr. Frank's and he was obsessed with black and white films, plus (and I realise I'm in a minority here of one) I wasn't really impressed by the photos in the book either. Though I did like the cover! Anyway, there was a big difference between seeing Chris Lee's hideous visage as The Creature in black and white photos in books and mags and seeing it on the screen – the moment where the camera moves in to show the bandaged monster, teetering slightly, then reaching up to tear the wrappings from its face, followed by a zoom in as The Creature's one good eye fixes on Frankenstein, is a stand-out moment in horror cinema. The subsequent strangling of the Baron by his creation is made even more horrible by the sight of The Creature's truly ghastly features contorted in an attempted grin, showing its hideously rotted teeth!

From this point on, the film maintains its grip and ends with The Creature falling into a vat of acid, Frankenstein's flashback/story being disbelieved, and the Baron being led to the guillotine. I wonder what happened next?

The Revenge of Frankenstein showed us, following very quickly in 1958. This film is the weakest of the series, but it's still a great film. Frankenstein escapes execution with the help of his previously-unseen assistants and sets up a medical practice in a nearby town where he attracts the attention of a young medical man (played by Francis Matthews) who wants to be his assistant – and not in the hospital either! The monster here is basically an ordinary-looking feller who ends up injured after being bashed about and becomes a bit twisted – literally. He also turns to cannibalism, though this being 1958 that element is very subtle. The end of the film is anything but, as Frankenstein is beaten to death by the inmates at the hospital where he's been working (they find out who he is and what he's been doing with their discarded body parts) and his brain is transplanted by Matthews into an identical body!

Peter Cushing and Francis Matthews in
The Revenge of Frankenstein *(1958)*

The Evil of Frankenstein (1964) ignores the continuity of the two previous films, so perhaps it should be regarded as an 'alternate universe' version. This Frankenstein (who, despite the film's title, is an old softy) has created life in the form of a Creature (Kiwi Kingston) that's meant to look like the old Universal Monster but I don't see much of a resemblance frankly. The Creature escapes into the mountains and gets shot, and that seems to be that. Except that Frankenstein and his assistant Hans (Sandor Elès) decide to return to the castle, expecting it to be fully furnished. Unfortunately, its been gutted by the Burgomaster and the Chief of Police, and Frankenstein himself is equally gutted – I love the bit where the Baron contemptuously kicks a rock out of the way as he strides towards his ruined hallway – only a truly great actor like Cushing could make such a simple act so entertaining and funny!

The Creature is found in a block of ice (a nice tribute to the old Universal horrors) but once revived, it doesn't say or do much, until it falls under the spell of a sinister hypnotist called Zoltan (Peter

Woodthorpe) who uses it to steal gold and kill the Burgomaster. Frankenstein isn't pleased when he finds out, Zoltan is kicked out on his ear and subsequently stabbed to death by The Creature, and the film ends with a rousing fire engulfing the castle and presumably both Frankenstein and his creation perish – but not for long, in the former's case. *Evil...* is an entertaining film but not one of the best of the series, though it's an improvement on its predecessor.

Frankenstein Created Woman (1967) is a fairly low-key film, though it deserves acclaim for being so different – Frankenstein seems to take a back seat in this one, and the 'Monster' is certainly unusual. *Frankenstein Created Woman* deserves recognition for its sheer off-the-wallness – who'd have guessed we'd see a Frankenstein's Monster wearing striped tights and a dress? But it isn't one of the better entries in the series. Soul transference is the theme here, with Frankenstein and his bumbling assistant Hertz (Thorley Walters) 'transplanting' the soul of a wrongly-beheaded feller called Hans (Robert Morris) into the body of his girlfriend Christina (Susan Denberg), who then uses her/his feminine wiles to kill the three top-hatted work-shy toffs who committed the murder that Hans was executed for in the first place.

The film is enjoyable but again, not one of the best and it ends in a strange fashion with Christina/Hans throwing her/himself into a river, while Frankenstein looks on, then walks sadly away.

Frankenstein Must be Destroyed (1969) is my favourite of the series. This stands head and shoulders above most other Hammer horrors, and is on a par with *Scars of Dracula* and *The Devil Rides Out* (see other chapters).

There's so much that's great about this one – a fantastic cast, a lively intro showing Frankenstein slicing a passerby's head off with a scythe then terrifying a tramp who breaks into the abandoned house that the Baron has been using as his lair, and perhaps best of all, a truly magnificent script – I'll just mention the 'lapels' speech and leave it at that.

Frankenstein is a right evil swine in this one – apart from murder, he ends up blackmailing a young couple into helping him, delights in the fact that the young man Karl (Simon Ward) has inadvertently committed murder, and later attempts to ravish Karl's fiancée Anna (Veronica Carlson). Most Hammer fans have it that the Baron actually rapes her but I'm not so sure as his trouser remain on, it is over in seconds, and Anna seems relatively unaffected the next day. The film revolves around brain transplants and the 'Monster' is Freddie Jones with a bald and horribly scarred bonce! Jones' performance is sublime and when I first saw this one as a very little kid in the mid-'70s, I got a bit confused – the fact the Baron wears a horrible bald-headed latex mask to scare that tramp off at the beginning had me thinking that it was the same bald-headed character I'd seen in stills (I'd totally forgotten that Frankenstein whips that mask off to reveal his own features), who comes later on in the film!

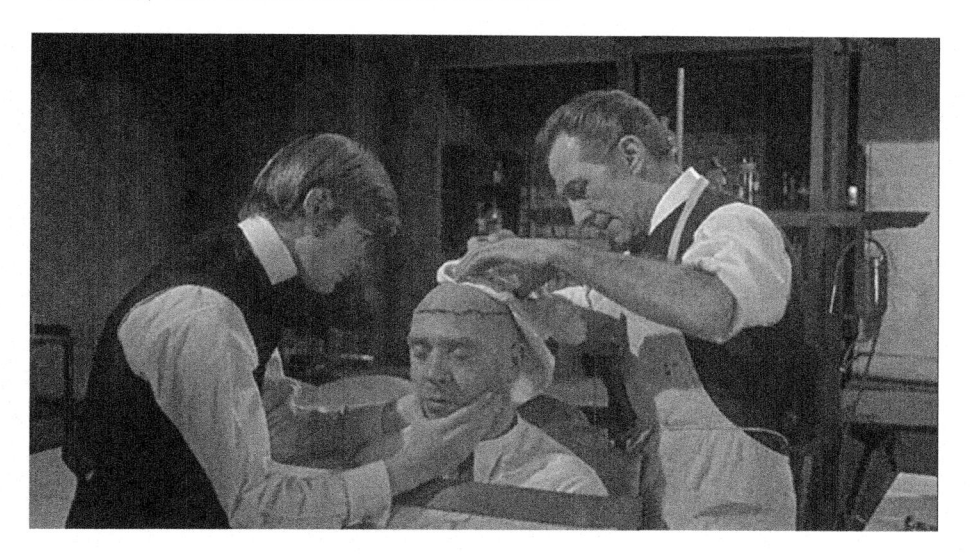

Simon Ward, Freddie Jones and Peter Cushing in
Frankenstein Must Be Destroyed *(1969)*

By the end anyway, everyone is dead or about to die and the closing credits run over a shot of a blazing mansion. Strangely, most of the credits appear at the end of the film rather than at the beginning. Anyway, this film is definitely the best of the series and a good intro if you haven't seen the first one.

The Horror of Frankenstein was made back-to-back with the equally unloved in some quarters *Scars of Dracula* from 1970, and is just as entertaining. The film has a great cast which includes Ralph Bates as Baron Frankenstein (Hammer considered Peter Cushing to be too old at the time and were seeking to replace him), as well as Dennis Price, Bernard Archard, Veronica Carlson and Kate O'Mara, with Dave Prowse as The Monster.

The film starts the story again from scratch so it's the only example of a Hammer reboot, and it works very well. The sets are a bit cheap, but so what? The film is fun, with a nice vein of black comedy running through it – I love the bit where Frankenstein sits down to dinner with his prospective fiancée Elizabeth (Carlson) and prospective father-in-law (Archard) and sees in his imagination a big number 1 on his host's forehead (Frankenstein has the parts of his creation all numbered and the brain is number 1)!

The Monster is introduced quite late in the film but, although not speaking or even grunting at all, it still has a sinister presence and makes short work of villagers with an axe, stopping off to have a quick bite of a dead bird!

When The Monster's end comes, it's both unexpected and a bit obvious, though it's a pity in a way they didn't do a sequel as Bates is excellent in the role.

Kate O'Mara in The Horror of Frankenstein *(1970)*

Though Ralph Bates didn't return, Dave Prowse did. This time, Prowse's creation is a horrible-looking Neanderthal-type thing in *Frankenstein and the Monster from Hell* (1974). This would return Cushing to the role of Frankenstein, this time set up in a lunatic asylum that he was sentenced to life imprisonment in but has managed to take over the place, after blackmailing the director who Frankenstein knows tried to rape his own daughter.

The Monster's creation is lovingly detailed, with quite gruesome brain transplant scenes that I find almost unwatchable! Once brought to consciousness, the Monster has a penchant for playing violins and trying to shove broken glass in people's faces. It doesn't end well for the Monster either, as the other inmates rip it apart and play with its guts while it's implied that Frankenstein has finally lost his marbles. The final image of the asylum is quite chilling – Frankenstein and his unwilling assistants in their own private bubble of madness in the building, left alone to do what they want. Unfortunately, it turned out to be the last of the series but at least it went out on a high.

Shane Briant and David Prowse in
Frankenstein and the Monster from Hell *(1974)*

HORROR!
MOST TERRIFYING STORY THE SCREEN HAS EVER TOLD!
DANA ANDREWS
CURSE OF THE DEMON
SCEPTICAL? Don't make up your mind till you see this masterpiece of the macabre!
co-starring PEGGY CUMMINS and NIALL MacGINNIS
Screen Play by CHARLES BENNETT and HAL E. CHESTER · Directed by JACQUES TOURNEUR
Based on the story "Casting the Runes" by MONTAGUE R. JAMES · Produced by HAL E. CHESTER · A HAL E. CHESTER PRODUCTION · A COLUMBIA PICTURE

CHAPTER 16

NIGHT OF THE DEMON (1957)

"Night of the Demon" by Randy Broecker

Directed by: Jacques Tourneur.

Written by: Charles Bennett (screenplay), Hal E. Chester (screenplay), Montague Rhodes James (story "Casting the Runes") and Cy Endfield (uncredited).

Starring: Dana Andrews, Peggy Cummins, Niall MacGinnis, Maurice Denham, Athene Seyler, Liam Redmond and more.

Studio: Sabre Film Production.

CASTING THE RUNES AND I'LL COME TO YOU...

THIS CLASSIC BRITISH film is probably the single best 1950s film of the fantastique, apart from Hammer's *The Curse of Frankenstein*. Based on a story called 'Casting the Runes' by M.R. James (my all-time favourite author of tales of the supernatural), the film has a lot to live up to and certainly delivers the goods... in the same way that the villain of the piece delivers his pieces of paper that lead to the deaths of his enemies!

Dana Andrews stars as Dr. John Holden, an American psychologist who travels to England to investigate the death of his friend and colleague Professor Harrington (Maurice Denham), who, in the first ten minutes of the film, is graphically killed by a fearsome demon from Hell! We can see that the film isn't going to rely on the more subtle scares that James used so successfully in his tales, but that doesn't matter one jot, and outside of Hammer, it makes a glorious change to see something so graphic and 'in your face' in a '50 British film, especially so early on before the characters have had a chance to be properly introduced.

After this first visitation, the demon remains in the background for the bulk of the rest of the film, the main on-screen villainy being provided by Julian Karswell (Niall MacGinnis), the exponent of the Black Arts who 'sicced' the demon on the hapless Harrington in the first place. The glamour in the film comes from Peggy Cummins, who plays Harrington's niece, and who joins forces with Holden to discover the truth about her uncle's demise.

The tone of the film is kept deadly serious, the only bits of 'comedy' coming from a mild bout of levity on board the plane heading for London, where Holden can't get comfortable in his reclining seat, and later during a séance with a batty old coot of the sort you always get in '40s and '50s British films.

Maurice Denham in Night of the Demon *(1957)*

I first saw this classic film in the 1980 *Horror Double Bills* season on BBC2, where (along with *The Ghoul*, from 1975) it started the season off, *Radio Times* cover and article and all! I've still got that iconic issue all these years later, and can remember the giddy excitement of seeing the cover previewed in the previous edition, followed by the long wait to get that issue, and my ensuing delight at seeing the words "The films mentioned in this article which are followed by a date are all included in the *Horror Double Bills* season on BBC2" at the end of the feature!

The Saturday the season debuted saw my mates and I spending a heady day of excitement talking about the films coming that night – apparently my cousin had seen a clip from the film in a trailer which showed the demon walking through some woods whistling! Intriguing...

When it came time to watch the film at 10.30pm, my enjoyment was marred somewhat as there was a break in transmission about twenty minutes in, during which a photo from the film was shown accompanied by tuneless muzak. Generally though, I enjoyed this masterpiece and did so again when it was shown in the 1990s on Channel 4, then subsequently released on DVD. So highly regarded is the film that there's even a whole book devoted to it: *Beating the Devil* by Tony Earnshaw.

The cat and mouse game played out by Holden and Karswell involves a children's party taking a sinister turn, when Karswell, dressed as a clown, summons up a howling gale. Later, Holden breaks into Karwell's large country house and is attacked by a leopard – or, rather by a ragged piece of material covered in spots – and later, is chased through the woods by the demon in its pre-manifestation form as a sort of miniature thundercloud. The end of the film sees Karswell attempting to get away, before the now wise to the world of the supernatural Holden manages to pass back to him the slip of paper that will mean being killed by the demon. Karswell suddenly realises the paper has been slipped back to him as he prepares to leave on a train... but the demon is waiting!

Dana Andrews and Niall MacGinnis in Night of the Demon *(1957)*

We see a fair bit of the creature in the climax, apparently against the wishes of the director Jacques Tourneur (you'd think he would have learned his lesson about being *too* subtle with all those tepid Val Lewton films he was involved with) but it all works brilliantly – the demon looks almost cute, as it tears Karswell to bits in its claws, then throws what's left to the ground. The film, contrary to the James tale it is based on, isn't really scary – it won't give you a sleepless night but it will convince you you've had a horror cinema experience of the best kind.

Perhaps now would be a good time for a remake.

Dana Andrews and Peggy Cummins star in
Night of the Demon *(1957)*

WHO WILL
BE HIS
BRIDE
TONIGHT
?
HAMMER FILM PRODUCTIONS, LTD. PRESENTS
HORROR OF
DRACULA
ALL NEW! in Brilliant TECHNICOLOR!
starring PETER CUSHING · also starring MICHAEL GOUGH and MELISSA STRIBLING with CHRISTOPHER LEE as DRACULA
Screenplay by JIMMY SANGSTER · From the novel by BRAM STOKER · Directed by TERENCE FISHER · Executive producer MICHAEL CARRERAS · Associate producer ANTHONY NELSON-KEYS · Produced by ANTHONY HINDS
A UNIVERSAL-INTERNATIONAL RELEASE

CHAPTER 17

DRACULA (1958)
and
DRACULA: PRINCE OF DARKNESS (1966)
DRACULA HAS RISEN FROM THE GRAVE (1968)
TASTE THE BLOOD OF DRACULA (1970)
SCARS OF DRACULA (1970)
DRACULA A.D. 1972 (1972)
THE SATANIC RITES OF DRACULA (1973)

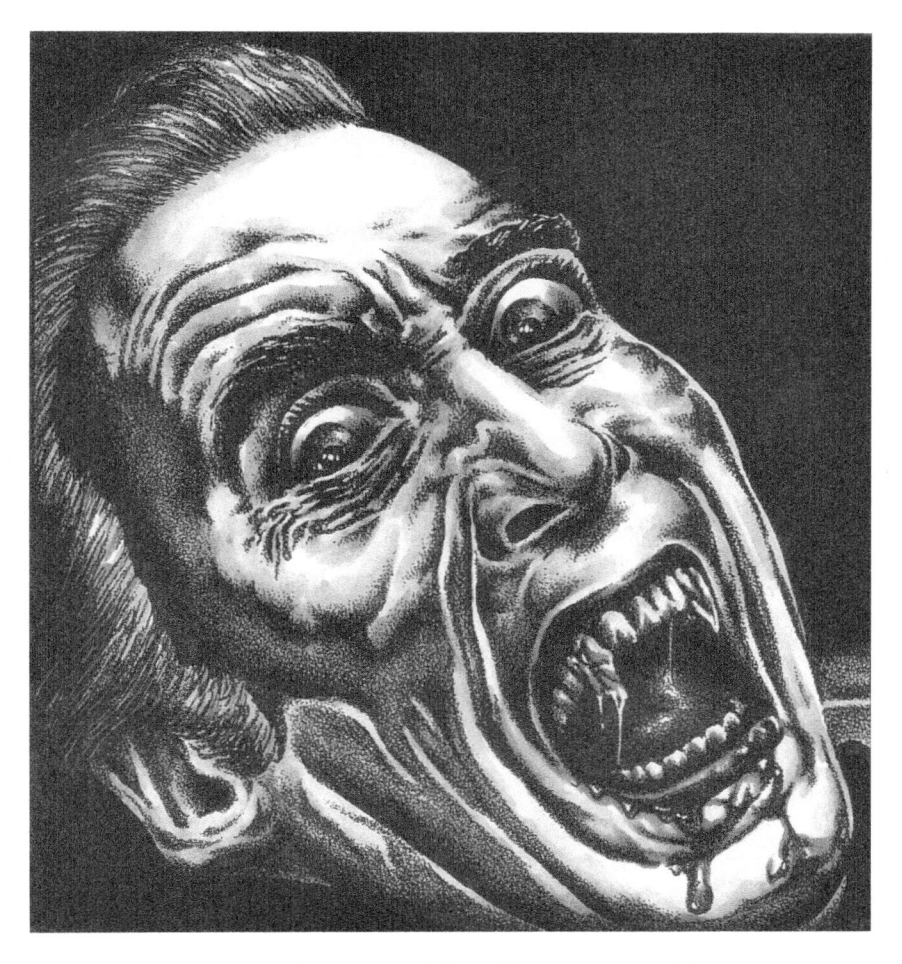

Dracula artwork by Allen Koszowski

DRACULA (1958):

Directed by: Terence Fisher.

Written by: Jimmy Sangster (screenplay) and Bram Stoker (novel).

Starring: Peter Cushing, Christopher Lee, Michael Gough, Melissa Stribling, Carol Marsh, Olga Dickie and more.

Studio: Hammer Films.

DRACULA: PRINCE OF DARKNESS (1966):

Directed by: Terence Fisher.

Written by: Jimmy Sangster (screenplay, as John Sansom), Anthony Hinds (from an idea by, as John Elder) and Bram Stoker (based on characters created by).

Starring: Christopher Lee, Barbara Shelley, Andrew Keir, Francis Matthews, Suzan Farmer, Charles "Bud" Tingwell and more.

Studio: Hammer Films.

DRACULA HAS RISEN FROM THE GRAVE (1968):

Directed by: Freddie Francis.

Written by: Anthony Hinds (screenplay, as John Elder) and Bram Stoker (based on the characters by).

Starring: Christopher Lee, Rupert Davies, Veronica Carlson, Barbara Ewing, Barry Andrews, Ewan Hooper and more.

Studio: Hammer Films.

TASTE THE BLOOD OF DRACULA (1970):

Directed by: Peter Sasdy.

Written by: Anthony Hinds (screenplay, as John Elder) and Bram Stoker (based on the characters by).

Starring: Christopher Lee, Geoffrey Keen, Gwen Watford, Linda

Hayden, Peter Sallis, Anthony Higgins and more.

Studio: Hammer Films.

SCARS OF DRACULA (1970):

Directed by: Roy Ward Baker.

Written by: Written by: Anthony Hinds (screenplay, as John Elder) and Bram Stoker (based on the characters by).

Starring: Christopher Lee, Dennis Waterman, Jenny Hanley, Christopher Matthews, Patrick Troughton, Michael Gwynn and more.

Studio: Hammer Films.

DRACULA A.D. 1972 (1972):

Directed by: Alan Gibson.

Written by: Don Houghton (screenplay).

Starring: Christopher Lee, Peter Cushing, Stephanie Beacham, Christopher Neame, Michael Coles, Marsha A. Hunt and more.

Studio: Hammer Films.

THE SATANIC RITES OF DRACULA (1973):

Directed by: Alan Gibson.

Written by: Don Houghton (screenplay).

Starring: Christopher Lee, Peter Cushing, Michael Coles, William Franklyn, Freddie Jones, Joanna Lumley and more.

Studio: Hammer Films.

THE BLOOD LIFE

Christopher Lee stars as the title role in Dracula *(1958)*

THE ORIGINAL 1958 HAMMER *Dracula* is a bit rubbish, really. There, I've said it. It's not a terrible film, just a deeply dreary and overrated one. For purposes of completeness though (you can't have a chapter looking at the Hammer Dracula series of films starring Christopher Lee and miss this one out!), I'm including it here, even though it's far from deserving of being in a Top 100 horror films list – Top 100 most overrated horror films, maybe!

I think the reason *Dracula* (aka *Horror of Dracula*) receives so much praise and attention is partly because it's the first Hammer/horror film many people saw, and they saw it at an impressionable age. If they'd seen say, *Taste the Blood of Dracula* instead, they would no doubt regard it as an all-time classic. Another reason is because, I suppose, many people have rotten taste and also, there's a herd-like mentality to many types of fandom, including this one – people are obliged to say they think *Dracula* is a supremely class act simply because (almost) everyone else does! I wonder how many of these people though *genuinely* think it's the best in the series?

The film starts well, with the first twenty-five minutes or so being very good. Harker (Jonathan Van Eyssen) arrives at Castle Dracula to take up his position as... er... the Count's librarian! This idea is very silly in itself – why would the Prince of Darkness seek to employ someone to arrange all his books? Did he ever read them? Was Harker's salary adequate? Anyway, in a nice twist, Harker knows his new boss is a vampire and is secretly planning to dispatch him. All well and good, but Harker is so utterly thick, he messes everything up (what sort of idiot would forget to bring a cross along with him, when preparing to confront a vampire?) and gets vampirised himself.

Ironically, bearing in mind he's such a superb and much-loved actor, the film grinds to a slow crawl as soon as Peter Cushing appears, and only recovers in the final two minutes – too little, too late. The battle between Dracula and Van Helsing (Cushing) is good but overrated (though I quite like the idea that, just before the climactic fight, Dracula is preparing to bury Mina and presumably dig her up to sample her blood later, like a dog with a bone!). Overall, nice sets, nice score, great performances from the two stars, but it results in a fairly tedious film, one that is bettered by every other film in the series. I'm not joking when I say that this film never fails to send me to sleep.

Dracula: Prince of Darkness (1966) is the belated sequel and it's an improvement on *Dracula* – just. It's still a fairly slow film (flashback sequence at the beginning aside, it takes over half an hour before we get to see the title monster), with characters who still seem fairly unengaging. I quite like the creepy Klove, but Charles and Diana (!) and Alan and Helen aren't particularly interesting, though the actors' performances are first rate.

The film takes its time introducing the main characters, with two couples on holiday in Transylvania, soon ending up at Castle Dracula where Dracula's servant Klove (Philip Latham) offers them a "damn fine dinner" and beds for the night, before cutting Alan's (Charles Tingwell) throat and allowing the blood to drain onto Dracula's ashes. Once revived, Dracula doesn't say a word but has a few good action scenes, as well as a bit lifted from the novel where he cuts his chest and offers Diana (Suzan Farmer) to taste the blood.

The hero of the film turns out to be Father Sandor (Andrew Keir), a crusty old monk with a Scottish accent who first meets the foursome in an inn and warns them not to go anywhere near Castle Dracula. Sandor is a good but overrated character, and wouldn't be anywhere near as watchable if played by anyone other than Keir. He destroys the Count in the end by the relatively novel means of water, and though

Dracula has no lines, he does at least get to give a hearty scream as he slides down a sheet of painted polystyrene and into a water tank. As I said, this film is an improvement on the first but it's no classic. It's too slow by half, and badly in need of an injection of the same life serum that made the next five films in the series so entertaining and watchable – again and again and again.

Barbara Shelley in Dracula: Prince of Darkness *(1966)*

Dracula Has Risen from the Grave (1968) was the first Hammer horror I ever saw all the way through, in the beloved Friday night film slot (11.05pm) on my local ITV station, Tyne Tees. I was chuffed that I'd managed to stay awake until that time – 11 o'clock at night seemed so far away when I was a kid – but as soon as I clocked the opening credits (I think it was coloured and treated footage of water, but my childish imagination – I was 9 – conjured up a million nameless horrors!) I had second thoughts about watching the film. I persevered though and in the end I was glad I did because I might have missed a classic film that knocks spots off the first two relatively dull and staid (though still included in this chapter for completeness) entries in the series.

Dracula Has Risen from the Grave gives the Count about the same amount of screen time as he had in the previous film, and Christopher Lee is still a great presence. The film has a priest (played by Ewan Hooper, who reminded me of stand-up comedian Mick Miller when I first saw this film) slipping on the ice, cracking his head open and letting his blood drip into Dracula's mouth. Though this scene has dramatic impact, it's clumsily staged, with paper-thin ice and a nasty head wound that completely vanishes as soon as Dracula (who's reflection is seen in the water) is up and about!

Veronica Carlson in Dracula Has Risen from the Grave *(1968)*

One aspect of the Dracula films that certainly improved as the years went by is the 'Hammer glamour' factor – Veronica Carlson, who plays the central female character in this film, knocks spots off the likes of Valerie Gaunt, Suzan Farmer and even Barbara Shelley in the previous films, and with Linda Hayden, Caroline Munro and Joanna Lumley to come, things kept getting better. Carlson plays Maria, girlfriend of Paul (Barry Andrews), a young lad who works in a bakery/tavern and turns out to be the film's hero.

Part of the reason the Hammer Draculas got a lot better as they went along is due to the fact that the supporting characters became a lot more interesting – in the 1958 film, the only characters of any interest are Dracula and Van Helsing. Here though, when Dracula isn't on screen (which is quite often), the viewer is kept entertained by the interactions of the other characters – Zena (Barbara Ewing), a flirty barmaid at the tavern who is vampirised and later killed by Dracula when he gets bored with her; the Monsignor (Rupert Davies) who starts all the bother when he exorcises Dracula's castle; the atheistic Paul; Maria and Paul's boss Max (the ubiquitous Michael Ripper, making his first appearance in a Hammer Dracula film).

The plot involves Dracula attempting to revenge himself on the Monsignor by vampirising his niece, and towards the end there is a surprising scene where Paul rams a wooden stake into Dracula's chest – but because he's an atheist, the Count has the power to pull the stake out and resume his reign of terror. This scene, when watched on the VHS release, was so dark you could hardly see what was going on! Christopher Lee reportedly objected heavily to this apparent disregard for basic vampire lore, but to no avail. And a good thing too – if the scene had been disregarded, we'd be missing one of the truly great moments in the series. The film ends not long after, as Dracula is impaled on a large cross which he falls onto – one thing I've never understood here is why, as the closing credits roll over the cross, with Dracula's cloak hanging off it and dripping blood, the cross is seen as a considerable distance away from the castle, unlike before! Anyone with the answer to this anomaly, please send it to me on the back of a fifty pound note c/o the *Phantasmagoria* address!

Taste the Blood of Dracula (1970) is even better. The first time I saw this one was in 1979 (guess where?) and it contained several scenes of nudity and gore that were missing from my next couple of viewings, most notably the very poor quality VHS release in the late '80s. The complete film though is a gem, with one of the best casts of the series: Linda Hayden, Martin Jarvis, Peter Sallis, John Carson, Ralph Bates, Roy Kinnear... even the bloke who played Lonely in *Callan* (Russell Hunter)!

Alongside the superb cast is a superb script, filled with memorable lines which myself and my horror film fan mates spent many hours quoting, when we first discovered our mutual love for these great films! The setting here is Victorian London, and the characters are all fascinating, with the three rich toffs who are ultimately responsible for the Count's resurrection being introduced, along with their families, in loving detail. Hargood (Geoffrey Keen) in particular is a fascinating character: a right hypocritical git who treats his wife and daughter like shit but then goes with his two mates to a brothel! It's heavily hinted that Hargood fancies his daughter (played by Linda Hayden), to the extent he treats her boyfriend and boyfriend's father badly too.

Dracula artwork by Allen Koszowski

Unfortunately, Hargood, Secker (John Carson) and Paxton's (Peter Sallis) night out comes to an abrupt and bloody end, when they have the misfortune of bumping into Lord Courtley (Ralph Bates), an even more depraved toff than they are. Courtley persuades them to buy Dracula's remaining artefacts and take part in an unholy ritual in a "de-sanctified" (has anyone ever heard or read that expression, outside of a Hammer film?) church. Thinking that drinking Dracula's blood will turn them into vampires, Courtley instead is poisoned – the others thoughtfully try to help by kicking him to death before he can choke – and after they have fled, his corpse turns into Dracula (the special effects are a bit ropey here but the scene has undeniable dramatic impact).

The only slight let down with this film is that, once Hargood has been killed (shovel to the bonce!), the film seems to lack something. Secker and Paxton are dispatched before too long (knife in the ribs, and stake in the chest respectively) and from then it's straight to the finale and Dracula's demise. Because the three toffs are such despicable characters, it has the unusual effect of making Dracula seem like a hero and it's a pity he has to be destroyed as well.

Scars of Dracula is my favourite of the series. Ironically, it's also the least favourite of many other Hammer fans. Quite often it tends to be the more pompous and humourless 'wooden-stake-up-their-arse' Hammer fans who look down on this one. These people are easy to spot – they also hate *Horror of Frankenstein*, *Lust for a Vampire*, and the *On the Buses* films – says it all. They hate any Hammer film that has a generous quotient of the 'fun factor', but cream themselves into a froth over the opulent sets and production values of relatively dry and dull fare like the 1958 film and some others from the same period, none of which come close to capturing the entertainment value of any of the above mentioned films (for what it's worth, I rate Hammer's Golden Age as being from 1966 to 1973).

Scars... gets off to a lively start when a vampire bat dribbles blood onto Dracula's ashes, reviving him. This is interesting for two reasons. Firstly, it doesn't follow on from where the previous film left off, thus breaking the previous strong continuity. Secondly, this marks the first appearance of a bat in a Hammer Dracula film, *The Brides of Dracula* notwithstanding – that one's a Dracula film in name only and therefore doesn't count (chuckle)! Contrary to the thoughts of many other fans, I like the bats in this film. I can't see anything wrong with them, and there are some great sequences – the aftermath of their attack on the women and children in the church, for example. Hammer's previous attempts at depicting bats on screen had been utterly awful – the tatty furball on visible strings in *Brides...* is almost eclipsed by the cartoon variety on display in the climax to *The Kiss of the Vampire* – but the ones in *Scars...* are a huge improvement.

The film revolves around a jack-the-lad character (i.e. a complete prat) who sleeps with one questionable lady too many and ends up being chased for his life, ending up spending the night at Dracula's castle. Paul (Christopher Matthews) is fun to watch, though it's hard to see why every woman in the film virtually drops her knickers at first sight of him! His ultimate fate remains a mystery until near the end, but his brother Simon (Dennis Waterman) and Simon's fiancée Sarah (Jenny Hanley) investigate, falling foul of Dracula and Klove (Patrick

Troughton). Klove is once more Dracula's servant but he has none of the dignity he possessed in *Dracula: Prince of Darkness* – he falls in love with Sarah having seen her in a cracked-glass photograph, then gets whipped (off-screen) by his master for letting her escape. Later on, a gory highlight of the film comes when Dracula applies a red-hot sword to Klove's already horribly slashed back! Once revived, Dracula remains within his castle for the rest of the film and his interactions with the rest of the cast are entertaining (but let's be honest – Jenny Hanley's character is boring and a wet lettuce. If it wasn't for her being so fanciable she'd drag the film down), especially when he offers the faintly wooden Waterman a glass of either blood, or drugged wine (it's not made clear)!

Christopher Lee and Dennis Waterman in Scars of Dracula *(1970)*

There's a great deal to enjoy in this film, which also has a different sort of 'look' to it than other Hammer films of the period. Dracula has become so evil and powerful here that it looks as if he's going to remain unscathed, but God lends a hand... it wasn't the best idea to have a stuntman in a plastic Dracula mask staggering around the set once the Count has been struck by lightning and set on fire, but the scene still packs a punch and overall this is the best film in the series, in my opinion. It even gives Hammer stalwart Michael Ripper one of his best and most entertaining roles.

Having seemingly exhausted the Gothic time period, the next film in the series, *Dracula A.D. 1972* (1972), is set in the then present day. I haven't seen this one for a good many years but I remember it well. It's a pity Hammer didn't see fit to make any more films set in the nineteenth century, but we get a lively prologue here, with Dracula and Van Helsing (Peter Cushing, making a welcome return to the series) bouncing about on top of a runaway coach which crashes, killing them both. Dracula ends up revived in the twentieth century, but gets stuck in a ruined old church for the duration of the rest of the film, while Van Helsing's modern day descendant (Cushing again) teams up with Scotland Yard to track him down.

I remember being surprised by the use of the word "bastard" (how rude!) when I first saw this film in the (you guessed it) Friday night film slot in 1978, but for the rest of it, I enjoyed matching up what I saw onscreen with the pictures on the *You'll Die Laughing* bubblegum cards which depicted scenes from some of the films accompanied by a corny (sometimes downright odd) joke. *Dracula A.D. 1972* isn't one of the best films in the series but it's fun. It even has some good songs in it.

The Satanic Rites of Dracula brought the Hammer series to an end in 1973, and it ended on a high. As well as having credits you can actually *read* (unlike on the previous film), *Satanic Rites...* is a much more exciting and action-filled film. As others have commented, it seems almost like a gory version of the TV show *The Avengers*, or to be more accurate, *The New Avengers* (which was still a few years in the future when this was made) – with Peter Cushing as Steed (Van Helsing), Michael Coles as Gambit (Inspector Murray) and Joanna Lumley as... er, Purdey (Jessica Van Helsing)! Director Alan Gibson returns, having helmed the previous film, and does an even better job here, with a fantastic cast. I've always enjoyed Freddie Jones' OTT performances and he's terrific value here, as a professor who's been broken by the pressure of his work to create a virus to destroy humanity! "Evil rules" he gibbers, before going on to extol the virtues of "the thrill of disgust!" and "the beauty of obscenity!" to a horrified Van Helsing, shortly before he gets shot.

Behind the plan to create the virus is Dracula himself – curiously, we aren't privy to his resurrection this time round, he's just there, and wishing to bring his undead existence to a permanent close while plotting to bring about the end of humanity with the aforementioned virus at the same time. Lee gets a bit more dialogue than in the previous film and his ultimate end involves him getting his foot caught on a hawthorn bush, before being staked by Cushing! Ah well, I'm sure many cinema-goers at the time thought he'd be back before too long, but sadly he wasn't. Lee departed Hammer horror – and the

UK – for good several years later, stopping only to make the fairly naff *To the Devil... a Daughter* in 1976. It was the end of an era.

Dracula artwork by Allen Koszowski

NERVE-SHATTERING TERROR!
HER HONEYMOON TURNED INTO A NIGHTMARE OF HORROR!
THE ALLIGATOR PEOPLE
WILL MAKE YOUR SKIN CRAWL!
CINEMASCOPE
STARRING
BEVERLY GARLAND • BRUCE BENNETT
LON CHANEY • GEORGE MACREADY
and
FRIEDA INESCORT · RICHARD CRANE · DOUGLAS KENNEDY
PRODUCED BY
JACK LEEWOOD
DIRECTED BY
ROY DEL RUTH
SCREENPLAY BY
ORVILLE H. HAMPTON
PRODUCED BY ASSOCIATED PRODUCERS, Inc.
20th CENTURY-FOX

CHAPTER 18

THE ALLIGATOR PEOPLE (1959)

The Alligator People *(1959)*

Directed by: Roy Del Ruth.

Written by: Orville H. Hampton (screenplay and story), Charles O'Neal (story) and Robert M. Fresco (uncredited).

Starring: Beverly Garland, Bruce Bennett, Lon Chaney Jr., George Macready, Frieda Inescort, Richard Crane and more.

Studio: Associated Producers (API).

CROC OF GOLD

ONE OF MY favourite SF/horror films from the 1950s, this is definitely the best such film to revolve around alligators also, and it's a film I first became aware of during the mid-to-late 1970s.

A friend of mine had called round one Thursday teatime, excitedly brandishing a book his mother had returned with after a shopping trip in Bishop Auckland. The book was a slim paperback titled *Monsters of the Movies* and I eagerly grabbed it from his hands and examined the cover.

Now, when I first saw that cover, with its artwork depictions of Dracula, Frankenstein's Monster, King Kong and other horrors, it made my blood run cold when I saw the dreaded name of Denis Gifford! Gifford had been the perpetrator of a hefty tome about horror films that I had purchased a few years previously. Now, that book, *A Pictorial History of Horror Movies*, is one that is held in very high regard by many horror fans of a certain age who got it as children in the 1970s – as indeed I did – but unlike those other horror fans I don't regard the book very highly at all. Even as a relatively uncritical eight-year-old, I thought Gifford's book was a bit rubbish – all unlikeable stills from many unlikeable films, on naff quality paper and written in an awful jokey style. Not to mention Gifford's dislike of any film made after 1950. The cover was the best part of Gifford's book, in my opinion and the whole work wasn't a patch on the Alan Frank book that I also had in my possession. Anyway, *Monsters of the Movies* actually turned out to be a lot better than Gifford's earlier book. It was filled with two-page entries on a wide range of film monsters, always including one photo. Now, the first entry was *The Alligator People* and, as with every other entry in the book, at that time, it was a film I'd never seen. But the film went on to occupy my thoughts for the following few months as it gave me a cunning plan – I was going to beat Mr. Gifford at his own game, and compile my own A-Z horror film guide! Which would, naturally, be a hundred times better than his. I intended to start off with *The Alligator People*, but I had a slight problem. I'd never seen it and couldn't recall what I'd briefly skimmed when I first perused my mate's copy. So, I made it up: my entry on the film had a synopsis in which a scientist discovers a way to make people live forever by making them eat discarded alligator skin (Me: "Mother, do alligators shed their skin?" Mother: "Of course, Son – why?" Me: "Oh, I'm just writing a book"). Unfortunately, this has the awful side effect of transforming them completely into alligators. In my synopsis, there were loads of alligator people in the film – men, women and children – and it all ended with one of them eating a nuclear bomb and blowing the scientist's house up! The scientist escaped, of course, and swore never to meddle with alligators again.

Soon after writing that, I acquired my own copy of the book (I stole my friend's when he wasn't looking – I did slip a copy of *Doctor Who and the Sontaran Experiment* in it's place though!), and whilst reading it I realised my own description of the film was a little off the mark. I put my second entry for my book – *Count Yorga, Vampire* – on hold indefinitely.

Fast-forward to 2010. I'm on Amazon, looking through the DVDs, and typing in as many interesting titles gleaned from *The Dark Side*'s never-ending horror guide as I can remember, when *The Alligator*

People crosses my mind. Before I know it, I've bought the film. It seems to take ages for it to arrive but eventually it does, and I do what I always do – I put the unopened parcel with all the others that I'm saving for Christmas! So, sometime in early 2011, I watch the film, on a Sunday night.

It is an excellent film and I loved it straight away. It's definitely, as I said above, one of the best horror/SF/fantasy films of the 1950s, ranking on a par with such movies as *The Hound of the Baskervilles* and *The Mummy* from Hammer, not to mention all those great SF films (*Forbidden Planet, This Island Earth, Invasion of the Body Snatchers*) that the decade is best remembered for, and light years ahead of stuff like *I Was a Teenage Frankenstein, The Werewolf, The Vampire, Monster on the Campus* and a hundred other penny dreadfuls.

Richard Crane and Beverly Garland in The Alligator People *(1959)*

The story involves a scientist, played by George Macready who genre fans might recognise from *The Outer Limits* episode "Production and Decay of Strange Particles" (1964) and the *Night Gallery* pilot (1969), carrying out experiments in restoring victims of terrible injuries and accidents back to full health from his laboratory in the Louisiana swamps, using a serum derived from alligators. Paul Webster (Richard Crane) is one such specimen, and, after being tracked down by his bride Joyce (Beverley Garland) to the scientist's house, starts to mutate, gaining hard, scaly, reptilian skin. There are other victims of the experiments hidden away in the house, but the main focus is on Paul. A seemingly-sozzled Lon Chaney Jr. is one of the film's stand-outs, playing a "Gator Hater" (that phrase was in my mind when I first saw the film, and I then discovered it on one of the scene selections points!) called Manon, who has had a thing about them after one of them bit his hand off. He has a hook there now, and when he's not drinking and trying to "hook" up with women, he spends his time shooting alligators in the nearby swamps. When Mrs. Garland is being driven by Manon through the swamps to the scientist's house, you can see there was limited space to film in, as the truck passes the same tree stump twice.

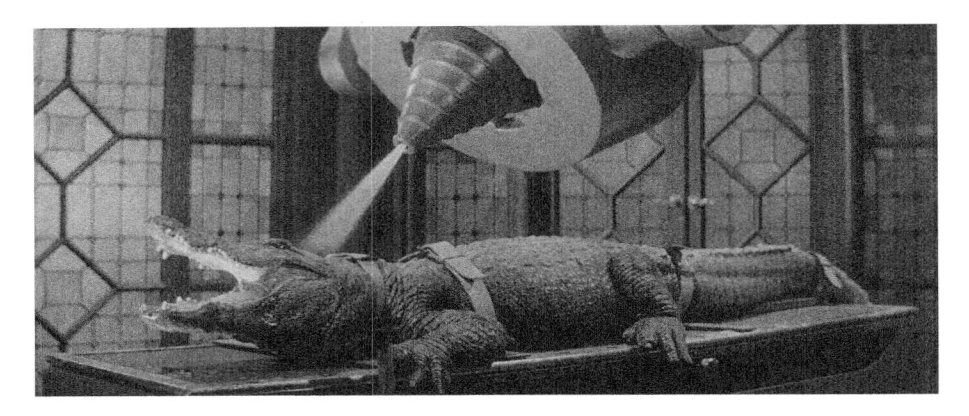

The Alligator People (1959)

When Joyce arrives at the house, the suspense is maintained as she, and the audience, knows something is wrong. We get brief glimpses of the deformed Paul, and the film's title lets us know it must have something to do with our scaly friends. Later, we get a weirdly iconic, science fictional image of an alligator strapped to a table, with a laser beam trained on it. Macready prepares one last desperate treatment to cure Paul, but doesn't have much hope of success, and he turns out to be quite right.

After the concluding treatment has been thoroughly sabotaged by Chaney Jr., bursting in looking for "that two-legged 'gator, Paul!", poor Paul emerges with the head and body of a humanoid alligator. I've never read any articles or reference works on this film so I have no idea how it is regarded overall but I'll bet there are plenty of disparaging comments about this costume – well, there shouldn't be, as it looks okay. Not perfect, but it does the job. It even bears up when Paul is wrestling with a real alligator in the swamps. I won't reveal the ending for those who haven't seen the film, but it's quite surprising.

So there you have it, an underrated and neglected little gem. You don't even have to like alligators to enjoy it, so get onto Amazon and buy a copy – and make it snappy (sorry, couldn't resist)!

Boyd Stockman in The Alligator People *(1959)*

Note: A version of this chapter first appeared in *We Belong Dead* magazine.

The CURSE OF THE WEREWOLF
in Eastman COLOR
Starring CLIFFORD EVANS · OLIVER REED · YVONNE ROMAIN · CATHERINE FELLER
Screenplay by JOHN ELDER Directed by TERENCE FISHER Produced by ANTHONY HINDS Executive Producer MICHAEL CARRERAS
A HAMMER FILM PRODUCTION · A UNIVERSAL-INTERNATIONAL RELEASE

CHAPTER 19

THE CURSE OF THE WEREWOLF (1961)

Oliver Reed in The Curse of the Werewolf *(1961)*

Directed by: Terence Fisher.

Written by: Anthony Hinds (screenplay, as John Elder) and Guy Endore (novel).

Starring: Clifford Evans, Oliver Reed, Yvonne Romain, Catherine Feller, Anthony Dawson, Josephine Llewellyn and more.

Studio: Hammer Films.

HAIR OF THE DOG

AS MENTIONED EARLIER in the book, *The Curse of Frankenstein* is where Hammer horror properly began, back in 1957. The studio had trifled with science fiction films earlier on in that doomy decade – *Four Sided Triangle* and *Spaceways*, for example – and sort-of-horror/SF films like *The Quatermass Experiment*,

Quatermass 2 and *The Abominable Snowman*, but the Frankenstein film was their first real stab at the horror genre. And they hit the bullseye with bottled lightning straight away, producing a classic that became a phenomenon, leading to two decades worth of similar such horrors, and a rash of imitators which ranged from the excellent (Amicus and Tigon) to the execrable (90% of everything else). They also made big screen stars of Peter Cushing and Christopher Lee, and, reportedly, saved Universal Studios in the USA from bankruptcy.

Hammer quickly set about planning more horror productions, most of which were remakes, or re-interpretations, of old '30s and '40s horrors. *Dracula* (1958) was an even bigger success than the Frankenstein film, though, in my opinion, time has not treated it kindly. It's certainly not a bad movie – it's well-acted, well-directed and has some impressive sets and effects – but it's just not entertaining and once the first twenty-three minutes are up, you may as well settle back in your favourite chair and turn up the gas. The film isn't blessed with an abundance of the "fun factor", and it becomes a picture where, for the entire middle section, Peter Cushing is the sole reason to keep watching. Now, Cushing was a brilliant actor, much beloved by horror film fans and tea-shop proprietors alike, but more than just his presence alone is needed to make a film watchable and entertaining, as *Corruption* (1968) (and some would add *The Blood Beast Terror*) proved. For example, a bit of action and gore wouldn't go amiss. *Dracula* is the only slight misstep from that late '50s horror film period though.

Into the 1960s, and Hammer brought back Dracula – sort of – in *The Brides of Dracula*, an excellent little film which, despite its title, isn't actually a Dracula film. Instead, it stars David Peel as Baron Meinster, and brings Van Helsing (Peter Cushing) back to the fold. But before that, Hammer made *The Curse of the Werewolf*...

I always wondered why this 1960 film was Hammer's only stab at the werewolf sub-genre (I've since discovered why – it was a box office flop), however its uniqueness makes it one of Hammer's best and most memorable films. Director Terence Fisher loved storylines that spanned a long period of time and this one spans three generations, beginning in 18th century Spain when a beggar (Richard Wordsworth) goes to the castle of the The Marques (Anthony Dawson) who has just gotten married. The beggar expects some charity but instead he is made a fool of in front of the asshole Marques and his stupid wife, and all the assembled guests. It looks as if the beggar might get away with mere public embarrassment but he goes too far with some saucy innuendo and gets thrown into a dungeon, where he spends the next twenty or so years slowly becoming more and more unkempt, and like an animal. The Marques tries it on with his serving wench – his own wife having being sent to "an early grave' by his asshole-ness – and when she rejects the depraved old sod's advances, he has her thrown into the same cell as the beggar who promptly rapes her (in a rather unpleasant detail – it's implied the exertion of the rape kills the beggar).

The girl (Yvonne Romain) manages to escape and ends up in the care of a woodsman (Clifford Evans) and his wife, but not for long, as she dies on Christmas Day not long after giving birth. Leon grows up to be a strange kid, killing sheep and howling at the moon, but definitely not as strange as the unmistakeably English accents sported by all the cast who are supposed to be Spanish (a highlight here is when the shepherd Pepe [Warren Mitchell] finds the remains of his flock and utters the classic line "'Ere, what's all this, then?")!

As Leon grows to adulthood and Oliver Reed takes on the role, the film starts to become a little more interesting though it still takes forever before we get to see the monster – a common thing in the '50s/'60s Hammer films. When the werewolf is finally revealed in all its grey-haired glory, it's certainly no disappointment – I remember seeing a clip of the bit where Leon, in a cell with a drunken derelict played by Hammer stalwart Michael Ripper, starts to transform on the ITV children's cinema show *Clapper Board* in the late '70s and being fascinated. The werewolf slowly advances on the terrified Ripper, and then suddenly lunges with its teeth bared – great stuff, though it's a pity we have to wait until the film is almost over before we get to scenes like this.

The werewolf's climactic rampage across the town's rooftops ends when Leon's adoptive father turns up and shoots it with a silver bullet, leading to some spectacular gymnastics on Oliver Reed (or his stuntman!)'s part as he throws himself around before finally perishing.

Overall, this film reminds me a little of Hammer's 1958 *Dracula* – a great beginning, then the bulk of the rest of the film is too slow-paced for its own good, but a great climax. This film scores higher though, because of its one-of-a-kind (for Hammer) monster, and the fact it has a sense of humour that the po-faced earlier film lacks.

"THE PHANTOM OF THE OPERA"
Eastman COLOR
The Greatest THRILL CLASSIC of All Time!!!
STARRING
HERBERT LOM · HEATHER SEARS · ALSO STARRING THORLEY WALTERS · MICHAEL GOUGH
Screenplay by JOHN ELDER Directed by TERENCE FISHER Produced by ANTHONY HINDS
A HAMMER-FILM PRODUCTION • A UNIVERSAL-INTERNATIONAL RELEASE
50th ANNIVERSARY
Universal International

CHAPTER 20

THE PHANTOM OF THE OPERA (1962)

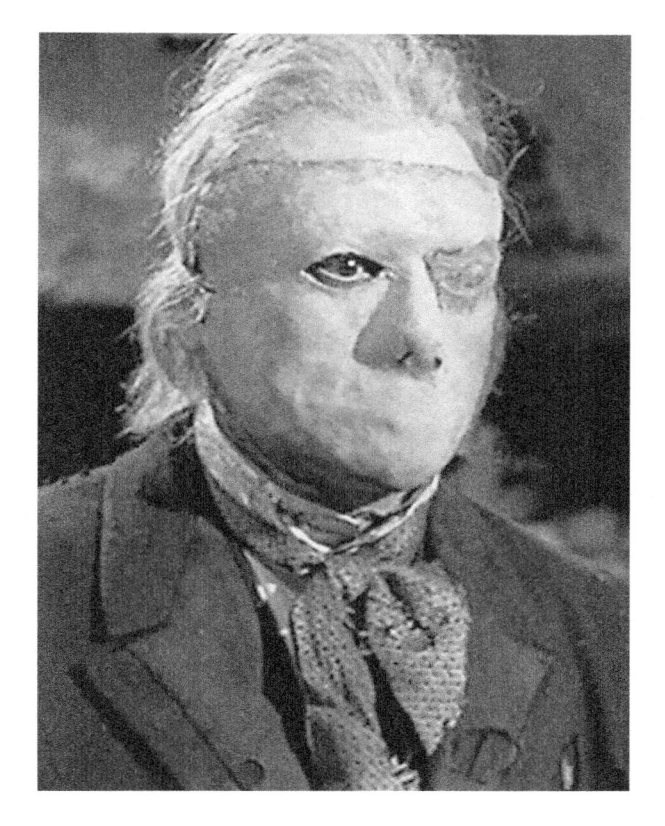

Herbert Lom in The Phantom of the Opera *(1962)*

Directed by: Terence Fisher.

Written by: Anthony Hinds (screenplay, as John Elder) and Gaston Leroux (composition).

Starring: Herbert Lom, Heather Sears, Edward de Souza, Thorley Walters, Michael Gough, Harold Goodwin and more.

Studio: Hammer Films.

ORGAN REPLACEMENT

I'VE ALWAYS HAD a soft spot for this one – a swamp at the bottom of the garden! No, seriously, I think that this neglected Hammer horror is a minor gem and often overlooked. It's definitely superior to the flaccid 1943 film with Claude Rains (which so emphasised the setting over the character, it should have been called "The Opera of the Phantom") and ranks better, in my opinion, than certain rather overrated Hammer horrors – this film is definitely more fun than the 1958 *Dracula*, *Curse of the Mummy's Tomb*, *The Hound of the Baskervilles* and the dreary and overrated *Taste of Fear*!

The film is essentially a remake of the 1943 Universal film, rather than the silent 1925 version. Apparently, Cary Grant (Cary Grant!!) was slated to play the title villain, after popping into the Hammer offices one afternoon and declaring himself to be a huge fan of the company's output. This led to an agreement that Grant would star in a future film, but – surprise! – when the time came, he pulled out. Good thing too, he would have been rubbish. Herbert Lom instead plays Professor Petrie, a rather mild music composer who approaches the lecherous and self-serving Lord Ambrose d'Arcy (Michael Gough) with a complete opera he has written, based on Joan of Arc.

Unfortunately his work gets sold for a pittance and d'Arcy claims ownership of the whole thing, leading to the embittered Petrie attempting to burn all copies at the printer's. He ends up getting splashed in the face by acid, horribly disfigured and takes up residence, so to speak, in the catacombs under the London streets – oh, sorry, did I forget to mention this film is set in 19th century London, rather than Paris?

The film builds up its main characters – we have the reliable Edward de Souza as the hero, Heather Sears plays the Phantom's platonic interest, and there's a nice turn from Thorley Walters as the harassed manager of the opera house (incidentally, when this film was released on video in the late '80s, the solitary picture on the packaging was of Walters' character, which confused me a bit back then!). The most interesting character though is the slime ball d'Arcy. I gather Michael Gough isn't generally considered to be a particularly great actor. I beg to differ – he's always good value in all of his appearances. Yes, he's a bit dull in *Dracula* but he's the least of that film's problems. I remember laughing my way through *Konga* (1961) due to Mr. Gough's hammy performance which was appropriate for that film, and he's perfectly fine in the dozen or so other horror films he graced, including this one. His sleazy attempt at seducing Sears, his contemptuous dismissal of Petrie and his later irritation at the fact that it's his "first opera and I'm let down at every turn!" are all enjoyable moments and it's a shame his character just disappears very quickly after seeing the Phantom's scarred fizzog and is not seen again.

There's a fair bit of opera footage and, like all opera, it's a load of tuneless, unexciting and unengaging noise to me, but pretentious people love it. Fortunately, there's plenty of action too, largely provided by the Phantom's dwarf henchman (Ian Wilson) – a rat catcher (pre-*Doctor Who* Patrick Troughton) gets stabbed, and we see someone swinging through the scenery with a rope around their neck in the middle of a performance, all thanks to the unnamed dwarf!

The Phantom isn't really portrayed as a villain, and it's this relative restraint that led to the film being a box office flop. The Phantom wasn't the sort of character who would return in half a dozen sequels though, so it didn't really matter.

After forming a sort of bond with the sympathetic Phantom, Sears and de Souza are released and the opera goes ahead. The best bits are saved till last with this one – the climactic falling of the chandelier and the unmasking of the Phantom are entwined in the same scene and certainly don't disappoint, bringing the curtain down on the sad tale of Professor Petrie and a very fine film.

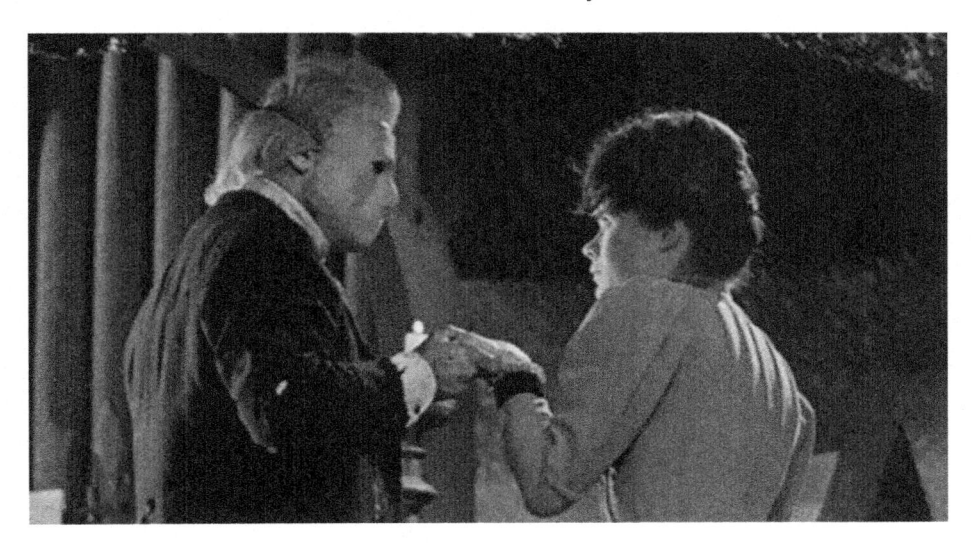

Herbert Lom and Heather Sears in
The Phantom of the Opera *(1962)*

A TRILOGY OF SHOCK AND HORROR!
AMERICAN INTERNATIONAL presents
EDGAR ALLAN POE'S
TALES OF TERROR
in COLOR
and PANAVISION
STARRING
VINCENT PRICE
PETER LORRE
BASIL RATHBONE
DEBRA PAGET
"...and there was an oozing liquid putrescence ...all that remained of Mr. Valdemar." --POE
"I had walled the black monster up within the tomb!" --POE
Produced and Directed by
ROGER CORMAN
Screenplay by
RICHARD MATHESON
Executive Producers
JAMES H. NICHOLSON · SAMUEL Z. ARKOFF
An AMERICAN INTERNATIONAL PICTURE

CHAPTER 21

TALES OF TERROR (1962)

Vincent Price, Peter Lorre and Basil Rathbone star in
Tales of Terror *(1962)*

Directed by: Roger Corman.

Written by: Richard Matheson (screenplay) and Edgar Allan Poe (based on the stories by).

Starring: Vincent Price, Peter Lorre, Basil Rathbone, Debra Paget, Maggie Pierce, Leona Gage and more.

Studio: Alta Vista Productions/American International Pictures (AIP).

THE RISE OF THE HOUSE OF CORMAN

I'M A BIG fan of the series of Edgar Allan Poe films made by American International Pictures (AIP) in the 1960s, and this one is my favourite. *House of Usher* started it all off in 1960, turning a fairly humdrum short story into an entertaining film, complete with hammy Vincent Price, wooden supporting actor (Mark Damon), tinted flashback dream sequences, shock appearance by a tarantula and footage of a burning roof – all elements that would recur in the other seven films in the series.

Pit and the Pendulum (1961) ironically discards the original Poe story (which is one of his best) and substitutes an involving tale of murder, madness and revenge, complete with most of the elements listed above. *Premature Burial* (1962) is one of my favourites, and has Ray Milland replacing Price. *The Raven* in 1963 is a macabre comedy, with Price joined by Boris Karloff and Peter Lorre, as well as a young Jack Nicholson. *The Haunted Palace* in 1963 is one of the best of the series, although it's based on a Lovecraft story rather than Poe. *The Masque of the Red Death* (1964) is a good but slightly overrated film, and *The Tomb of Ligeia*, also in 1964, brings the series to an impressive end.

There's a high standard of quality running through all the films. *Tales of Terror* (1962) is my favourite simply because it's an anthology and therefore stands out. Like a lot of the films covered in this book, I first saw it as a kid, in 1977. The Friday night film slot on Tyne Tees showed it, and I spent the day excitedly hyping the film up to my equally horror-obsessed schoolmates. That night, as 11.05 drew near, I remember re-reading the paragraph allocated to the film in Alan Frank's *Horror Movies*... and, as the scheduled time at last came, I settled back – and almost literally shit myself in shock!

I don't know what I expected, but I certainly didn't expect the full-screen image of a beating heart, accompanied by the creepy tones of the film's leading man! I was utterly terrified, but forced myself to continue watching, with the rest of my family gathered round as usual. The opening story, "Morella", was the only one I saw that Friday night, as the telly was turned off after it finished, and I never got to see the entertaining turns of Peter Lorre and Basil Rathbone in the other two stories.

"Morella" has Price as Locke, an alcoholic recluse who lives in the same cliff top castle that appeared in *Pit...* and *The Raven*. He's a bitter old soak, who blames his grown-up daughter Lenora for the death of his wife, Morella. As it turns out, Morella blames her too and when Lenora comes visiting for the first time in years, her mother's vengeful spirit is aroused and neither Lenora nor Price survive the night.

Morella must have been a nasty, vindictive old witch – her dust-coated corpse is seen several times in the film, face contorted in a sneer, and there's the obligatory shock appearance (in close-up, this time!) by a creepy tarantula. Nice performances and a suitably fiery ending. Next!

The second story is a lot better and has Price in camp form as Fortunato, a suave wine taster who's imbibing more than a nice glass of Chardonnay, when he ends up having an affair with Lorre's wife. Lorre gives a great performance here, as a permanently-sozzled and bad-tempered little man, who spends his days and money in the local tavern, and his nights sleeping it off, until he discovers his wife is having an affair with Price, and is surprisingly sober enough to care. It ends in *Black Cat* fashion, with Lorre walling his victims up alive before the titular animal alerts the police, but despite the mediocre story, it's all directed and acted with such style and verve that it becomes a mini-masterpiece of the genre. There's a nice dream sequence too, in which the adulterous pair end up removing Lorre's head and throwing it around like a ball!

The final tale is very effective too, with Basil Rathbone as hypnotist Carmichael, a thoroughly despicable swine who puts Valdemar (Price) into a trance at the point of death and keeps him there for months, while he fiddles around with Valdemar's wife and generally takes over the house.

Before watching the film in that 1970s Friday night slot, this was the segment I was most worried/excited about, due to stills I'd seen in horror film reference books which showed Price "clasping Carmichael to him in a grip of slime" before fully liquefying, with Carmichael "dying of fright"! That's not quite as it appears onscreen – the picture goes a bit blurry, probably to conceal the deficiencies in the make-up, and it didn't look as if Rathbone's character was "dying of fright" to me. Nevertheless, an good ending. As with the second segment, though Price is supposedly the film's star, he is upstaged by his co-star here – Rathbone looks genuinely evil and sinister and he is a good example (like Lorre) of a horror star who should have been more recognised.

The second story is prefaced by the blood-red paw prints of a cat moving across the screen, the third by dripping blood, and all three stories end with a (inaccurate, in the case of the second story) quote from the relevant Poe story. A great showcase for AIP, and the talents of the returning cinema greats Lorre and Rathbone, *Tales of Terror* is the perfect early '60s bridge between the old and the new of American horror cinema.

"It could be the most terrifying motion picture
I have ever made!"—
"...and remember, the next scream you hear may be your own!"
ALFRED
HITCHCOCK'S
"The Birds"
TECHNICOLOR®
STARRING
ROD TAYLOR · JESSICA TANDY
SUZANNE PLESHETTE and Introducing 'TIPPI' HEDREN
Based on Daphne Du Maurier's Classic Suspense Story!
A Fascinating
New Personality
Universal Release
Screenplay by EVAN HUNTER · Directed by ALFRED HITCHCOCK

CHAPTER 22

THE BIRDS (1963)

Tippi Hedren (centre) in The Birds *(1963)*

Directed by: Alfred Hitchcock.

Written by: Daphne Du Maurier (from the story by) and Evan Hunter (screenplay by).

Starring: Rod Taylor, Tippi Hedren, Jessica Tandy, Suzanne Pleshette, Veronica Cartwright, Ethel Griffies and more.

Studio: Alfred J. Hitchcock Productions.

PECKING DISORDER

BACK IN THE mid-'70s, BBC1 showed *The Birds* (1963) at 9.30pm one Monday evening. I knew very little about it, other than that it was a horror film directed by someone with a very silly surname. I was barely out of short trousers back then, and kids at school had spent playtime talking about the film (which must have been shown on TV before) and it's merits, so when the time rolled around, I was sat with my family, excitedly revved up to watch what I assumed was going to be a very entertaining and enjoyable film. I was wrong.

The opening credits freaked me out for a start, with all those birds flying past and screeching, although the gentle scenes after that put me at ease... but not for long. The film is very clever in that respect – the opening "Doris Day/Rock Hudson"-type rom-com between Tippi Hedren and Rod Taylor certainly doesn't tip off to the viewer that a thoroughly nightmarish vision of the end of the world is coming. Because that's what the film is all about – it's essentially doomsday.

Tippi Hedren and Rod Taylor in The Birds *(1963)*

I have to say, I'm no fan of the overrated Alfred Hitchcock but he does his best work here, delivering a body blow to the unsuspecting viewer's complacency. After about thirty minutes of being suckered by all the light romantic comedy stuff, we see a man lying dead on the floor of his bedroom, surrounded by dead birds and with his eyes pecked out! From that moment on, the film becomes a nightmare in which the viewer is trapped along with the characters. The scene with all the kids, running from school pursued by the birds illustrates the nightmarish feel perfectly – kids at school, singing in class, then looking forward to going home, a perfect example of ordinary everyday life becoming sour and horrible. The scene of Rod Taylor's character Mitch boarding up the windows of the house in preparation for the next bird attack rams home the feeling that everyday life has become a surreal and strange nightmare.

More horror comes in the café scenes, with adults casually chatting about the threat posed by the birds. The feeling I had as a kid watching this was that I was there in the film myself, both a participant and an observer.

The bird attacks come in waves and there's no explanation for why they are doing it, and as a result, no possible solution either. The action is set in Bodega Bay, a small coastal town near San Francisco and, as the original idea for the film's ending would have made clear, the bird attacks would become widespread – onscreen, Melanie (Hedren) and Mitch (Taylor) make their way to the car and drive off. In the unused ending, they would have headed to San Francisco and seen the Golden Gate Bridge from a distance – covered with birds!

A real classic of the genre, this has a feel like no other horror film, and is truly disturbing. Perhaps the best indication of the film's effectiveness is that, after watching it as an adult, it makes you want to go outside and shoot as many of the feathered swines as possible!

Tippi Hedren in The Birds *(1963)*

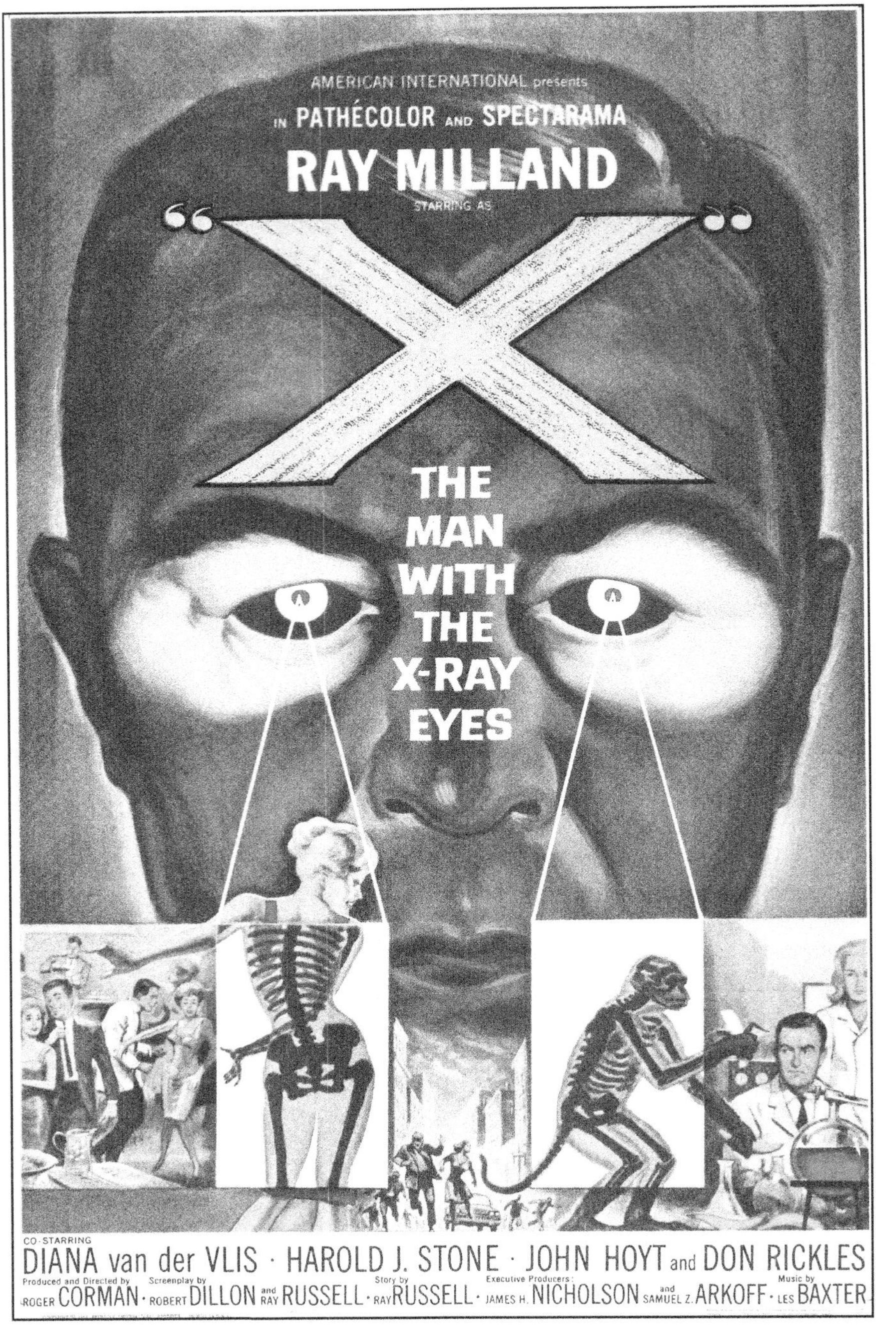
AMERICAN INTERNATIONAL presents
IN PATHÉCOLOR AND SPECTARAMA
RAY MILLAND
STARRING AS
"X"
THE MAN WITH THE X-RAY EYES
CO-STARRING
DIANA van der VLIS · HAROLD J. STONE · JOHN HOYT and DON RICKLES
Produced and Directed by ROGER CORMAN · Screenplay by ROBERT DILLON and RAY RUSSELL · Story by RAY RUSSELL · Executive Producers: JAMES H. NICHOLSON and SAMUEL Z. ARKOFF · Music by LES BAXTER

CHAPTER 23

X: THE MAN WITH THE X-RAY EYES (1963)

Ray Milland in X: The Man with the X-Ray Eyes *(1963)*

Directed by: Roger Corman.

Written by: Robert Dillon (screenplay) and Ray Russell (screenplay and story).

Starring: Ray Milland, Diana Van der Vlis, Harold J. Stone, John Hoyt, Don Rickles, Leon Alton and more.

Studio: Alta Vista Productions/American International Pictures (AIP).

X-RAYTED

MY GOD, THIS is a bloody unpleasant film! It was screened on BBC1 in 1975, in the Monday film 9.30pm slot but I just saw the trailer for it and nothing of the film itself. I then read about it in Alan Frank's seminal *Horror Movies* book but the author glossed over most of the film, just commenting on the ending.

Fast-forward to July 1978, and BBC2's horror double bill season. It's the second week and *The Fantastic Disappearing Man* (1958), a film I'd never heard of, is paired with the 1963 Roger Corman production. The *Radio Times* listings worried me a little and as that night rolled around and my family and I had returned from staying with relatives for a few days, I looked at the listing again and began to have, in the words of Han Solo, "a bad feeling" about watching this film.

The first film on the bill was okay, certainly not the bland "invisible scientist" type of film I expected but certainly not a classic either. Once it finished, the BBC2 announcer... err... announced that the second film was to be shown in a few minutes after the usual news bulletin. This announcement was made over the most god-awful photo/picture I'd ever seen in my life! The BBC often used to cobble together weird images to publicise these films – a bat with a human face for *Night Monster*, a *Doctor Who* Auton for *House of Wax*, and an indescribable image for *White Zombie*, for example! – but this one was the worst: an eyeball surrounded by nerves and blood vessels with a jagged streak of forked lightning coming from it. That image was so horrific it put me off the film there and then, but I struggled through it all, accompanied by my understanding, and equally spooked mum.

The film stars Ray Milland and is directed and produced by good ole' Roger Corman for good ole' AIP but the film has none of the cosy feel of the Poe-based horrors. It's set in the then-present day for a start and has a completely serious tone, with not a trace of spoofery. Milland plays Dr. James Xavier who has created a serum which, when dropped into the eye, gives a person the ability to see the radiation which is ever-present in the air around us, and in turn enables that person to see through things. This is all described in serious scientific tones and makes one really nervous about what lies ahead!

With his attractive assistant Diane (Diana Van der Vlis), Xavier wastes no time trying out the serum on a monkey which promptly has a heart attack, induced by the shock of what it sees. Xavier then decides to try out the serum on himself. The effects in the film aren't the best but they still have a certain something about them. When Xavier drops the serum into his eyes, he (and the viewers) see some cheap coloured effects, but the script is quite a different matter, as he describes a nightmarish "splitting of the world" that is filled with an intolerable light. Once this wears off, he discovers he can indeed see through things but at a relatively low level, so he decides to put another drop into each eye...

When Xavier recovers, we have a brief moment of "comedy" in which he's at a party and is delighted to see himself surrounded by a bunch of naked, jiving bodies! We don't see anything we shouldn't, as the camera focuses on legs, feet, bare backs and faces. Good thing too. I'm in a minority but I don't think there's anything at all sexy or attractive about a lot of pimply, pale, over or underweight, bodies writhing about! Women are much sexier when clothed. Anyway, Xavier is promptly escorted off the party premises by his disapproving assistant but the levity doesn't last long, and we get another horrific description of what his new sight is showing him, as he describes Diane as a "perfect, breathing dissection"!

Xavier ends up on the run, after accidentally killing his friend and colleague Sam (Harold J. Stone), getting a brief job in a carnival as a sort of all-seeing fortune-teller. Corman regular Dick Miller has a nice cameo as a heckler who gets shown up by Xavier, who it turns out, has a nice line in witty put-downs. Don Rickles plays a vendor who realises he's gotten hold of a metaphorical golden goose with Xavier, and the pair of them soon set up shop in a squalid apartment block, with Xavier looking into people's bodies and diagnosing their ailments.

These scenes again promise to be spine-chilling but the effects don't match up – perhaps a good thing. Upon gazing into the bodies of terminal cancer patients, we see a rather inept bit of artwork showing the inside of the body, though Milland's delivery of the sublime script convinces us that he's seeing something a lot worse. One aspect of the film that I didn't really take in when seeing it for the first time was the fact that Xavier kept on taking the serum, having become addicted to it. If he hadn't the effect would have worn off, but because he keeps dropping it into his eyes, it has a cumulative effect. So much so, that Xavier's vision becomes so powerful, he has to wear a pair of extra-thick dark glasses, behind which his eyes are permanently closed! One of the most horrific bits has Xavier, before retiring to bed for the night, putting more of the hellish serum into his eyes. In obvious distress, he can't help but open them but screams in agony and horror at the hellish light he sees.

The action then switches to Las Vegas, with Xavier reunited with

Diana, and trying to win a fortune by using his vision to cheat at cards. Unfortunately, his specs are knocked off during a fracas... This bit, when Xavier screams in horror and denial as he's confronted by a bunch of garishly-coloured skeletons has a definite frisson and it's scenes like this that make one have to keep reminding oneself that the film comes from the cosy stable of Price and Poe chillers like *Tales of Terror* and *The Raven*.

Don Rickles and Ray Milland in
X: The Man with the X-Ray Eyes *(1963)*

The film ends on a bleak note, with Xavier tearing his eyes out, having reached a point where the world is a mad kaleidoscope of colour and light which he can no longer tolerate. Watching the film at the age of twelve in 1978, I convinced myself that what I saw was Xavier's face covered in blood with two empty eye sockets surrounded by gore... what is actually seen on screen is a bloodless Xavier sporting a couple of red contact lenses (another sinister touch is that Xavier's eyes change colour over the course of the film, becoming gold and black)! The ending has impact though, with Xavier deciding that the weird pulsating image he can now see is God Himself looking at him. The ending would have been even more unsavoury if the original line about "I can still see!" had been included – I wonder if this was actually filmed or in the script, or is it just an urban myth sort of thing?

Anyway, a downright excellent, if disturbing and unpleasant SF/Horror – definitely not the sort of film you'd slip on if you fancied a cosy relaxing night's viewing. Back in July 1978, on the Monday after this film had been shown, I returned to school (last week before the six week summer holidays!) excitedly looking forward to chatting to my mates about the film and animatedly discussing all its scientific aspects and camera work and implied nudity... but none of them had seen it!

Ray Milland in X: The Man with the X-Ray Eyes *(1963)*

RUE MORGUE AND FANTASIA
JOSE MOJICA MARINS'
AT MIDNIGHT I'LL TAKE YOUR SOUL
COFFIN JOE
IN PERSON! VERY RARE APPEARANCE!
ONE NIGHT ONLY!
CLASSIC TRAILERS!
GHASTLY PRIZES!

CHAPTER 24

AT MIDNIGHT I'LL TAKE YOUR SOUL (1964)
and
THIS NIGHT I WILL POSSESS YOUR CORPSE (1967)

José Mojica Marins in At Midnight I'll Take Your Soul *(1964)* aka À Meia Noite Levarei Sua Alma *(original title)*

AT MIDNIGHT I'LL TAKE YOUR SOUL (1964):

Directed by: José Mojica Marins.

Written by: José Mojica Marins (story and screenplay) and Magda Mei.

Starring: José Mojica Marins, Magda Mei, Nivaldo Lima, Valéria Vasquez, Ilídio Martins Simões, Arildo Iruam and more.

Studio: Indústria Cinematográfica Apolo.

***THIS NIGHT I WILL POSSESS YOUR CORPSE* (1967)**:

Directed by: José Mojica Marins.

Written by: Aldenora De Sa Porto and José Mojica Marins.

Starring: José Mojica Marins, Tina Wohlers, Nadia Freitas, Antonio Fracari, Jose Lobo, Esmeralda Ruchel and more.

Studio: Ibérica Filmes.

JUST A GUY NAMED COFFIN JOE

I'M NOT BIG on Brazilian horror cinema so I came to these films cold, so to speak. I first became aware of Coffin Joe when I quickly perused the premiere issue of the *House of Hammer* magazine which had an article on Brazilian films (I think it was all of two pages), and then much later, it was in the DVD review section of *The Dark Side* when I read about it properly, in a very interesting piece from Vince Whatever-his-name-was. It was easy to recall this particular review as it was the only interesting one he did, preferring to review DVDs of really cheap and tacky, obscure rubbish that nobody would want to watch once, let alone buy!

At Midnight I'll Take Your Soul, however, sounded interesting. Apparently, the central character of Coffin Joe was a celebrity in Brazil and the actor José Mojica Marins was very famous out there, with his creation in Brazil's first real horror film and him ending up as something of a cultural icon and national bogeyman. It wasn't long before I purchased the boxed set of all the Coffin Joe films (all two) and associated stuff, like *Day of the Beast* and *The Strange World of Coffin Joe*, an anthology of three tales in which CJ acts as host (oh, and my mate Philip's wife is also named CJ, incidentally! I hope she has her nails cut...), so I then settled down to watch them late one Friday night many moons ago.

The first film straight away comes across as something a bit out of the ordinary, with it's sinister opening warning getting the viewer in an appropriately creeped-out mood. Filmed in black and white, Marins plays Coffin Joe, or "Zé do Caixão", to give him his real name, an undertaker who has a bee in his bonnet about God and his wife's inability to bear him a son. Proving that he also has a few bats in his belfry, so to speak, CJ sics a horrible-looking tarantula on his bound and captive wife, resulting in her death. CJ gets away with it though, as the authorities can find no evidence that he was behind the murder.

Coffin Joe is a nice chap – eating meat in full view of a holy procession on Good Friday, spouting abuse at the Almighty and getting involved in bloody altercations in the local tavern, he and his terribly long fingernails (which were apparently Marins' own) are regarded with fear by the inhabitants of the unnamed town where he lives and works, so much so that the creepy top-hatted figure thinks he can try it on with anyone. Unfortunately, CJ's advances towards his friend Antônio's fiancé Terezinha result in him being soundly rebuffed, which quickly leads to her subsequent rape, vicious beating and eventual suicide. But not before she vows to return from the grave at midnight, hence the film's title. To pass the time, CJ also drowns Antônio in a bathtub and then gouges out the eyes of the neighbourhood doctor (who suspects CJ isn't carrying a full coffin, so to speak) before setting him alight.

Things don't end well for Joe, who finds himself pursued by sinister ghostly apparitions which lead him to the crypt where Antônio and Terenzinha are buried and CJ's ghastly mutilated body is discovered not long after. Serves the bastard right. The film is a little slow at times, and Marins goes overboard at detailing the character's hatred for humanity, God and the universe, but ultimately this is a winner.

José Mojica Marins as Coffin Joe in
At Midnight I'll Take Your Soul *(1964)*

This Night I Will Possess Your Corpse was the charmingly-titled sequel from 1967. It seems CJ *wasn't* killed by the re-animated corpses at the end of the previous film but merely injured and recovering in hospital. Once discharged he wastes no time in returning to his old home town and proves his previous experience has done his sanity no favours when he promptly kidnaps six women overnight, bringing them to his lair where he subjects them to a seemingly-endless horde of spiders! The survivor of all of this, Marcia, is therefore deemed fit enough to bear Joe's offspring but before the unhinged undertaker gets the chance to drop his underpants Marcia is off, but she promises to keep quiet about what he's done (which also includes murdering the other five girls with a horde of snakes, an incident which nearly polished off an actress for real apparently)!

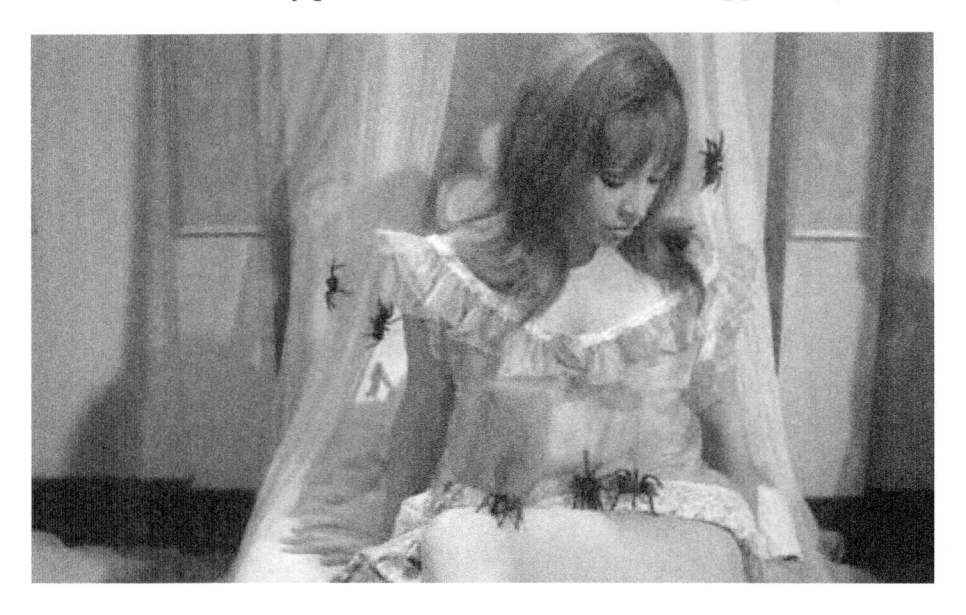

Scene from This Night I Will Possess Your Corpse *(1967) aka* Esta Noite Encarnarei no Teu Cadáver *(original title)*

Discovering later that one of the women he gleefully murdered was pregnant, Coffin Joe feels remorse for his actions but it's too late as he ends up getting dragged down to Hell, in what is the highlight of the film. *This Night...* is a gloomy monochrome film like the first but it blooms into glorious colour for the sequence set in Hell – which has strangely frozen over! No sign of any fires here, it's all ice and frost covering its victims. These scenes are quite repetitive after a bit with the same footage being repeated constantly, but it doesn't matter and if you'd been quietly nodding off prior to this section of the film then this segment will wake you right up! The sight of bare-assed demons waltzing about with whips and intermittent lightning bolts striking writhing souls encased in mounds of ice is an eye-opener, and the Devil himself has Joe's face!

After this, the film isn't as good but it leads to a good ending in which Joe is shot by the enraged townsfolk and ends up in a pond, before being persuaded to accept God by a friendly priest!

The film has the same problems as the first one, being a little slow-paced and with CJ's constant ranting about having a kid getting tedious after a bit – personally, I'd rather have a sandwich – but is an effective enough chiller to warrant investing in the DVD boxed set. I remember watching it with a couple of mates not long after and although they started to ridicule it at the beginning, they quickly came around (one moment of levity involved my choking on a piece of the burger I was chomping on at the time – I briefly became "Coughin' Joe"), drawn in by the film's mix of *Night of the Living Dead*-style 1960s B&W, mixed with graphic blood-letting and a nicely-judged note of blasphemy!

Marins died earlier this year but he left behind a lasting legacy as Brazilian horror cinema's best (only?) representative. The Coffin Joe saga is just crying out to be remade by an American studio – speeded up a bit and set in the present day with an English-speaking cast, these films would work a treat.

This Night I Will Possess Your Corpse *(1967)*

WHEN THE SKULL STRIKES
YOU'LL SCREAM!
THE SKULL
TECHNICOLOR
TECHNISCOPE
STARRING
PETER CUSHING · PATRICK WYMARK · GUEST STAR: CHRISTOPHER LEE
PRODUCED BY MILTON SUBOTSKY AND MAX J. ROSENBERG · DIRECTED BY FREDDIE FRANCIS · SCREENPLAY BY MILTON SUBOTSKY · BASED ON A STORY BY ROBERT BLOCH
AN AMICUS PRODUCTION
A PARAMOUNT RELEASE

CHAPTER 25

THE SKULL (1965)

"The Skull" by Randy Broecker

Directed by: Freddie Francis.

Written by: Robert Bloch (from the story "The Skull of the Marquis de Sade" by) and Milton Subotsky (screenplay by).

Starring: Peter Cushing, Christopher Lee, Patrick Wymark, Jill Bennett, Nigel Green, Michael Gough and more.

Studio: Amicus Productions.

BLOCH'S BONER

I'VE NEVER READ any Robert Bloch stories, but I've always intended to. This 1965 Amicus film is based on one such story, "The Skull of the Marquis de Sade", published in 1965. I don't know about the story but this is a bloody good film, make no bones about it!

I first saw the first 25 minutes or so in the mid-70, in (wait for it!) the Friday night film slot on Tyne Tees. I was impressed but also at that age where 11 o'clock at night was so far away and impossibly distant – the result being I began to yawn cavernously and so my mother carted me off to bed, resulting in me missing the bulk of what looked like being a very good horror film. Fast forward to 1980 – I'm 13 years old, can watch what I like on my portable TV in my bedroom (reception permitting!) and *The Skull* is being shown as part of BBC2's best ever horror double bill season – so good, in fact, that it was actually called *Horror Double Bill* for once – in week 9, paired with the Universal historical melodrama that always gets classed as a horror film, 1939's *Tower of London*.

I quite liked the 1939 film – the "warm-up", I suppose you could call it – and settled back as the glorious music of Elisabeth Lutyens filled my ears to the accompaniment of the opening credits, fully expecting to enjoy another classic British film in the same way I'd loved *Dr. Terror's House of Horrors*, *From Beyond the Grave* and *Night of the Demon* in the same season. I was bored rigid. Admittedly, it was only after the first 40 minutes or so that I began to get a bit restless – Peter Cushing and Christopher Lee (billed as "Guest Star", which surprised me, as this wasn't a US TV show) were as impressive as ever, in fact I think their roles in this one are criminally underrated and overlooked and the fact alone that they both end up dead makes this an atypical film in that respect – but so much of the action towards the end seemed to consist of the skull floating around, and a line-less Cushing looking frightened, that I began to lose interest. In later years, when recollecting this film, I wondered how they could make a movie where the last 30 minutes had no dialogue – I was actually misremembering it, as the actual amount of screen time with just the skull and Cushing towards the end is nowhere near as long as that.

Peter Cushing in The Skull *(1965)*

I saw the film again in the 1990s and was quick to video tape it. This time it was shown on a Friday night on Tyne Tees under the "Appointment With Fear" banner so beloved in the '70s, and which we in Geordie-land never got. The intro used in that earlier decade was replaced by a newer one, still very effective. It showed the faces of Cushing, Price, Lee, the Creature, Linda Blair's Regan, Chaney's Phantom and at least half a dozen others morphing into each other, until finally a skull changed into the logo. Anyway, I enjoyed the film very much on this occasion, finally seeing in it the classic qualities everyone else did. Getting the film on Blu-ray in 2012 cemented that opinion.

The Skull casts Peter Cushing as Christopher Maitland, a collector of the grotesque and the forbidden, and he certainly gets his money's worth here – the collection of statuettes of figures from the "Parliament" of Hell are bloody terrifying, even if they are made of stone, and they would have been amazing in any film in which these characters appeared in the flesh.

Bidding against him, and ultimately winning, is Christopher Lee playing another similarly-obsessed character, Matthew Phillips, with an interest in the occult. Talking of which, I remember reading an interview with Lee in the 1990s in which he admitted dabbling in stuff like this and the consequences put him off trying it again... Interesting. The two friendly rivals are joined in the film by a "somewhat shady individual" called Marco (Patrick Wymark) who supplies them both with items for their collections, at a hefty price. Marco's latest procurement is the skull of the Marquis de Sade, which still houses a sinister spirit – cue lots of death and destruction, after an impressive and lengthy flashback sequence to the skull's previous owners and what happened to them (the part featuring George Coulouris as a lawyer chappie who is influenced by the skull to commit murder was my main memory of this film from my 1970s viewing, with part of the scene being watched through the empty eye sockets of the skull itself, a trick repeated later on in the film).

Peter Cushing and Christopher Lee in The Skull *(1965)*

There's a great cast in this one – apart from the two horror stars and Wymark, Peter Woodthorpe plays Marco's landlord who has a smashing part – literally! – as he meets his end tumbling down through several sheets of glass in his boarding house. Jill Bennett plays Cushing's wife, Nigel Green has a small role as a detective, dear old Michael Gough has a small role as an auctioneer, and Bob

Todd-lookalike Frank Forsyth plays the sinister Marquis himself in a weird dream sequence in which Cushing is forced to play Russian Roulette with a loaded gun to his head. The scenes of the skull floating about aren't as effective on Blu-ray where the wires can clearly be seen, but the end still packs a punch and there's plenty of great dialogue to be had in the scenes where Lee and Cushing are discussing the skull and the evil influence it has (Cushing learned how to play snooker, during this scene apparently) – "Don't think I wasn't tempted", cautions Lee, as he tells Cushing of the sinister demonic beings that would come into his snooker room during a particular time of the year/night and try to get him to take part in their unholy ceremonies (snooker?)! All because of the skull, which he had in his possession at the time.

An excellent example of a non-anthology Amicus horror, *The Skull* exerts an influence on the viewer comparable to the influence the actual skull has on characters in the film – but without the murder!

April Olrich in The Skull *(1965)*

The dreaded curse of the Ourang Sancto turned her into a slithering snake!
THE REPTILE
COLOR BY DELUXE
Starring
NOEL WILLMAN · RAY BARRETT
Also Starring
JENNIFER DANIEL · JACQUELINE PEARCE
Produced by ANTHONY NELSON KEYS · Directed by JOHN GILLING
Screenplay by JOHN ELDER
A Seven Arts-Hammer Production Released by 20th Century-Fox

CHAPTER 26
THE REPTILE (1966)

"The Reptile" by Randy Broecker

Directed by: John Gilling.

Written by: Anthony Hinds (screenplay, as John Elder).

Starring: Noel Willman, Jennifer Daniel, Ray Barrett, Jacqueline Pearce, Michael Ripper, John Laurie and more.

Studio: Hammer Films.

HISSY FIT

THIS 1966 HAMMER CORNISH chiller was made back-to-back with the similarly "set in the land of the pasty" *The Plague of the Zombies*. It's hard to say which film is better but I have a soft spot for this one, having previously missed both films when they were shown in the late '70s *Dracula, Frankenstein and Friends!* double bill season on BBC2.

The comic strip of *The Reptile* appeared in issue 19 of *House of Hammer* magazine (or *Hammer's House of Horror* no. 1, if you prefer) and it was a stand-out, with the late Brian Lewis's excellent artwork – though funnily enough, it didn't grace the cover. I did finally catch up with the film in the mid-'90s with a rare TV showing, and it turned out to be as good as I expected.

Ray Barrett plays Harry Spalding, who comes with his wife Valerie (played by the very attractive Jennifer Daniel) to live in the small Cornish cottage recently vacated by his dead brother. The viewers already know because they've seen it in the film's effectively creepy prologue – that Spalding's brother was killed by some sort of venomous snake which left his face as black as boot polish and frothing at the mouth like an irate *Doctor Who* fan who has just discovered his time-travelling, two-hearted alien hero has become female.

It's not long before we are introduced to the suavely sinister Dr. Franklyn (Noel Willman, who had appeared with Daniel in Hammer's earlier *Kiss of the Vampire*) and his moon-faced daughter Anna (Jacqueline Pearce), who it turns out has paid for her father's nosiness and been transformed into a snake-woman by a sinister foreign tribe who worship such creatures. Typically for a '60s Hammer film, it takes forever before we actually get to see Anna in snake form but it's not disappointing, with some of Roy Ashton's best make-up work being given more weight by some of John Gilling's best direction – the reptilian Anna lurches from a doorway to sink her fangs into the hero's neck, but although the boot polish beckons, he manages to get the poison removed before it can take effect.

One element that I like very much is the character of "Mad Peter", the village's resident idiot, brought colourfully to life by John Laurie, an actor who would soon be swapping his mad Cornishman role for a mad Scotsman in the BBC *Dad's Army* series. Laurie has a great face for horror films and despite Peter being essentially a comic character, he still comes across as quite scary – especially when slouched against the Spalding's window, face blackened and desperately trying to get help after being bitten on the moors, and later, when his corpse is exhumed. Peter is the most entertaining character in the film, and I share the sentiments of Michael Ripper's landlord when he says "I, for one, will miss him".

The film comes to a standard fiery climax, with a large house on fire, which is also how Hammer films such as *Evil of Frankenstein*, *Plague of the Zombies* and *Frankenstein Must Be Destroyed* came to an end. Compared to Hammer's other snake-oriented female monster of the same period, *The Gorgon* from 1964, *The Reptile* stands up very well, despite the absence of either Cushing or Lee in the cast and though it's not as good as the company's very best films, it easily outdoes the worst.

Jacqueline Pearce in The Reptile *(1966)*

When in Southern California visit Universal City Studios
America's Funniest Family
in their FIRST FULL-LENGTH FEATURE
in TECHNICOLOR
MUNSTER, GO HOME
Herman races the world's fastest cars with his DRAG-U-LA special!
starring
FRED GWYNNE · YVONNE DeCARLO
AL LEWIS · BUTCH PATRICK and DEBBIE WATSON
also starring
TERRY-THOMAS · HERMIONE GINGOLD
SCREENPLAY BY GEORGE TIBBLES, JOE CONNELLY and BOB MOSHER
DIRECTED BY
EARL BELLAMY
PRODUCED BY
JOE CONNELLY and BOB MOSHER
A UNIVERSAL PICTURE

CHAPTER 27

MUNSTER, GO HOME! (1966)

Butch Patrick, Al Lewis, Fred Gwynne, Yvonne De Carlo and Debbie Watson in Munster, Go Home! *(1966)*

Directed by: Earl Bellamy.

Written by: Joe Connelly, Bob Mosher and George Tibbles.

Starring: Fred Gwynne, Yvonne De Carlo, Al Lewis, Butch Patrick, Debbie Watson, Terry-Thomas and more.

Studio: Universal Pictures.

UNIVERSAL LAUGHTER

I HAD A fair few crushes when I was a lad. The first was Daphne from *Scooby-Doo* (Editor Trevor Kennedy's first love as well!). Ah, how I remember my little fantasies about being Shaggy and impressing her with my bravery, humour, and sandwich-eating skills! These crushes later spread to various women from TV and films, the strangest being a chimpanzee, when I got an infatuation with Zira from the *Planet of the Apes* films!

By 1983, my crush on *Buck Rogers* babe Wilma had worn off but I didn't have much time to kick off my libido and relax before I got another mad infatuation – this time with a female vampiress in a 1960s sitcom...

The Munsters (1964-1966) featured a family of loveable monsters led by Fred Gwynne as Herman Munster, a Frankenstein's Monster-a like. Herman was, as his wife Lily pointed out once, a "real goofball". Grandpa (Al Lewis, who had starred with Gwynne in the earlier sitcom *Car 54, Where are you?*) was Count Dracula himself, capable of turning himself into a bat or a wolf and concocting all sorts of strange spells and potions in his laboratory. Eddie (Butch Patrick) was a werewolf, though we never see him in full wolf mode. The Munsters' niece Marilyn was a normal blonde, and was played by Beverley Owen in the first episodes and by Pat Priest for the rest of the series. The Munster family lived at 1313 Mockingbird Lane, in a ramshackle old house with a dinosaur called Spot in the basement!

My infatuation with Lily Munster (Yvonne De Carlo) came about when Channel 4 – previously shown on BBC2 in the '60s, Channel 4 had been screening it since November 1982 – screened the season two episode "Herman, the Master Spy" in June 1983. In this particular episode, the family go for a day out at the beach. While Herman goes off scuba diving (and gets caught by the crew of a Russian submarine!), Eddie builds sandcastles, and Grandpa, Lily and Marilyn decide to sunbathe. Lily normally always wore a white floaty shroud-like dress but here she wears a totally different outfit – the sight of Lily Munster in a mini-skirt and opaque black tights was such a turn-on for me as a hormonal teenager. She became my new crush and I devoured the *TV Times* article on De Carlo that appeared around Easter that year!

Fast-forward to 1986. Channel 4 have repeated the whole series and my crush on Lily/Yvonne De Carlo had worn off. But over Christmas, Channel 4 decided to screen the 1966 cinema spin-off film *Munster, Go Home!*, followed by the 1981 TV movie *The Munsters' Revenge*. I'd seen the 1966 film previously, when it had been shown on a Saturday morning around 1978 on my local ITV station Tyne Tees. But I couldn't really remember much about it, and I'd never seen the TV show at that point.

Munster, Go Home! was made directly after the TV show had finished, with its seventieth and last episode "A Visit from the Teacher" in May 1966. The film retained all the elements of the show, except that Pat Priest was replaced by Debbie Watson as a far cuter Marilyn, and of course there was no sound of audience laughter in the background.

Directed by Earl Bellamy, who had directed numerous episodes of the series, the film has the Munster family upping stakes and moving to England after Herman inherits Munster Hall following the death of his wealthy uncle. Terry-Thomas and Hermione Gingold (the liquid Ralph Dibney drank to become the Elongated Man in DC Comics!) play a couple of scheming crooks who want the estate to themselves and after their scare tactics of dressing up as spooks to frighten the Munsters away fail miserably – Herman and Lily enjoy the show! – they attempt to do away with lovable goof Herman during a drag car race, which is obviously filmed near the Hollywood Hills rather than in England's green and pleasant lands.

The humour in the film is the same as that in the show and, though I love the series, I never really found it laugh-out-loud funny, and that's the case here – the humour tends to be fairly obvious and twists everyday conventions on their heads with macabre and supernatural spins (i.e. Grandpa's sayings such as "never put the hearse before the horse" or the family thinking it's a beautiful day when it's raining and cloudy) but it was successful and it's a shame that the show only lasted two seasons before it had a chance to blossom into colour.

The film ends with the Munsters deciding to pack up and return to the States (and their pet dinosaur Spot!), and the last scene in the film was the final one filmed, with the family driving away in their converted hearse, the Munster Koach, to a future of continual re-runs, a large fan following, and several resurrections, none of which came close to achieving the charm and success of the original.

SHRIEK!!
warning:
to every creature of flesh and blood!
Beware
the beat of the cloth-wrapped feet!
Dead A Thousand Years
Now He Lives And Breathes
To Avenge An Ancient Curse---
To Strangle The Living...
Raise The Dead---
And Prey Upon Human Flesh!
Beware
"THE MUMMY'S SHROUD"
COLOR
BY DELUXE
STARRING
ANDRE MORELL · JOHN PHILLIPS · DAVID BUCK and ELIZABETH SELLARS · Also Starring CATHERINE LACEY
Screenplay by JOHN GILLING
From an Original Story by JOHN ELDER
Produced by ANTHONY NELSON KEYS · Directed by JOHN GILLING
A SEVEN ARTS-HAMMER PRODUCTION · A 20th CENTURY-FOX RELEASE

CHAPTER 28

THE MUMMY'S SHROUD (1967)

Eddie Powell in The Mummy's Shroud *(1967)*

Directed by: John Gilling.

Written by: John Gilling (screenplay) and Anthony Hinds (from an original story by, as John Elder).

Starring: André Morell, John Phillips, David Buck, Elizabeth Sellars, Maggie Kimberly, Michael Ripper and more.

Studio: Hammer Films/Seven Arts Productions.

BEWARE THE BEAT...

DEFINITELY THE BEST of the four Hammer Mummy films, the cycle began with 1959's *The Mummy* and ended in 1971 with *Blood from the Mummy's Tomb*. *The Mummy* is a great film and it cleverly remakes the five Universal Mummy films in one film, with a great performance by Christopher Lee and some stunning set-pieces. *The Curse of the Mummy's Tomb* (1964) is a good film but the weakest of the bunch, and doesn't really bring much that's new to the table, as well as having a distinctly no-star cast (Dickie Owen as the Mummy, anyone?). *Blood...* is a great film but not really, despite it's title, a Mummy film. So, *The Mummy's Shroud* it is.

I once persuaded a fellow Hammer/horror fanatic to watch the film at his house one night, back in 1999. He wasn't keen but I managed to talk him round, though the film's beginning certainly didn't help – ten minutes of seeing a bunch of extras stumbling around a beach in Buckinghamshire and pretending they're in ancient Egypt! Once past that though, the unwary Hammer fan who hasn't seen this one is in for a treat...

After Dickie Owen – bit of a tongue-twister, that name – the role of the bandaged one fell to the equally unknown Eddie Powell for this film. Powell, like Owen, was a stuntman and no real acting was required for the part so Powell lumbered around, arms outstretched as good as anyone. The film has the usual plot: group of archaeologists break into a tomb, of boy Pharaoh Kah-to-Bey and there is soon hell to pay, as they are pursued by a murderous Mummy and the Pharaoh's bodyguard Prem (played by Dickie Owen!). What sets this one apart are the details – Michael Ripper, for instance, in one of his best roles, plays Longbarrow, the nervous and obsequious secretary to the financier of the expedition, Preston. Longbarrow is constantly harping on about getting back to England and is constantly disappointed, culminating in his death at the hands of the Mummy.

Talking of which, the Mummy murders here are another strong reason for the film's success. André Morell plays Sir Basil Walden, an important member of the expedition who is overworked to the point of collapse. The evil and lazy, glory-hogging swine Stanley Preston (John Phillips), depicted as a man who is happy to sit on his arse swigging back whiskeys and sodas while the rest of the team are breaking their backs, breaking into the tomb, has Basil put in an Egyptian asylum but he soon escapes. Taking temporary refuge in a creepy fortune teller's tent, the sinister old crone predicts death – just as the Mummy comes in behind Walden and crushes his head! We don't see this but we hear it, as the camera focuses on the old crone's gloating eyes.

Another victim gets done in by the Mummy in a laboratory, when it smashes a bottle containing acid all over the poor sod who is cringing on the floor. Longbarrow is killed by Prem in his hotel room – he breaks his glasses, can only blurrily see the monster bearing down on him and when he does realise what it is, it's too late! Longbarrow's demise is both funny and sort-of-frightening, as the Mummy bundles him up in blankets from his bed, then throws him out of the window and into a trough.

When Preston gets his just desserts, it's disappointingly routine with no frills. Pity – a more elaborate end for the swine would have been better than just being quickly dispatched in a street. The murderous Prem is destroyed when the words from the titular shroud are read backwards and it crumbles to dust. David Buck and Maggie Kimberly are the heroes here, and future *Doctor Who*'s The Master actor Roger Delgado plays a sinister character who is in cahoots with the aforementioned fortune teller and the Mummy, and who gets shot in the finale.

This was the last Hammer film made at Bray Studios, synonymous with the Hammer name. It was the end of an era.

Maggie Kimberly in The Mummy's Shroud *(1967)*

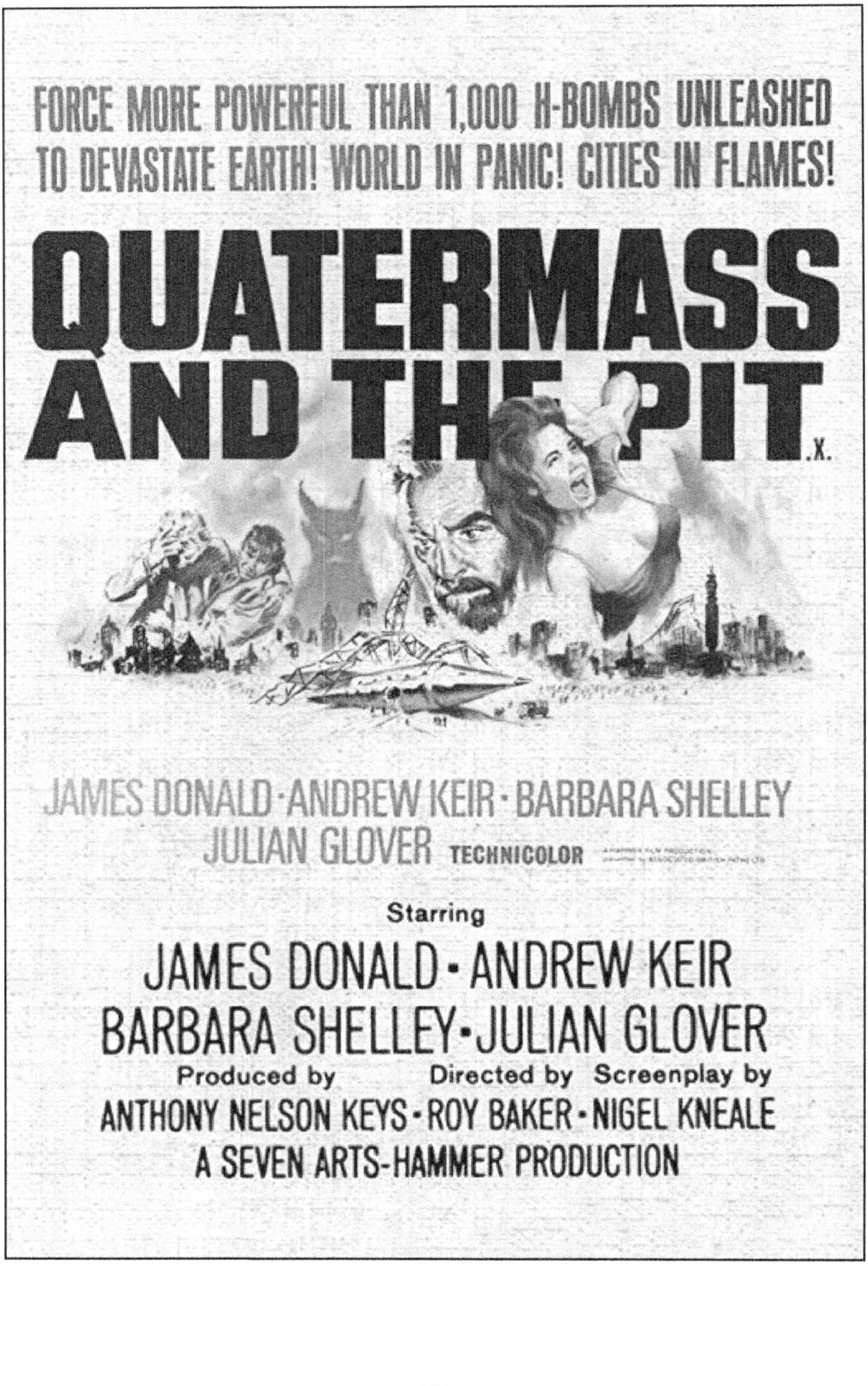
FORCE MORE POWERFUL THAN 1,000 H-BOMBS UNLEASHED
TO DEVASTATE EARTH! WORLD IN PANIC! CITIES IN FLAMES!
QUATERMASS
AND THE PIT
X.
JAMES DONALD · ANDREW KEIR · BARBARA SHELLEY
JULIAN GLOVER TECHNICOLOR
Starring
JAMES DONALD · ANDREW KEIR
BARBARA SHELLEY · JULIAN GLOVER
Produced by Directed by Screenplay by
ANTHONY NELSON KEYS · ROY BAKER · NIGEL KNEALE
A SEVEN ARTS-HAMMER PRODUCTION

CHAPTER 29

QUATERMASS AND THE PIT (1967)

Andrew Keir in Quatermass and the Pit *(1967)*

Directed by: Roy Ward Baker.

Written by: Nigel Neale (original story and screenplay).

Starring: James Donald, Andrew Keir, Barbara Shelley, Julian Glover, Duncan Lamont, Bryan Marshall and more.

Studio: Hammer Films/Toho Company.

HELL IN HOBBS LANE

IT'S BEEN A very long time since I last saw *The Quatermass Xperiment*, Hammer's 1955 film version of the 1953 BBC serial. I've got the DVD of the three Quatermass serials but only the first two episodes of the 1953 serial survive, and watching them for the first time, I found them to be incredibly slow to the point of being unendurable. Watching them the second time, I enjoyed them quite a bit more but it's a pity the other four episodes are lost. *Quatermass II* was the 1955 follow-up and I think it's by far the best of the three BBC productions. *Quatermass and the Pit* followed in 1958 and it's good but overrated.

The 1955 Hammer version of the first serial I remember as being a very good film, and light years ahead of other Hammer SF like *Four Sided Triangle* and *Spaceways* (both 1953). Hammer did *Quatermass II* full justice, with their 1957 film version which is oddly disturbing at times. I also have to admit I like Brian Donlevy as Quatermass – true, a loud-mouthed American in a mac isn't the average picture of an English professor, but Donlevy is oddly interesting in the role – though creator and writer Nigel Kneale didn't think so, branding him "dreadful" (Kneale was notoriously difficult to please).

Donlevy's services were not utilised by the time Hammer got around to adapting the third serial *Quatermass and the Pit* in 1967, instead opting for Scottish actor Andrew Keir who'd been Father Sandor in Hammer's *Dracula: Prince of Darkness*. Personally, I think Keir is a tad overrated in the role – yes, he's more like what you'd expect an English professor to be like but he's not particularly impressive and also doesn't receive top billing – instead James Donald (Doctor Roney) oddly gets the credit.

The film is in colour which makes it stand out from the first two monochrome entries. Some changes are made to the story, with the original BBC six-parter involving building work on a street (Hobbs Lane, Hob being an old name for the Devil), while this one takes place in the London Underground. A nice cast is assembled including familiar Hammer faces such as Barbara Shelley, Duncan Lamont and Robert Morris, while *Doctor Who* fans will recognise Edwin Richfield and Julian Glover from their appearances in that iconic BBC show.

The film revolves around a building extension in the Underground, with workers finding a human skeleton millions of years old, followed by what the Army thinks is an unexploded bomb but is actually an ancient spacecraft from Mars. Nice performance from Julian Glover as Colonel Breen, a pompous military idiot who sticks to his pet theory that the Martian ship is a Nazi weapon, and the weird alien insects contained within it are designed to freak out us Brits! Quatermass comes in to investigate and gets the chance to let rip at the narrow-minded military and governmental idiots he's surrounded by and who block his attempts to find out the truth at every turn. Strangely though, Quatermass isn't really the hero of the film – along with James Donald as Doctor Matthew Roney getting top billing, it's Roney who saves humanity at the end, at the cost of his own life.

The film has some nicely ripe performances – I love it when Duncan Lamont's workman Sladden gets "possessed" by the sinister forces from the spaceship, and it's obvious Lamont loved it too! Just the right side of OTT, the sight of Lamont being merrily buffeted along by a paranormal wind, causing a burger van to be demolished in his wake, is quite hilarious! The feeling of race memory fear caused by the ship's discovery and activation is well evoked, with sweaty policemen and hysterical female scientists, and getting the idea across that the Martians have influenced mankind's development and evolution for millions of years. Talking of sweat, there's plenty of it on Colonel Breen's face when the literally-stinking Martians are removed from their ship, and he looks at them with revulsion, partly from the bizarre sight of the unearthly insectoids and partly from gagging disgust at their putrid pong – "Like rotting fish!"!

The Martian insects are effective and much better than the ones in the BBC serial, thought the "wild hunt" scenes set on Mars don't quite come off as they should and run the risk of being close to silly. When the climactic chaos properly comes, it's well-directed by Roy Ward Baker, with cameras, cables and the general public being hurled in all directions as the spaceship starts to oddly glow – nice special effects throughout the film, courtesy of Les Bowie, though Nigel Kneale felt the effects let the film down. He was being rather harsh as usual as the effects are fine, with some nice model work, and the image of the "Devil" looming in a red sky over London at the film's climax is one of the most chilling images from Hammer, and I imagine that's a scene that would have been quite petrifying on a cinema screen.

I first saw this one in 1979, as it was the final film in BBC2's *Masters of Terror* season (I don't think Andrew Keir counts as a horror star/Master of Terror though...) and I didn't like it much, surprisingly. I've since changed my mind, of course, as this was one of those Hammer films that seemed to be shown on TV every other year in the '80s and '90s.

This is the best of the Quatermass films and definitely, along with *Quatermass 2*, the best example of Hammer science fiction. When Hammer next turned to the subject of outer space, it was with *Moon Zero Two*... You may judge for yourself how well that turned out.

Alternative poster and title for The Devil Rides Out *(1968)*

CHAPTER 30

THE DEVIL RIDES OUT (1968)

Nike Arrighi and Charles Gray in The Devil Rides Out *(1968) aka* The Devil's Bride *(alternative title)*

Directed by: Terence Fisher.

Written by: Richard Matheson (screenplay) and Dennis Wheatley (novel).

Starring: Christopher Lee, Charles Gray, Nike Arrighi, Leon Greene, Patrick Mower, Gwen Ffrangcon Davies and more.

Studio: Hammer Films/Associated British-Pathé/Seven Arts Productions.

GET MOCATA

I'VE NEVER READ anything by Dennis Wheatley (from whose novel this film was adapted) but he has a reputation as being a very stiff and boring author, or at least, writes very stiff and boring books. I can't comment on that but this film is not boring at all. It was released by Hammer in 1968, but it doesn't feel like a Hammer film. It's genuinely frightening and disturbing and a world away from the cosy castles, bubbling laboratories and nineteenth century cobbled streets and coaches of most other Hammer films of the period.

The first time I saw this was back in 1979, as part of *Masters of Terror*, that summer's season of horror double bills on BBC2. This was screened in the third week, paired with *Night Monster* (1942) and my mother and I were staying at my older brother's while he and his then wife were gallivanting abroad. Come Saturday and I was hyped up as ever (I must have seen the BBC2 trailer for these films – "I'd rather see you dead than meddling with black magic!" – at least ten times!) and couldn't wait for 10.15 pm to roll around.

Night Monster isn't a favourite of mine but it's a perfectly fine film (I even wrote a piece about it for some book by someone whose name escapes me) and set the right mood for the second helping of cosy Hammer horror that evening – an orange-tinted picture of Christopher Lee as the Duc de Richleau was followed by a five minute news bulletin and then by the film itself...

Within seconds of it starting, my mother and I turned and looked at each other in utter horror – we both enjoyed horror films to an extent but anything involving the Devil was a different thing... unlike vampires, werewolves and Bad Baron Frankenstein, there is a *chance* the Devil and demons may exist so any film involving them created a frisson for us. Which in itself was strange because I certainly, at the age of 11, hadn't seen many horror films revolving around Old Nick – only the 1973 TV movie *The Devil's Daughter* springs to mind. Anyway, the opening of this film seriously spooked us and I was having second thoughts about sitting through it all.

Part of the reason the film lacks the usual cosy sort of Hammer feel is because it isn't set in the usual nineteenth century Europe locale but instead takes place in 1930s England... and with Christopher Lee as the hero! Lee is utterly excellent in this film, sending out authority in waves and making it his best performance ever, in my opinion.

The Devil Rides Out involves the Duc and his friend Rex (Leon Greene, dubbed by Patrick Allen) trying to save their friend Simon (pre-*Emmerdale* Patrick Mower) and a girl called Tanith (Nike Arrighi) from the clutches of a cult of Satanists, led by Mocata (Charles Gray). The film, once past the terrifying intro/credits, settles down slightly and focusses on character(s), until a chilling scene in Mocata's house, where the two heroes are confronted by a grinning demon emerging from a hole in the floor. The effect is terrifying and totally successful.

Later, we see a more elaborate creation in the form of the Goat of Mendez – the Devil himself! This is a very realistically-depicted character, being half man and half goat seated on a throne. Though the Devil doesn't get to speak, his presence is all-powerful, and the fact he only appears briefly doesn't lessen the impact.

One thing I never understood as a kid, and still don't now – why would anyone worship the Devil? To put it bluntly, that bastard (if he exists, and Dennis Wheatley firmly believed he did) will do you no favours. So why worship and devote your life to someone who, sooner or later, is going to kill you and cannot be trusted? Satanists, eh? Can't live with them, can't do a terrifying 1960s British horror film without them...

The film moves from location to location, but always with a palpable sense of dread. The climactic scenes in the house of Richard Eaton (Paul Eddington), his wife Marie (Sarah Lawson) and daughter Peggy (Rosalyn Landor), as the assembled heroes surround themselves with a protective chalk circle while Mocata subjects them to supernatural attacks designed to lure them out of the circle, are hair-raising in their intensity. Arachnophobes such as myself won't appreciate the part where a giant tarantula comes crawling into the room (some fuzzy lines around the creature at one point, but overall the effect is a good one), and this is surpassed by the nightmarish visitation of the Angel of Death, a skeleton in armour on a winged horse. When this character appears, the combination of Lee's performance, the sound effects, editing and direction combine to create a masterly moment, one of the very best in Hammer horror.

The film has an unusual ending in which time is reversed, but the evil-doers get their comeuppance (though, worshipping the guy with the horns, they would have sooner or later anyway). The film is a massive success, and it led to the later Wheatley adaptation of *To The Devil a Daughter* in 1976 (which was more a case of "To Hammer a Mediocre Movie"), plus *The Satanist*, another Wheatley novel which was on the cards but never came to fruition.

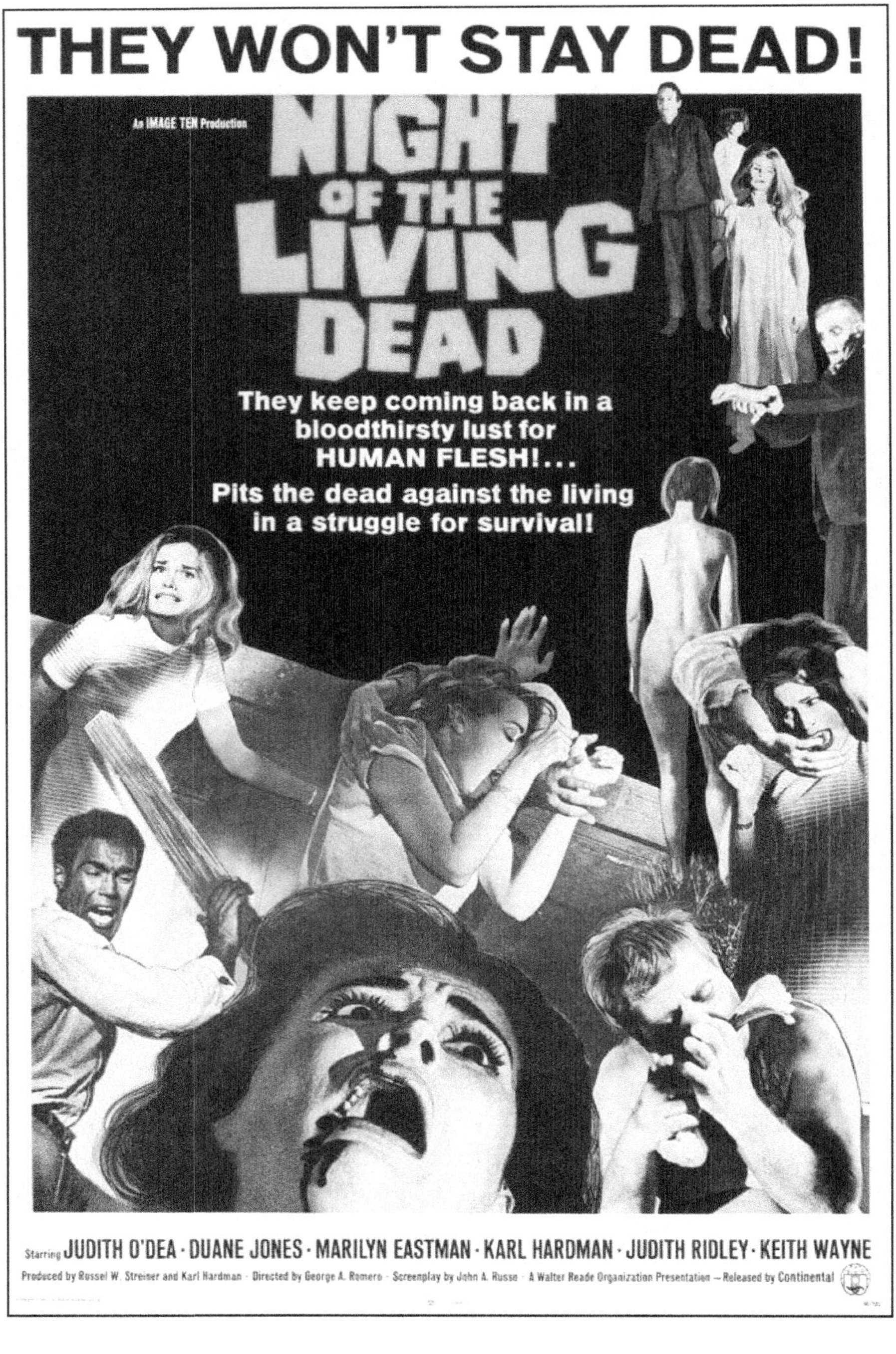
THEY WON'T STAY DEAD!
An IMAGE TEN Production
NIGHT OF THE LIVING DEAD
They keep coming back in a bloodthirsty lust for HUMAN FLESH!...
Pits the dead against the living in a struggle for survival!
Starring JUDITH O'DEA · DUANE JONES · MARILYN EASTMAN · KARL HARDMAN · JUDITH RIDLEY · KEITH WAYNE
Produced by Russel W. Streiner and Karl Hardman · Directed by George A. Romero · Screenplay by John A. Russo · A Walter Reade Organization Presentation — Released by Continental

CHAPTER 31

NIGHT OF THE LIVING DEAD (1968)

Night of the Living Dead *(1968)*

Directed by: George A. Romero.

Written by: John A. Russo (screenplay) and George A. Romero (screenplay).

Starring: Duane Jones, Judith O'Dea, Karl Hardman, Marilyn Eastman, Keith Wayne, Judith Ridley and more.

Studio: Image Ten.

DON'T WATCH THIS FILM IF YOU'RE EASILY SCARED AND YOUR NAME IS BARBARA...

I'M NOT A big fan of George Romero films but this and *The Crazies* (1973) are top notch. Well, almost. This film is in black and white (not a problem) but looks cheap and fairly tacky, only slightly removed from the likes of *Plan 9 from Outer Space*. However, this opening salvo in Romero's ongoing zombiethon is definitely worthy of your time...

Filmed on an estimated budget of $114,000, the film went on to make around $30m at the box office, over 250 times that budget. Shot in Pittsburgh, the film has become a cult classic, leading to several sequels and the film being preserved in the National Film Registry. Not bad for a black and white (relatively) cheap B movie!

The film begins with a couple, siblings Barbra (Judith O'Dea) and Johnny (an uncredited Russell Streiner) visiting their father's grave and encountering the first of many flesh-craving zombies. Exit Johnny (and a good thing too, he's a right annoying bastard!). The action switches to a remote farmhouse which remains the setting of the action for the rest of the film, with the seven central figures holed up there as night draws on... and the living dead converge!

Barbara is soon joined by the Coopers, Harry (Karl Hardman, who was also one of the producers of the film) and Helen (Marilyn Eastman), who have sought shelter in the farmhouse along with their daughter Karen who is ill after being bitten by a zombie. Tom and Jerry... er, Judy (Keith Wayne, Judith Ridley) are a couple of teens, also seeking refuge in the farmhouse and the seven are completed by the hero of the film, Ben (Duane Jones) who just happens to be passing.

The most annoying character in the film, however, is Harry Cooper whose stupid insistence on holing up in the basement lost him any respect from me within a few minutes. Obviously, it would be the worst place to get trapped in, as there's only one way out – and the zombies never give up, in their endless lust for food i.e. people, or more specifically, peoples' brains!

One of the most frightening and disturbing scenes for me in any horror film is the sight of the zombie girl (played by Marilyn Eastman, who also plays Helen Cooper) eating a centipede from a tree! Romero worked wonders on a low budget here, with the black and white of the film adding an atmosphere that would have been probably lost in colour.

The film of course led to several sequels, none of which in my opinion are as good as the original – the main clue to this film's superiority being in the title: *Night*... If you're facing an unstoppable horde of undead ghouls, then night would be the worst time to face them. There's a small clue given via a TV News report as to the cause of the outbreak, with unexplained radiation from a space probe affecting the dead but this is not dwelt on.

The film has a downbeat ending, as all the main characters end up dead, and worse, as reanimated corpses! Nice to see that asshole

Harry getting eaten by his daughter though...

As for the zombies themselves, they firstly appear as people with a bad hangover, the make-up getting more gruesome as the film proceeds. Too gruesome I would venture for the film's première which was actually shown in an afternoon matinee slot, with kids in attendance – the film's stark and unfunny horror being entirely unsuitable for the stunned and horrified six and seven-year-olds who were watching!

I have to admit, I've never seen the colourised version of the film, but I don't really want to. The film gains a large part of it's frightening atmosphere from the monochrome picture and the colour would make it more accessible and more like horror films of recent years. Now, we're used to genuinely scary stuff from horror films of the '70s right up to the 2000s and 2010s, but an unsettling horror in black and white is different (as entertaining as the Universal etc films of the '30s and '40s were/are, they can't really be described as frightening), as it gets us while we're unprepared, just as those weeping kids in 1968 were!

Similarly to the colourised versions, I've not seen the remake from 1990: being a 1990s film is a strike against it from the start as it's very likely to be crap! One of George Romero's finest hours (along with *The Crazies*), this is a *Night* to remember.

Duane Jones and Judith O'Dea in Night of the Living Dead *(1968)*

CURSE OF THE CRIMSON ALTAR
The Master of Evil in his last and most shocking role!
BORIS KARLOFF
CHRISTOPHER LEE
terror fills the night
as she stalks her prey!
MARK EDEN · BARBARA STEELE · MICHAEL GOUGH
VIRGINIA WETHERELL · RUPERT DAVIES ·
GP
COLOR
VERNON SEWELL · MERVYN HAISMAN and HENRY LINCOLN · GERRY LEVY · TONY TENSER · LOUIS M. HEYWARD
TIGON BRITISH AMERICAN INTERNATIONAL
AMERICAN INTERNATIONAL

CHAPTER 32

CURSE OF THE CRIMSON ALTAR *(1968)*

Barbara Steele in Curse of the Crimson Altar *(1968)*
aka The Crimson Cult *(alternative title)*

Directed by: Vernon Sewell.

Written by: Mervyn Haisman (screenplay by), Henry Lincoln

(screenplay by), Jerry Sohl (from a story by), Lewis M. Heyward, Gerry Levy (uncredited) and H.P. Lovecraft (story "The Dreams in the Witch House", uncredited).

Starring: Boris Karloff, Christopher Lee, Mark Eden, Barbara Steele, Michael Gough, Virginia Wetherell and more.

Studio: Tigon British Film Productions.

GREEN-SKINNED WITCH AND A CRIMSON ALTAR

I LOVE THIS film, one of the great Tigon horrors of the '60s/'70s. Tigon was a British company that made, and distributed, films and Tony Tenser was the guy in charge, responsible for gems such as this one and the severely-underrated *The Blood Beast Terror* (1968) and *The Haunted House of Horror* (1969), as well as the cultified *Witchfinder General* (1968).

I'd be very interested though, if someone could explain what the film's title has to do with the film itself: there's no curse to speak of, and no altar either, crimson or otherwise. The film is based on a Lovecraft tale, "The Dreams in the Witch House", but, I imagine, rather loosely. It's not a scary sort of horror film, it definitely won't give you sleepless nights... but it's a nicely *cosy* type of horror, the type you'd come in from the pub and watch while propped in your favourite recliner chair while eating your body weight in sandwiches and cold slices of pizza.

I first saw the film on a Saturday night in 1979, as part of a mini season of horrors (which also included *Psychomania* [1973], Hammer's rarely seen – and rightly so, as it's rubbish – *Crescendo* [1970], and *The Wicker Man* [1973]) on Tyne Tees. I didn't particularly warm to the film on this screening, but it wass one of those films that seemed to be shown on telly every three or four years back in the '80s and '90s, and I caught up with it on each of its subsequent screenings and ended up being quite a fan.

Director Vernon Sewell assembled quite a cast here for his modest little horror opus – Christopher Lee in understated form, playing a seemingly mild-mannered character who turns out to be the main villain; Barbara Steele, who plays the strangely jade-coloured Lavinia and who is generally wasted; Boris Karloff, who steals the show; Michael Gough, in a small role as a dishevelled butler, and, fresh from being almost throttled by Patrick McGoohan while working on *The Prisoner* and quite a few years from his successful turn in *Coronation Street* as the evil tram-baiting Alan Bradley, Mark Eden.

The story revolves around Eden's character, an antiques dealer called Robert Manning who is trying to trace his missing brother. The trail leads to the creepy town of Greymarsh, which is one of those '60s/'70s English towns you always wanted to find yourself in, after seeing them in films like this as a kid. Craxted Lodge is the imposing manor house where Manning finds himself pitched up for the night, after questioning Morley (Lee) about his missing sibling.

Lee is good as ever but it's not one of his best performances and makes one wonder if he felt a little intimidated at the presence of the great Boris Karloff. Talking of whom, there's a nice little in-joke where Manning, being given a tour of the house by Morley's sexy niece Eve (Virginia Wetherell, who was Ralph Bates' wife and whom *Doctor Who* fans will remember from the first Dalek story in 1963/4), comments that it's the sort of creepy place where you expect to see Boris Karloff pop up at any moment... and then he does!

Karloff is fun in one of his last roles – I love the part where he gives a withering response to Manning's "good stuff" summation of the vintage brandy Marsh (Karloff) has turned up with, and a few moments later his gleeful "instruments of torture", after Manning has asked what his hobby revolves around. Marsh supplies some info on the sinister Lavinia, who is Morley's ancestor and who carried out human sacrifices and such in the very walls of the house. It seems the green-skinned witch was something of a celebrity in these parts, and the town of Greymarsh celebrates the death of Lavinia every year, in a sort of occult version of Bonfire Night – which would have been fun for everyone but Karloff, who reportedly died after contracting pneumonia during the cold night shoots.

Not a lot happens for the rest of the film, but it's fun anyway. Manning suffers a few creepy bouts of nocturnal wanderings, in which he encounters the sinister Lavinia, and then tries to get help at the local police station! Rupert Davies pops up too in a virtual cameo as Greymarsh's vicar. But the film is fairly tame, and doesn't really dispense much in the way of shocks or chills, as it meanders its way to a genteel sort of climax in which the laughing figure of Lavinia briefly appears prior to Craxted Lodge being burnt down with Morley perishing in the flames, but it's not dwelt on. The ending is quite abrupt, and unlike the Manning character the film doesn't outstay its welcome.

Overall, a very entertaining, but not really scary, horror film, one that all lovers of '60s and '70s British horrors should have in their collection – a mixture of Lee, Karloff, Steele, Gough and Lovecraft is too good to miss.

IF YOU DARE...
taste the deadly passion
of the BLOOD-
NYMPHS!
CAUTION
Not for the
mentally
immature!
The
Vampire
Lovers
R
AN AMERICAN INTERNATIONAL
HAMMER FILM PRODUCTION
STARRING
INGRID PITT · GEORGE COLE · KATE O'MARA and PETER CUSHING as "THE GENERAL"
GUEST STAR DAWN ADDAMS
SCREENPLAY BY TUDOR GATES · DIRECTED BY ROY WARD BAKER · PRODUCED BY HARRY FINE · CO-PRODUCER MICHAEL STYLE
COLOR BY MOVIELAB

CHAPTER 33

THE VAMPIRE LOVERS (1970)
and
LUST FOR A VAMPIRE (1971)
TWINS OF EVIL (1971)

The Vampire Lovers *artwork by Allen Koszowski*

THE VAMPIRE LOVERS (1970):

Directed by: Roy Ward Baker.

Written by: Joseph Sheridan Le Fanu (story "Carmilla"), Harry Fine (adaptation), Tudor Gates (adaptation and screenplay) and Michael Style (adaptation).

Starring: Ingrid Pitt, George Cole, Kate O'Mara, Peter Cushing, Dawn Addams, Pippa Steel and more.

Studio: Hammer Films.

LUST FOR A VAMPIRE (1971):

Directed by: Jimmy Sangster.

Written by: Tudor Gates (screenplay) and Joseph Sheridan Le Fanu (based on characters created by).

Starring: Barbara Jefford, Ralph Bates, Suzanna Leigh, Yutte Stensgaard, Michael Johnson, Helen Christie and more.

Studio: Hammer Films.

TWINS OF EVIL (1971):

Directed by: John Hough.

Written by: Tudor Gates (screenplay) and Joseph Sheridan Le Fanu (characters created by).

Starring: Peter Cushing, Dennis Price, Mary Collinson, Madeleine Collinson, Isobel Black, Kathleen Byron and more.

Studio: The Rank Organisation/Hammer Films.

SEX MARKS THE SPOT

THE VAMPIRE LOVERS (1970) was the first film in a new trilogy from Hammer Films, revolving around the female vampire Carmilla Karnstein. It's also the weakest film in the trilogy, but is still a good movie in and of itself. The overrated Ingrid Pitt plays Carmilla, who, using the pseudonym Marcilla, worms her way into the household of General von Spielsdorf (Peter Cushing) and his family, leeching the young Laura (Pippa Steel) of her blood and having lesbian interludes with her in the process.

One nice imaginative touch is that Laura has nightmares of being attacked by a giant cat, while all this undead sex stuff is going on. Marcilla/Carmilla tries the same sly trick upon moving into the household of one Roger Morton (played by George Cole) and draining the blood of Emma, Morton's daughter (Madeline Smith), casually getting rid of anyone who suspects she's a wrong 'un. Another nice touch in this and the next film, is the presence of a sinister feller in black who watches grinning, as each atrocity takes place.

Kirsten Lindholm, Pippa Steel, Kate O'Mara, Madeline Smith and Ingrid Pitt in The Vampire Lovers *(1970)*

Peter Cushing is rather wasted in his brief role of General von Spielsdorf, but this may have been filmed around the time of his wife's illness so he couldn't commit himself to a larger slice of screen time. Never mind, it's still good to see him and his character gets the honour of disposing of the villain at the end – having discovered Marcilla is really the undead Carmilla, and taking no chances, he stakes her then chops her head off. Overall *The Vampire Lovers* is a good little film but it would have had much more impact if it had been the only Karnstein film the company had made. Unfortunately for everyone involved with *TVL*, they went on to make two more films revolving around this family of the undead.

Lust for a Vampire followed in 1971 and is a much better film. Yutte Stensgaard, who plays Carmilla/Mircalla, is much better than Ingrid Pitt, and the film is generally much more fun. I even like the "Strange Love" musical interlude, so sue me.

This one has would-be horror star Mike Raven playing Count Karnstein, who resurrects Carmilla who in turn promptly enrols in an exclusive girls' finishing school, finishing off effeminate tutor and secret depraved devil worshipper Giles Barton (Ralph Bates) before long. The school itself seems quite high-tech for the time and it's bizarre to see a typical run-down sort of village more or less next door, with an inn presided over by a surly landlord (who I recognised as Killer Karminski from *The Prisoner* episode "The Girl Who Was Death") who warns the sort-of hero not to approach Castle Karnstein. Needless to say, the he does and it isn't long before he has become smitten with the beautiful Mircalla/Carmilla, leading to the "Strange Love" song which many Hammer fans can't live with for some strange reason... maybe they just don't like music?

Yutte Stensgaard and Judy Matheson in Lust for a Vampire *(1971)*

The film occasionally cuts back to the sinister Count Karnstein, who seems to have borrowed Count Dracula's eyes for the occasion! It all ends with the sort of "lets all go off and destroy the vampires by setting fire to their castle" rousing mob scenes that make one almost envious of the villagers – it would have been great fun to have participated in one of these blazing nights out! Overall, a very enjoyable and entertaining film. To heck with all the so-called Hammer fans who diss this one – it's got more enjoyment in ten minutes than the whole of most Hammer horrors from the '50s/early '60s, and the fact that Jimmy Sangster reportedly disliked it too proves that everyone has an off day.

It's a curious phenomena that many of my fondest horror film memories of the 1970s – the decade I grew up in – relate to films I didn't actually see. *Bride of Frankenstein* is a good example: shown in May 1975, in the Friday Night film 11.05 pm slot on Tyne Tees (and mentioned a lot in this book!). I'd spent the day looking forward to it greatly – they even had the good sense to show a clip of the Monster and the blind hermit just before the local news at 6 pm, which had gotten me very hyped up. But when it came to seeing the actual film itself, I fell asleep long before 11, and missed the thing! This happened quite a few times – I have fond memories of not seeing such gems as *Dracula Has Risen From the Grave* (in 1975, anyway, it was repeated a few years after, and I saw it then), *The Haunted Palace, Curse of the Mummy's Tomb, The Creeping Flesh* and *Tales from the Crypt*. One of my favourite memories of not seeing a film came in 1977, when I didn't see Tyne Tees' showing of Hammer's *Twins of Evil* (1971). I was in a relative's house (RIP Aunt Martha) just over a week before, and picked up and perused a copy of the *TV Times* that had Purdey from *The New Avengers* on the cover, and as usual, I turned straight to the Friday page to see what the film was that night... and it was *Twins of Evil*, a film I'd read about, knew was a Hammer with Peter Cushing in it, and so, it must be good! I had my place on the settee booked from that moment on... sofa, so good!

However, as the Friday night rolled around, never one to break tradition, after waiting for it all day and hyping it up to other kids at school, I dutifully fell asleep and completely missed it. So, at the age of ten, I never did get my fix of the Collinson twins, Gustav Weil (Cushing's character), Dennis Price, and some bad dubbing. Instead, I had to wait a mere sixteen years to see the film, when it was shown on the BBC, as part of the first *Dr. Terror...* season.

The film is the best of the trilogy, which goes from good to excellent and maintains that standard throughout. For both of you who haven't seen the film, it's basically about a group of religious fanatics, the Brotherhood, and their leader, Gustav Weil, whose idea of a good night out is one where they ride to some isolated cottage in the woods and end up burning pretty young girls to death at the stake. Gustav has two sexy nieces, one of whom, Maria, is vampirised by the depraved Count Karnstein, the other, Freda, is the nicer of the two and has a thing for the local schoolmaster Anton. It all builds to a gory climax, with Gustav axed in the back, Count Karnstein staked (very impressive effect, as Karnstein gradually loses all his hair and eventually becomes a skeleton), and the evil Maria getting her head chopped off.

Mary and Madeline Collinson (Freda and Maria) came to the UK from Sweden, and appeared on the cover of *Playboy* magazine, attracting the attention of Michael Carreras, Hammer's head man. The twins are a good example of how the women in Hammer horror films ramped up the sex appeal of their female stars as the years passed, more so than in their '50s/early-mid '60s movies. In the late 1960s though, things began to change – Susan Denberg for example, and then we got Veronica Carlson, Linda Hayden, Ingrid Pitt, and Yutte Stensgaard in quick succession – more than enough to steam up anyone's glasses! Lynne Frederick is also one of the many high points in *Vampire Circus*, and Stefanie Powers is the only good thing in the otherwise woeful *Crescendo*. Madeline and Mary Collinson are the cream of this crop, however, and it's a pity they didn't make any more horror films either separately or together. They are dubbed throughout the film too, which is a pity.

Mary and Madeline Collinson in Twins of Evil *(1971)*

This is one of Peter Cushing's best performances, in my opinion, made all the more memorable by the fact that he isn't actually acting, or doesn't seem to be! This film was made shortly after Helen Cushing's death, and you feel while watching it that Peter is still affected by his loss at this stage. Such moments as the part where he confronts schoolteacher Anton (David Warbeck) stand out.

The film features two sets of villains – Gustav and his "merry band", as Count Karnstein refers to them, and the vampires themselves. Character actor Dennis Price appeared in a few horror films for Hammer, starting with *The Horror of Frankenstein* in 1970, and he gives a nice performance here as Karnstein's toadying lacky. Roy Stewart plays Joachim, Karnstein's mute servant, and can also be seen in two *Doctor Who* stories as well as the James Bond film *Live and Let Die* (1973).

There's a nice rousing music score, and one scene set in the schoolhouse would have involved Anton and the girls belting out a song, similar to "Strange Love" in *Lust For a Vampire*, but the scene was cut. The film has all the usual sturdily-built sets you would expect from Hammer, and nice location filming around the Black Park forest area seen in many a Hammer horror.

One of the best Hammer horror films then, definitely in my Top Ten, and maybe, the Top Five as well, if it can edge *The Devil Rides Out* out!

Madeline and Mary Collinson star in Twins of Evil *(1971)*

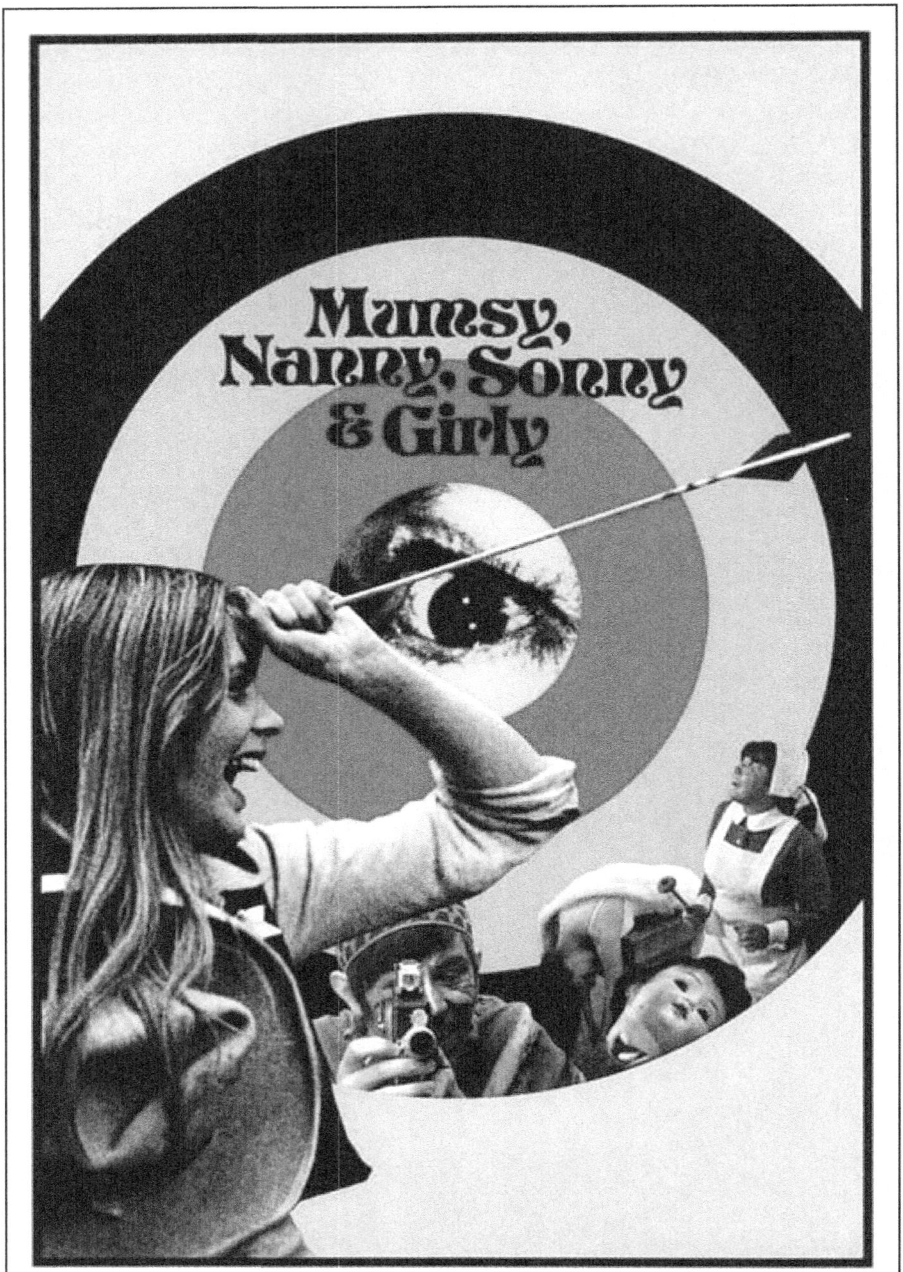
Mumsy, Nanny, Sonny & Girly

CHAPTER 34

MUMSY, NANNY, SONNY & GIRLY (1970)

Howard Trevor, Vanessa Howard, Pat Heywood and Ursula Howells in Mumsy, Nanny, Sonny & Girly *(1970) aka* Girly *(alternative title)*

Directed by: Freddie Francis.

Written by: Brian Comport (screenplay) and Maisie Mosco.

Starring: Michael Bryant, Ursula Howells, Pat Heywood, Howard Trevor, Vanessa Howard, Robert Swann and more.

Studio: Brigitte/Fitzroy Films Ltd./Ronald J. Kahn Productions.

HAPPY FAMILIES

WELL, DARLING READERS, I hope you're all sat tucked up nicely in bed, with a mug of lovely hot chocolate by your side, and a copy of *Midnight Treasury* in your hands. Maybe you're alone, or maybe you have a friend lying next to you, and maybe another friend in the room next door. These might be old friends, or they might be new friends. Anyway, I hope you're following the rules and have your electric buzzer, or maybe an alarm clock, set to go off at a certain time to indicate when you can start to read the book...

RRRRRRRRRRIIIIIINNNNNGGGGGGGG! Oh, there it is! You can start to read the book now! I bet you're excited! You might have thrilled to articles on *Count Yorga*, or *The Alligator People*, and you might even have read about horrors from Italy (fancy!), or Spain!! The next part you'll be reading might be about a demon from Hell, or about an abominable doctor called Phibes and some lusting after a vampire. Oh, it makes me shiver just to think about it!

But anyway, dears, I want to tell you all about our new friend. But first, lets have some tea and toasted scones... try not to get crumbs all over the sheets, won't you? I just changed them this afternoon, and I'll be so cross if they get dirty. RRRRIIINNNGGG! Okay, kiddies, you can start eating now. Raise your hands if you want seconds.

Well, that was nice wasn't it? Time to go to the toilet now – I hope nobody has put a jack-in-the-box in the bowl like our new friend did last week. I don't suppose he will do that again, as we sent him to the angels on Friday. He looked ever so nice, in his smart suit – Girly wanted to dress him up in a Red Indian costume but we thought that would have been inappropriate for such a solemn occasion. Anyway, our new friend in room 6 is a writer – fancy! He's mainly connected with articles about horror films – nasty stuff – and has written features on Hammer's *Dracula* films, BBC2 horror seasons, the TV show *Night Gallery*, Amicus anthology films, and that *Exorcist* film (Sonny and Girly went to see that, and came home terrified!! They had to sleep with Mumsy and me in our nice old four-poster bed, with the rose coloured sheets. Girly ended up being sick, and we had to give her some castor oil. She coughed and retched so much, we thought she was dying!). Anyway, he has written this very book – lots of articles, one about some very strange Alligator People living near a swamp (imagine that!), one about a house dripping blood, and another about a man who gets sent to the angels but they send him back – hanging upside down on a rope! Wearing a cheap rubber mask!! Fancy! Some people have no sense of decorum...

Anyway, our new friend, the writer, was noseying around our lovely home, wanting to get material for another feature he was writing – or so he said! We soon saw through him, and before too long Girly had him wrapped around her little finger. I think Mumsy took a shine to him as well. I don't fancy him at all really – they're welcome to him! Anyway, he enjoyed it when Girly kitted him out in one of Sonny's spare school uniforms – he said it reminded him of something an actor called Patrick McGoohan wore in an old TV show about prison or something. It might have been *Porridge*, but I don't remember any piped blazers in that... Our friend, the writer stuffed his face with jelly and ice cream, and then wanted to leave... something about not missing a deadline... but Girly persuaded him to stay. She can be very persuasive when she wants to be...

Ursula Howells and Vanessa Howard in
Mumsy, Nanny, Sonny & Girly *(1970)*

He's been here for about a week now. He's sat in room 6 most of the time, with his nose in a laptop, writing, writing, writing... the only time I've seen him come out at night is when he sneaks into Girly's room when he thinks nobody is looking. There's been some strange noises coming from that room – Girly says they just sit around talking about films and playing "Doctors and Nurses", but I think there's something going on. Anyway, he came and sat on the porch with me and Mumsy last night. We sat knitting, and he started talking about films. He talked about a director called Freddie Francis, and about an actor called… Trevor Howard, I think. He was very famous years ago… or it might have been Howard Trevor, who was very unknown years ago… and probably still is. Our friend the writer told us about an actress called Vanessa Howard, who was considered something of a catch back in the late '60s and early '70s, but dropped out of acting when her film projects were unsuccessful. Oh dear… our friend also started talking about an actress called Ursula Howells, who he said Freddie Francis cast in another film he made after he'd worked with her in a movie where she played a werewolf's wife! I think he was making that up just to impress Mumsy – who would ever believe a woman called Howells appearing in a film about a werewolf?! Anyway, our friend can get a bit boring, droning on about films so much, so we slipped some sleeping tablets into his cornflakes, and he drifted off to sleep soon after. Bless…

Well, I'm getting a bit sleepy myself now, kiddiewinks, so I'm going to hand over to Mumsy. Night, night, sleep tight, don't let the bedbugs bite…

RRRIIINNNGGG!!! Ah, it's my turn to talk. About time, Nanny has used up most of the allotted time for this article – she's such a stuffy old windbag. Anyway – hello, children! It's Mumsy here, and I have to tell you that Nanny was probably telling naughty old stories when she said that she wasn't interested in our new friend in room 6. I've seen her face, when he's telling us his endless stories about films – she can't get enough of him! I think Sonny dislikes him though – he probably feels he's had his nose pushed out of joint, poor lamb. I think Girly is very pleased that our new friend has come to join us – she was getting a bit bored with the friends in rooms 7 and 8 – they just didn't know how to make a convincing cup of tea! Anyway, apart from his stories about films, our new friend has other things in his favour. I think it'll be a while yet before we decide to send him to the angels. Anyway, our pet… RRRIIINNNGGGG!!!! Oh, there's the doorbell. It'll be the milkman, I expect…

Now then, it's Girly here… Mumsy has left us for a bit, so I'm going to quickly tell you about our new friend, the writer in room 6. Nanny was talking nasty old rubbish, with her stories about him and me being naughty at night… we just sit chatting about films, obscure British horrors from the late '60s/early '70s mostly, and sometimes play at shopkeeping. Another thing about him is that he likes playing with dolls, and so that's fine with me. Nanny was very cruel and nasty to me about it all, saying he was just pretending to like dolls so that he could get me to be naughty, so I told her to go and boil her head…

RRIIINNNNNGGGG!!! Oh well, there we are, kiddiewinkles, we've come to the end of our little chat. We hope you've enjoyed yourselves and will buy your own copy of this book rather than just reading someone else's. Our friend, the writer, was a very naughty boy this morning, and managed to climb over the wall and get away... we'll catch him though. And, even if we don't, we can easily get another new friend to replace him – who knows, it might even be you...

The main cast of Mumsy, Nanny, Sonny & Girly *(1970)*

VAMPIRES! VOODOO! VIXENS! VICTIMS!
TERROR WAITS FOR YOU IN EVERY ROOM IN
THE HOUSE THAT DRIPPED BLOOD
From the author of "Psycho"
Cinerama Releasing presents
THE HOUSE THAT DRIPPED BLOOD
Starring Christopher Lee Peter Cushing
Nyree Dawn Porter Denholm Elliott Jon Pertwee
Joanna Dunham Joss Ackland John Bennett John Bryans
Wolfe Morris also starring Tom Adams and Ingrid Pitt as "Carla"
Executive Producers Paul Ellsworth and Gordon Wescourt
Produced by Max J. Rosenberg and Milton Subotsky
Written by Robert Block
Directed by Peter Duffell
Colcr
GP
ALL AGES ADMITTED
FROM CINERAMA RELEASING CORPORATION
71/89

CHAPTER 35

THE HOUSE THAT DRIPPED BLOOD (1971)

Ingrid Pitt in The House That Dripped Blood *(1971)*

Directed by: Peter Duffell.

Written by: Robert Bloch and Russ Jones (segment "Waxworks", uncredited).

Starring: Christopher Lee, Peter Cushing, Nyree Dawn Porter, Denholm Elliott, Jon Pertwee, Ingrid Pitt and more.

Studio: Amicus Productions.

VAMPIRES! VOODOO! VIXENS! VICTIMS!

I LOVE CREEPY old houses, and the first time I saw this film I was staying in one – sort of. My older brother and his then wife were on holiday in Belgium, and my mother and I had the fun of staying in the house for two weeks while they were away. It was the beginning of the summer holidays in 1978, and I was thoroughly excited and hyped up – staying in someone else's house and watching a horror film late that Friday night was too exciting for words.

The film was shown on my local ITV station Tyne Tees (again!) – once again showing a horror film every Friday night at 11.05, in the Friday night film slot. I feel sorry for people who lived in other areas, as ITV stations like Anglia and HTV seemed to have shown absolutely bugger all when it came to horror films. Oh well… I was still, as an eleven-year-old, envious of people who got ITV regions like Yorkshire, as their horror film slot was called "Appointment With Fear". I had actually discovered, at an early age, that "Appointment With Fear" even had its own specially-filmed intro! Staying at a relative's house sometime in 1975, I managed to stay up late for that night's horror film…. but the film was preceded by a montage of images of monsters – Dracula, Mummy, Wolfman etc – followed by the faces of birds of prey and wildcats! The final face was that of Karloff's Frankenstein's Monster, and the sequence seemed to go on forever. My memory is that it was all tinted yellow/green but it might be cheating me. Anyway, I never saw the intro again, and I'm inclined to think that my relative's TV was able to receive other stations (such as Yorkshire), so it was actually "Appointment With Fear" on Yorkshire I was watching, rather than the Friday night film on Tyne Tees (which never had an intro sequence to any film I saw after that)!

Back to that Friday night in July 1978 – the atmosphere was electric as 11 pm started to get closer, my mother spooking me for a few minutes by suggesting we didn't talk too much about horror films as we might get properly scared! As soon as the film started though, I knew I was going to enjoy it. The opening credits are beautiful, showing the exterior and interior of the titular house, to the accompaniment of Douglas Gamley's atmospheric score. This was the first of the seven Amicus anthology horrors I'd ever properly seen – I'd seen most of *Dr. Terror's House of Horrors* a few years previously, but that was too much for me back then – and I was looking forward to it.

These films always featured a "framing sequence" and this one was one of the best. John Bennett plays a surly detective from Scotland Yard who comes to a small town to investigate the disappearance of famous horror film star Paul Henderson. Inspector Holloway's enquiries at the local police station take us into the first two stories, and his interactions with the estate agent Stoker (John Bryans) lead into the other two.

The stories are all based on works by Robert Bloch again (as with *Torture Garden*), with "Method for Murder", first published as a story in 1962, leading things off. Denholm Elliott (who I recognised straight away but couldn't say from where) plays Charles Hillyer, a writer of horror stories who moves into the isolated titular house with his wife Alice (Joanna Dunham). Charles' latest tale concerns a sinister character known only as Dominick, who roams the night, searching for women to strangle! Charles even has a very nicely drawn piece of art of Dominick (which he scrunches up and throws in a river later, sadly), and gloats to Alice how this character is going to make them rich.

Joanna Dunham and Denholm Elliott in
The House That Dripped Blood *(1971)*

    The first time Charles sees Dominick in the flesh is very effective, and excellently directed, with Charles having a quick drink by a mirror and suddenly seeing the sinister, unshaven character he's been writing about looking down at him from the top of the stairs, in the reflection. After that, Dominick is sinister enough to even be frightening when seen in broad daylight, never mind the part where Charles (but not his wife) can see him in the dark corner of his study. Apparently, the film's director Peter Duffell thought that Dominick had the look of the Karloff Frankenstein's Monster about him, but I can't see it myself – a tall figure, dressed in black and that's about it for any resemblance. It soon becomes clear that Alice knows more than she is letting on – and indeed, she's having an affair with some actor guy who is playing the part of Dominick, the plan being to drive Charles crazy. Unfortunately for all three, the guy playing Dominick (Tom Adams) is a nutter and not being content with killing just Charles, he kills his (Charles') psychiatrist as well and then Alice. Watch out for the scene where Adams takes off his Dominick wig and false teeth – he pulls the stubble off his face at the same time...

Peter Cushing in The House That Dripped Blood *(1971)*

"Waxworks' next, based on a Bloch story first published in 1939. Peter Cushing brings a touch of class to the film, with his performance as Philip Grayson, retired stockbroker, who is the house's next tenant. Grayson seems to enjoy his new life of looking through old photos and listening to music, though it would help if he had more than just the one record in his collection – "Death and the Maiden" by Schubert, apparently. He plays this over and over, and it's while he's listening to it that he spies a photo of an old flame in his box of memoirs, and later, when visiting the town and being drawn into a waxwork chamber of horrors, he sees a figure called Salome, who reminds him of his lost love. Salome must have some supernatural power to affect men's thoughts and make them see their love reflected back at them, as the wax figure looks nothing like the woman in Grayson's photo (which Grayson later tears up – shades of what Denholm Elliott's character did to that rather nice drawing of Dominick in the first story). Anyway, Grayson becomes obsessed with the figure and, while listening to the same record again one night (it's strange that none of the tenants in the four stories have a TV set!) is visited by an old chum Neville (Joss Ackland) who also had a thing about the girl in the photo and who, upon visiting the waxworks, becomes similarly smitten.

The story ends predictably but it's a delight overall, with much fun to be had seeing these two late middle-aged men in love, pining over a woman. Nice direction, especially during a haunting scene where we see Grayson's fairly empty daily routine – when he's not listening to that same record – of standing looking into a river, going for a walk round the small town, looking in shops, walking through a graveyard...

The two main characters both wind up as part of the waxworks display themselves – though it's hard to stifle a laugh, as the wax head of Ackland in particular looks ridiculous, and the Cushing one is only slightly better.

The third story is "Sweets to the Sweet" and is based on a tale Bloch had published in 1947. This is the weakest of the four stories, in my opinion. It's good, but the other three are better. It's hard to say what this one lacks – maybe it should have come first in the film where it might have had more impact. Christopher Lee gives a good performance as a pompous and humourless character who comes to live in the house with his lovely little daughter, Jane (Chloe Franks). It soon becomes clear that Jane has the same effect on her dad as Tom has on Jerry, and he is terrified of her.

Stories in the fantasy/horror genre onscreen involving kids can go either way – you can end up with a classic (*The Exorcist*, *Star Trek*'s "Miri", *The Innocents*), or something not so great (*The Omen*, *Doctor Who*'s "Night Terrors", *Curse of the Cat People*), or something downright rubbish (*Children of the Damned*, *Children of the Corn*). Fortunately this segment falls somewhere between being great and merely okay. It turns out little Jane is a witch and, after her dad has chucked a doll given to her by her governess (Nyree Dawn Porter) onto the fire, the battle lines are drawn and you know it's only a matter of time before Lee gets his comeuppance. Which he does at the end, after Jane chucks a wax image of him on the fire, with a close-up of the melting wax accompanied briefly by a loud scream from him upstairs – a sequel to this segment might have been a good idea, showing how a grown-up Jane was getting along...

"The Cloak" is the final segment and the best is certainly saved 'til last. This is a brilliantly entertaining horror comedy, with a first-rate performance from *Doctor Who* star Jon Pertwee, playing a big-headed horror film star (who, unlike a certain other apparently big-headed horror film star who has appeared in the segment immediately before this, actually enjoys the genre he is famous for!) who buys a strange cloak from a creepy backstreet shop. Geoffrey Bayldon, who should really have been a horror star himself – *Catweazle* terrified me as a kid! – gives a great turn here as the shop's creepy proprietor. Modelled on '30s actor Ernest Thesiger (see the *Bride of Frankenstein* entry), Bayldon is simultaneously creepy and funny and he should have appeared in many more similar roles in '70s British horrors. Anyway, after Bayldon convinces Pertwee to buy the cloak (interesting to see these two here and think that a few years later, they'd be famous on TV again – Pertwee's Worzel Gummidge was a loveable character, while Bayldon's Crowman in the same show was as quietly sinister and creepy as his earlier Catweazle), the actor soon finds that, when worn, the cloak transforms the wearer into a real vampire, leading to some scenes which once again masterfully mix the ghoulish with the funny, when Henderson puts the cloak on at midnight in the house, sprouts fangs and levitates (this was Pertwee's own idea, apparently)!

Jon Pertwee in The House That Dripped Blood *(1971)*

    One subtly nice touch is that the interior of the house changes with each change of tenant, and we see different rooms – in the third story, we see a bedroom for the only time in the film, while in this tale, Pertwee has tarted the place up with some of his film memorabilia, including a painting of himself which seems to be creepily watching what's going on! The overrated Ingrid Pitt is actually good for once here, playing an actress called Carla who, it turns out, is already a vampire and wants to initiate Henderson into the ranks of the undead. The story ends a bit abruptly, but the film isn't quite over yet... there's a nice little coda in which Holloway goes to the house alone, at night!

After a search of the place, he comes under attack in the cellar from Henderson, now a fully-fledged vampire. He manages to dispose of Henderson but there's still Carla waiting in the (bat's) wings!

The film ends, as most of the other Amicus anthologies do, with a character addressing the audience – in this case, it's the estate agent Stoker who explains the house's modus operandi of reflecting the personality of its owner. That being the case, it seems a bit harsh that such awful fates were meted out to the relatively harmless characters in the first two stories in particular, but such is life...

Overall, a great film – yes, there's no blood but this is a thoroughly enjoyable and atmospheric old horror, and one of Amicus' best properties in more ways than one. Also, thank God the director didn't get his own way and call the film "Death and the Maiden"...

Ingrid Pitt in The House That Dripped Blood *(1971)*

a CHILL-FILLED Festival of HORROR!
THE BLOOD ON SATAN'S CLAW
DENNIS FRIEDLAND AND CHRISTOPHER C. DEWEY PRESENT "THE BLOOD ON SATAN'S CLAW"
STARRING PATRICK WYMARK AND LINDA HAYDEN • EXECUTIVE PRODUCER TONY TENSER
PRODUCED BY PETER L. ANDREWS & MALCOLM B. HEYWORTH • DIRECTED BY PIERS HAGGARD
A TIGON BRITISH / CHILTON FILM PRODUCTION • COLOR • A CANNON RELEASE
R RESTRICTED Under 17 requires accompanying Parent or Adult Guardian

CHAPTER 36

THE BLOOD ON SATAN'S CLAW (1971)

"Blood on Satan's Claw" by Randy Broecker

Directed by: Piers Haggard.

Written by: Robert Wynne-Simmons (original screenplay) and Piers Haggard (with additional by).

Starring: Patrick Wymark, Linda Hayden, Barry Andrews, Michele Dotrice, Wendy Padbury, Anthony Ainley and more.

Studio: Tigon British Film Productions/Chilton Films.

CHILDREN OF THE DAMNED

I REMEMBER SEEING this excellent Tigon offering in the Friday night film slot at some point in the late '70s but I must have been underwhelmed, as I could only really recall the scene where a character gets some skin cut from her leg. Seeing the film in the same slot a few years later, I was impressed and remain so to this day. I know Tigon's *Witchfinder General* is considered to be their best film, but for me, this little gem surpasses it.

An all-star cast which includes actors familiar from *Doctor Who*, *Catweazle* and the later *Some Mothers Do 'Ave 'Em* get their collective teeth stuck into a spine-tingling tale of witchcraft and devilry in eighteenth century England. Described by writer Mark Gatiss as an example of the sub-genre of "folk horror", the film begins with Ralph Gower (Barry Andrews) discovering a strange skull while he's ploughing a field. The furry skull disappears soon after, and the film's original plot involves the Devil ('twas his skull, you see!) possessing the children and teens of the area and getting them to re-animate him by rebuilding his body!

The great cast I mentioned earlier includes the voice of Mr. Kipling's cakes himself James Hayter, who gives an exceedingly good performance as the local out-of-his-depth Squire Middleton. Patrick Wymark (who had earlier experience with a strange skull for Amicus) plays The Judge, but he isn't in the film for very long, departing early and returning in time for the finale. Simon Williams, of *Upstairs, Downstairs* fame (or would be, in a few years) appears as Peter, who moves in with his fiancée Rosalind into the house of his disapproving aunt, but it all goes pear-shaped: Rosalind is driven mad by something that happens during the night and Mistress Banham (Avice Landone) becomes ill after being struck by the screeching Rosalind.

The film appears a bit disjointed at times, but that's because it's basically three stories joined together (in a similar fashion to the Devil being stitched together in the course of this movie!), with the business of the strange goings on in Mistress Banham's attic and Rosalind's insanity being originally considered a different story to the main plot of the satanic Angel Blake and her minions. The attic-centred story is very effective though, especially when Peter returns to investigate further and is attacked by a furry-clawed creature which leads to him hacking its hand off only to discover it's his own appendage he's missing!

Linda Hayden (right) in The Blood on Satan's Claw *(1971)*

Directed by Piers Haggard, who I always remember as the director of the 1979 ITV *Quatermass* serial, *The Blood on Satan's Claw* is heady stuff, probably more horrific than the Hammer films on offer at the time, and similar to Tigon's earlier *Witchfinder General* (1968). The main card Haggard plays is the casting of Linda Hayden as Angel. Hayden is one of the best of the '70s UK horror film stars. It's a pity Hayden didn't make more horror films, as she has great screen presence which she makes full use of here. Once Angel has been taken over by the evil infesting the village, the other kids start to cop it – the good ones, anyway.

Robin Davies, best known as Carrot from the first series of *Catweazle*, is the first to go: his character Mark gets lured into a game of blind man's bluff, which leads to him being throttled and his corpse stuffed in his family's woodshed. Mark's sister Cathy (Wendy Padbury) is killed soon after – Padbury was best known as Zoe, one of the second Doctor's companions in the BBC's *Doctor Who* and somewhat ironically, her character of Cathy is lured to her death by another ex-companion of the good Doctor: Roberta Tovey had played Susan opposite Peter Cushing's doddery, seemingly piles-afflicted, Dr. Who in the two 1960s films, and an unaccredited Tovey here lures Cathy to the Angel Blake gang who proceed to rip her dress, rape her and then finally, she is killed. The children have been growing hair on their bodies which belongs to the demon and shortly before Cathy's rape (a disconcerting scene this for a *Doctor Who* fan, as it's hard to watch it without thinking it's actually Zoe who is being violated!), hair is revealed on her back which is removed.

The Blood on Satan's Claw *(1971)*

Michele Dotrice ("Ooh, Betty!") is also growing hair on her leg and this is removed shortly before she escapes, pursued by hounds, but finds herself rejected by Angel, as she no longer has the Devil's fur growing on her. Captured and interrogated by Wymark's returned Judge, Margaret spills the beans on Angel's cult and not only is Angel herself killed in the lively finale, but the Devil ends up being re-animated for only a short time before the Judge impales him on a sword. End of film.

A very fine film though. Apart from the great cast I've mentioned, future Master from *Doctor Who* Anthony Ainley plays the school teaching Reverend, who is arrested on suspicion of sexually molesting Angel, (the bit where she strips off in front of him is a highlight of the film) but is later released. Black Beauty's aunt (or whatever) Charlotte Mitchell also has a role in the film, playing the distraught mother of

Mark and Cathy, and Howard Gooney is another, soon to be familiar face. He never became a star but he's a familiar presence in TV shows like *Into the Labyrinth* and *Only Fools and Horses*.

Released in America under Haggard's preferred title of *Satan's Skin*, the film proved to be a box office flop, which is a shame. *The Blood on Satan's Claw* is definitely one of the best British horrors of the 1970s, and the best "folk horror" film ever made.

Linda Hayden in The Blood on Satan's Claw *(1971)*

Love means
never having to
say you're ugly.
JAMES H. NICHOLSON and SAMUEL Z. ARKOFF present
VINCENT PRICE
JOSEPH COTTEN
the abominable
dr. phibes
also starring
HUGH GRIFFITH and TERRY-THOMAS
presenting
VIRGINIA NORTH
as Vulnavia
JAMES WHITON and WILLIAM GOLDSTEIN · LOUIS M. HEYWARD and RONALD S. DUNAS
SAMUEL Z. ARKOFF and JAMES H. NICHOLSON · BASIL KIRCHIN · ROBERT FUEST
GP
ALL AGES ADMITTED
COLOR BY MOVIELAB
An AMERICAN INTERNATIONAL Picture

CHAPTER 37

THE ABOMINABLE DR. PHIBES (1971)
and
DR. PHIBES RISES AGAIN (1972)
COUNT YORGA, VAMPIRE (1970)
THE RETURN OF COUNT YORGA (1971)
BLACULA (1972)
SCREAM BLACULA SCREAM (1973)

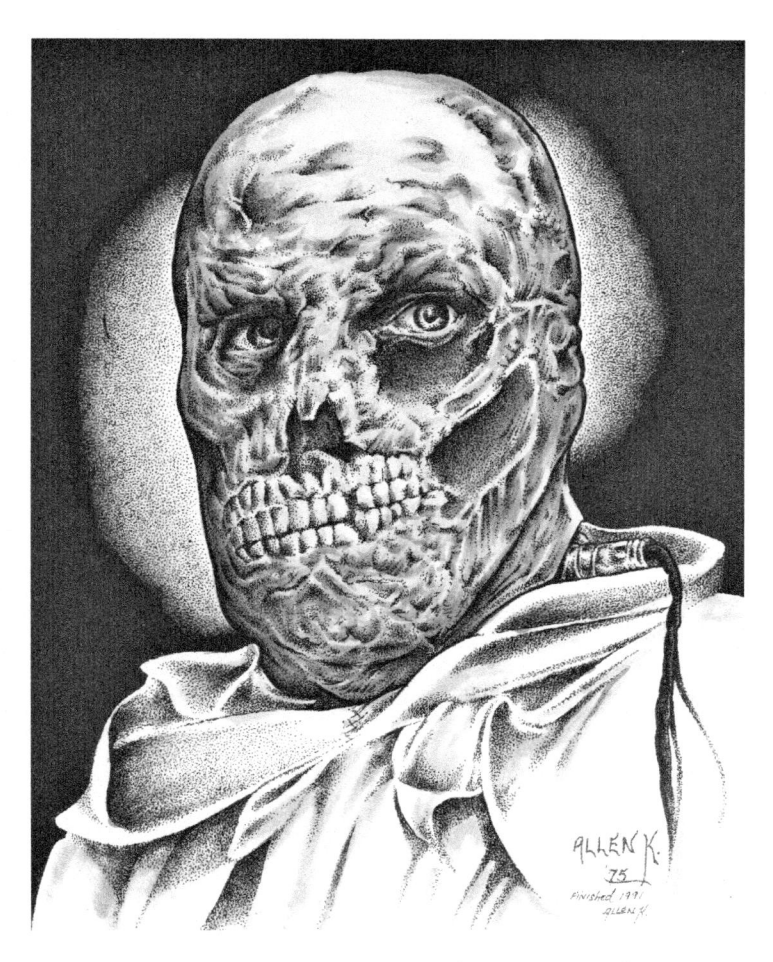

Dr. Phibes artwork by Allen Koszowski

THE ABOMINABLE DR. PHIBES (1971):

Directed by: Robert Fuest.

Written by: James Whiton and William Goldstein.

Starring: Vincent Price, Joseph Cotten, Virginia North, Terry-Thomas, Sean Bury, Susan Travers and more.

Studio: American International Pictures (AIP)/Amicus Productions.

DR. PHIBES RISES AGAIN (1972):

Directed by: Robert Fuest.

Written by: Robert Fuest, Robert Blees, James Whiton (based on characters created by) and William Goldstein (based on characters created by).

Starring: Vincent Price, Robert Quarry, Valli Kemp, Hugh Griffith, John Thaw, Keith Buckley and more.

Studio: American International Pictures (AIP)/Amicus Productions.

COUNT YORGA, VAMPIRE (1970):

Directed by: Bob Kelljan.

Written by: Bob Kelljan.

Starring: Robert Quarry, Roger Perry, Michael Murphy, Michael Macready, Donna Anders, Judy Lang and more.

Studio: Erica Productions Inc.

THE RETURN OF COUNT YORGA (1971):

Directed by Bob Kelljan.

Written by Bob Kelljan (screenplay) and Yvonne Wilder (screenplay).

Starring: Robert Quarry, Mariette Hartley, Roger Perry, Yvonne Wilder, Tom Toner, Ruby De Luca and more.

Studio: Peppertree Productions Inc.

BLACULA (1972):

Directed by: William Crain.

Written by: Joan Torres (screenplay) and Raymond Koenig (screenplay).

Starring: William Marshall, Vonetta McGee, Denise Nicholas, Thalmus Rasulala, Gordon Pinsent, Charles Macaulay and more.

Studio: American International Pictures (AIP).

SCREAM BLACULA SCREAM (1973):

Directed by: Bob Kelljan.

Written by: Joan Torres (screenplay and story), Raymond Koenig (screenplay and story) and Maurice Jules (screenplay).

Starring: William Marshall, Don Mitchell, Pam Grier, Michael Conrad, Richard Lawson, Lynne Moody and more.

Studio: American International Pictures (AIP).

THE UNHOLY THREE FROM AIP

"THE INCREDIBLE LEGENDS of the abominable Dr. Phibes" first appeared in 1971, in AIP's *The Abominable Dr. Phibes*. Starring Vincent Price in perhaps his signature role, the film is a very effective horror comedy, set in the 1920s and with an all-star cast.

Phibes is a surgeon who gets horribly burned and disfigured in a car crash, resulting in him looking like a walking skeleton. His appearance is made slightly more palatable by the fact his skeletal mug is kept largely hidden under a Vincent Price look-a-like mask, but he loses points for normality by the fact he has to speak and eat through a device in his neck! Anyway, Phibes isn't happy that his wife Victoria died during surgery, and blames the team of surgeons, setting out to kill them in a variety of Bible-inspired ways.

I have to admit, I find the character of Phibes to be fairly irritating and unlikeable – not because he commits one murder after another, with a blatant disregard for human life but because he's such a clever bastard! Phibes proves to be an expert on music and sound, cooking (though, I imagine it doesn't take a genius to boil some Brussels sprouts), clockwork mechanisms, theology, the construction of ice-making machines...

Vincent Price (left) in The Abominable Dr. Phibes *(1971)*

The murders are nicely inventive and gruesome, my favourite being the mechanical frog mask that gradually crushes the head of its unfortunate wearer – a psychiatrist who describes himself as a "head-shrinker"! Death by bees, death by bats, death by a unicorn horn... A nurse is killed when Phibes drips boiled sprouts onto her sleeping face, then unleashes a horde of locusts into the room... A guy in a plane is killed by rats... Terry-Thomas gets his blood drained.. .(this was the point, incidentally, at which the telly was turned off and I had to go to bed when I first saw the film, in 1978 in the Friday night film slot on Tyne Tees)...

The film ends with Phibes putting himself into suspended animation with the corpse of his rotten wife, who was indirectly to blame for everything anyway! Peter Jeffrey and Norman Jones are the two faintly comedic policemen trying to catch Phibes, and failing. The film didn't fail to be a success though, and *Dr. Phibes Rises Again* followed in 1972.

The sequel isn't as good as the original but it's still a very fine film and I have a soft spot for it, as it was the first horror film I ever captured on (audio) tape, back in early 1981. Beginning with a series of clips from the first film and an explanatory voice-over from Robert Quarry, the film has Phibes (still alternately looking like an evil Salvador Dali or Skeletor) emerging from his hibernation with the intention of travelling to Egypt to find an elixir to bring Victoria back to life (in photos of the late Mrs. Phibes, we see Caroline Munro giving her best performance – Ms. Munro was strikingly attractive and a very nice person by all accounts, but she couldn't act for toffee, or at least she couldn't in any of the dozen films I've seen her in). Biederbeck (Robert Quarry) is a literally immortal scientist and he has survived by taking a life-giving serum. He also intends to travel to Egypt with his lover to find a "River of Life", and the film is basically a race to see who can get there first between Quarry and Price.

One of the parts I loved re-listening to over and over again on my worn-out C-90 tape was the electronic organ music that Phibes would play every so often, accompanied by a clockwork band. Another part I enjoyed listening to was the death of Biederbeck's manservant, whose game of billiards is snookered by invading mechanical snakes and then a telephone spear which shoots right through his head and out the other side!

The film features its share of lively murders (none of which are justified) with death by sand, hawk, scorpions, crushing, and being stuffed in a giant gin bottle... There's even time for a nice cameo appearance by the great Peter Cushing as the ship's captain. The film ends with Phibes punting along the River of Life, singing "Somewhere over the Rainbow" as Biederbeck ages to death behind him. Generally considered to be not as good as the first film but okay in its own way, it is a fine sequel and it's a pity the mooted third film never got made.

Count Yorga, Vampire or, *The Loves of Count Iorga, Vampire* (USA alternate title) before the name was changed and it became more of a horror as opposed to a soft porn, appeared in 1970 and as much as I love the Phibes films, I love the Count Yorga films more. Set in modern-day Los Angeles, Robert Quarry makes a very effective vampire and it's a pity he didn't appear in a longer series of CY films rather than just the two.

The film begins with a séance, which is presided over by the Count, and which most of the attendees aren't taking seriously. Later, two of the group, Erica and Paul, drive Yorga home to his eerie hillside mansion but after leaving, their camper van gets stuck in the mud and they prepare to spend the night at the bottom of Count Yorga's driveway. The atmosphere here is marvellously spine-chilling, especially when we realise someone is creeping about outside the van, in the dark. We hear a crescendo of crickets, just before Erica looks out of the window and sees the frightening face of Yorga looking in at them...

Vampire attack in Count Yorga, Vampire *(1970)*

I remember this film and the sequel being shown within weeks of each other on TV back in the late '70s and one bit that brought a reaction from my usually unconcerned dad was the part where the now-vampiric Erica eats her pussy – literally! I still laugh when I think of my dad staring at the screen in disgust and horror at that moment – looking at it now though as an adult, the moggy model is incredibly realistic.

The hero of the film is Roger Perry, better known to me as a huge *Star Trek* fan, as Captain Christopher from the time travel episode "Tomorrow Is Yesterday". Here Perry plays a Dr. Hayes, who gets some of the best scenes in the film – suspicious that Yorga is indeed one of the undead, Hayes and several others pay him a late night call and attempt to keep him up until sunrise by plying him with questions about the occult and asking for more brandy! I also love the double-take Perry gives when he catches sight of the gruesome mug of Yorga's huge and disfigured servant, Brudah!

The film's cat and mouse battle of wits between Hayes and Yorga ends with the former dead at the fangs of Yorga's vampire harem, and Yorga himself staked. A great film in itself, and a nice snapshot of 1970s LA, the film led to *The Return of Count Yorga* in 1971.

In *The Return of Count Yorga*, still keeping the slightly contemptuous and superior amusement towards dim-witted humans that he possessed in the first film, Robert Quarry returns in a film set in San Francisco this time. The film has a beginning that creeped me out, along with a few dozen other school kids who saw it back then in 1978, when a mute kid form an orphanage is playing with his ball as night starts to draw in. Yorga's vampire brides rise from the grave, just as the kid Tommy runs into the waiting Yorga – in a nice bit of stock footage from the first film of his creepy face!

Quarry again gets some great lines here – during a fancy dress party/competition at the orphanage (in which someone dressed as a white-faced Dracula wins), someone asks Yorga, "Where are your fangs?", to which he replies, "Where are your manners?", beaten only by the subtly magnificent, "Only when played well", when quizzed about his liking for piano music by an enthusiastic teen at the aforementioned party.

Roger Perry returns for this sequel but with a beard and playing a different character. He ends up badly at the conclusion again, which is a similar ending to the first film's – here it's Perry's character who is revealed to have become a vampire after despatching the villain and briefly getting the girl. Mariette Hartley is the girl, Cynthia, a teacher at the orphanage who Yorga falls in love with, despatching her family during a very creepy and *Night of the Living Dead*-ish sequence, in which Yorga's vampiric harem breaks into Cynthia's house at night. Cynthia is then spirited away to Yorga's mansion and it's up to her boyfriend David (Perry) to save her, with the help of a pair of slightly humorous cops, both of whom also end up dead sadly.

The two Yorga films are brilliant, in my opinion far surpassing Hammer's similar modern-day vampire opus *Dracula A.D. 1972*, which was apparently inspired by Yorga's success, but didn't come close to equalling it. Talking of Hammer, there's a nice part in *Return...* where we see Yorga watching a foreign language version of *The Vampire Lovers* on telly. Nice!

AIP's two Blacula films are like the Count Yorga ones but with a smooth-talking black man as the vampire. William Marshall is a superb actor with a great voice and screen presence and it's a crying shame he didn't become a fully-fledged horror film star. *Blacula* (1972) begins in the eighteenth century, with Prince Mamuwalde (Marshall) visiting Count Dracula to enlist his help in abolishing the slave trade. Dracula turns out to be as racist as he is undead, insulting Mamuwalde and making lewd remarks towards the former's wife. It all ends with Dracula making Marshall one of the undead, christening him "Blacula" and poor Blacula ends up stuck in a coffin until the 1970s...

Once revived in present day LA, Blacula makes short work of two gay removal men and demonstrates an eerie ability to change his appearance, sprouting extra hair when he's in full-on vampire attack mode. Blacula takes a shine to a young lovely who reminds him of his late wife, and spends the film trying to get her into his clutches while the rest of the predominantly black cast try to stop him.

William Marshall stars as Blacula

There's lots of entertainment to be had here, with the hilarious '70s fashions and the scenes with Blacula at a club where he looks ridiculous standing there with his Shakespearian accent and his cloak, to a background of jiving and gyrating! Watch for the great and very funny scene where Blacula is sent flying by a taxi driving into him, and the sassy black female driver's response when he calls her an "imbecile" (she soon regrets it).

Blacula artwork by Allen Koszowski

Blacula's despatch is very effectively done, as he exposes himself to sunlight having realised his existence is futile, and his visage quickly disintegrates into a maggot-infested skull!

Scream Blacula Scream followed in 1973 and mixes the vampire stuff with a voodoo plotline, involving a Mama Loa who chooses Pam Grier as her replacement and thus pisses her son Willis (Richard Lawson) off enough that he buys the bones of Mamuwalde, using voodoo to resurrect the smooth-talking vampire.

Blacula becomes smitten again, this time with Lisa (Grier) and she tries to use voodoo to help him lift his vampire curse but it all goes wrong, naturally. Blacula sets up house in a groovy pad, with Mama Loa's son Willis who Blacula bit as soon as Willis resurrected him. Nice bit of humour as the vain Willis realises he will never be able to admire himself in a mirror again, now that he is undead! There's also a very nicely humorous scene as Blacula is accosted by two hustlers on the streets of after-dark LA who threat to kick his ass if he doesn't part with his bread! Just hearing the mellifluous tones of Marshall uttering the line "...and, as for kicking my ass..." makes this a stand-out scene in the film.

Pam Grier and William Marshall in Scream Blacula Scream *(1973)*

As with the Yorga films, it's a pity only two Blacula films were made, as the character was strong enough to support a series of seven or eight such entries. We last see Mamuwalde/Blacula screaming in pain as the doll made in his image is stabbed by Lisa, a nicely ambiguous ending. Described by some as the worst blaxploitation film ever made, it gets my vote as the best.

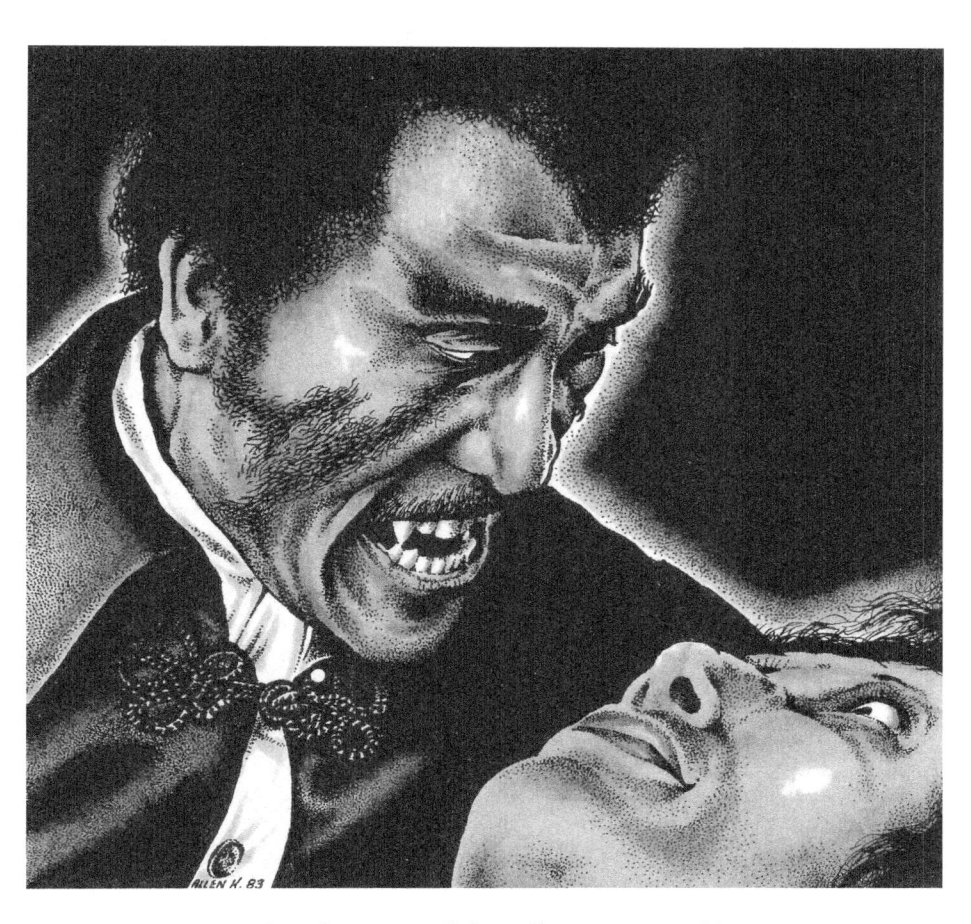

Blacula artwork by Allen Koszowski

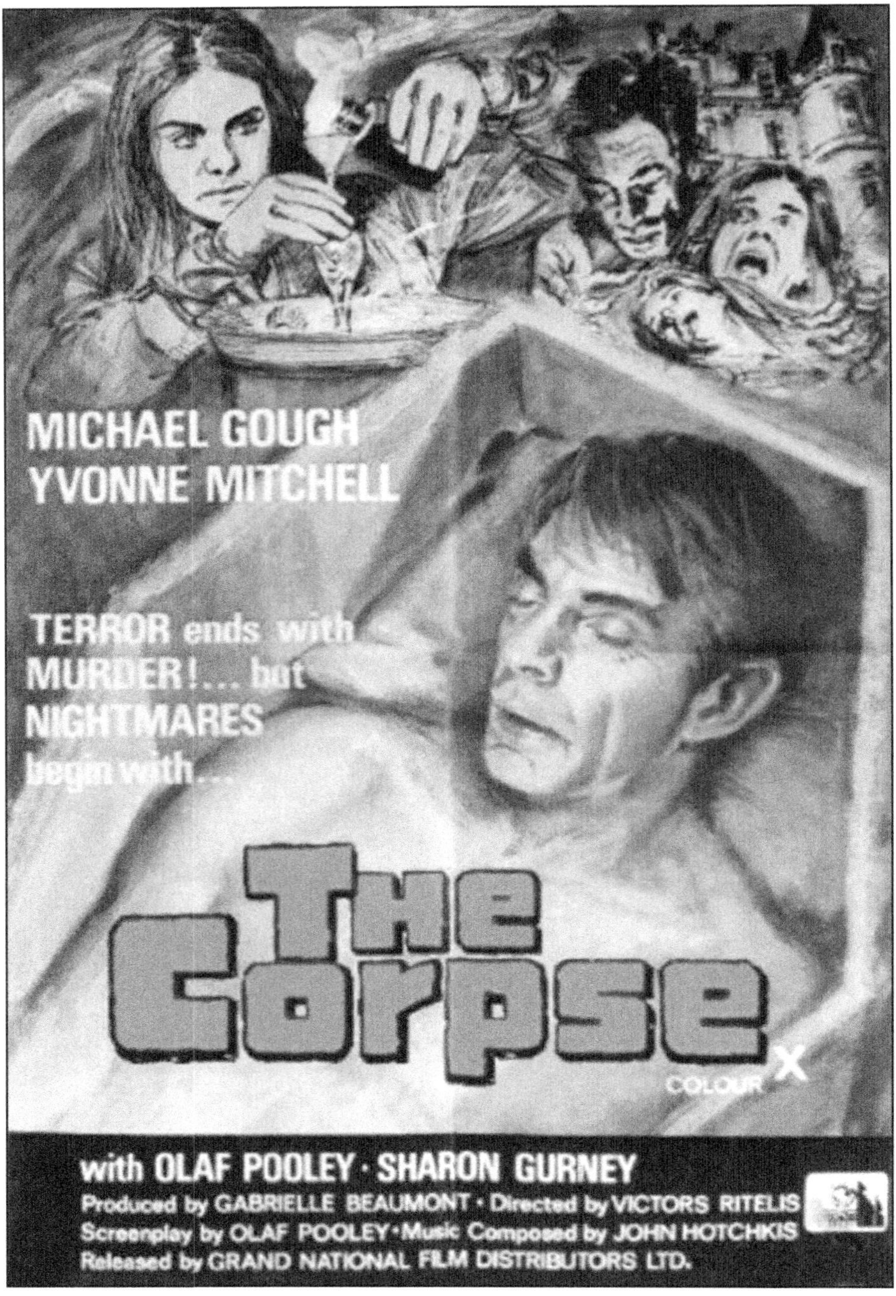
MICHAEL GOUGH
YVONNE MITCHELL
TERROR ends with MURDER!... but NIGHTMARES begin with...
THE Corpse
COLOUR X
with OLAF POOLEY · SHARON GURNEY
Produced by GABRIELLE BEAUMONT · Directed by VICTORS RITELIS
Screenplay by OLAF POOLEY · Music Composed by JOHN HOTCHKIS
Released by GRAND NATIONAL FILM DISTRIBUTORS LTD.

CHAPTER 38

THE CORPSE (1971)

Michael Gough in The Corpse *(1971) aka* Crucible of Horror

Directed by: Viktors Ritelis.

Written by: Olaf Pooley.

Starring: Michael Gough, Yvonne Mitchell, Sharon Gurney, Simon Gough, David Butler, Olaf Pooley and more.

Studio: Abacus Productions/London-Cannon Films.

DIGGING THE CORPSE

THE CORPSE IS a 1970 British film that I wanted to see ever since I read about it in an issue of *Shivers* magazine. It was never shown on

TV, and I never saw it on VHS either, but it was finally released on DVD under its US title of *Crucible of Horror*. I ordered it as quickly as possible, and couldn't wait for it to arrive! When *The Corpse* did finally arrive, it wasn't exactly fresh – the picture quality was a step down from awful, looking variously like the film was shot through a pair of tights or a wine bottle, and the sound wasn't very good either. Another niggle is that, because it was a US disc, it had the US title – maybe the US distributors thought a film called *The Corpse* would stiff at the box office, who knows? Well, at least it became available, even with the wrong title and an inferior print. Anyway, I got hyped up to watch the film. It was a special movie that I'd waited a long time to see, so it couldn't be just slapped into the player and watched any old time – it was definitely an eleven o'clock on a Friday night (preferably with a day or two off work afterwards) affair. However, I got sick of waiting and decided to watch the film at eight o'clock on a Thursday instead. Oh well, it was still an exciting time as I was about to watch a film that is definitely on the obscure side and which Jonathan Rigby – in that *Shivers* piece – made sound like one of the greatest horror films ever.

The Corpse was directed by Viktors Ritelis, a director I have been unable to find little info on, and appropriately for a film revolving around a dysfunctional family, it's a family affair in itself – Michael Gough is the star, with his actual son, Simon, and Simon's wife/Michael's daughter-in-law Sharon Gurney in the cast. The screenplay is by Olaf Pooley, an actor who has the rare honour and distinction of having both *Doctor Who* and *Star Trek* on his CV, and he also appears in the film itself. The other main player is Yvonne Mitchell, playing the older Gough's wife, Edith.

The film begins around what posh folk call dinner time, but which normal folk call tea time. Walter Eastwood (Michael Gough) returns from a hard day's work sitting on his arse shuffling papers and washes his hands, ready for tea... I mean dinner. His son Rupert (Simon Gough), who like his dad is permanently welded into a suit, arrives not long after. The downtrodden mother Edith (Yvonne Mitchell) is there, and the sixteen-year-old Jane (Sharon Gurney, who was older than sixteen) tries out an endearing wig for dinner. As dinner goes on, the male Eastwoods, subtly and unsubtly, take the piss out of not only the two female members of the family, but women everywhere. The pudding is interrupted by someone from the golf club arriving to plant a smacker on Jane when Walter's back is turned, and then accuse her of stealing a nice big wodge of green and white paper from the club safe! Afterwards, Walter teaches Ann a lesson by giving her a sound thrashing!

The direction of this scene has always tickled me, with Rupert listening to some fancy classical music in his bedroom and swinging his arms around as if conducting an orchestra, while in his sister's bedroom, Walter's arms are swinging wildly as he whips his daughter's ass – literally! It's this punishment that causes Walter's wife to decide to kill him. Unfortunately, things don't go according to plan...

Yvonne Mitchell and Sharon Gurney in The Corpse *(1971)*

The film, it must be said, gets a bit slack at certain key points. It would have benefited from a scene showing mother and daughter concocting their plan to do away with Walter, but instead they just turn up at Walter's country cottage retreat and get down to business. These scenes are intercut with flashbacks, showing Walter giving his daughter a good spanking after she disobeys his instructions not to go for a swim. Once Walter has been forced to drink poison, he gets dragged upstairs and the two women take his trousers off, then later he gets his corpse shoved into a large crate.

There are some tense, suspenseful scenes when Olaf Pooley's character turns up for a nose around, and his equally nosey dog nearly unearths Walter's dead body in the crate. After that, the women take said crate in the boot of their car and chuck it into the sea...

One thing that might annoy some viewers is the fact that nothing is actually properly explained. Was Walter really killed? Or was the whole thing a dream? If it really happened, then how did he survive the poison, and how did his body move from one spot to another? The final part, with someone swinging upside down from a rope whilst wearing a Michael Gough mask, is the closest the film gets to a proper shock horror film moment. It's strangely effective though it only takes a few moments to realise it's not Gough himself (pity, that would have been quite funny!). The guy in the Gough mask is not the only one to be left hanging, as the film ends shortly afterwards with a "back to square one"- type scene, with the two misogynistic men being seen to be just as harsh in their treatment of the women (Walter skittily reads aloud a letter sent to Jane by a young man who has taken a fancy to her and who wants to go on a date, before tearing it up), and that for Edith and Jane, there is no escape. Oh, well.

Yvonne Mitchell and Sharon Gurney in The Corpse *(1971)*

I must say, I like the film's ambiguity. It's one of those breed of strangely pointless films, a category where stuff like *Neither the Sea Nor the Sand* (1972), or *Symptoms* (1974) fall into, as if someone with pretentious leanings had recently acquired a large amount of money and decided to blow it all on making a film without hiring a screenwriter. Maybe Olaf Pooley was a family friend of the Gough clan, and they all concocted the idea for the film between them one drunken evening? Or maybe Gough himself just wasn't thinking straight, after most of his brain cells had melted away during his appearance in *Trog* (1970)? It's certainly an entertaining, and most definitely unsung, horror film, so some good came out of it.

If you like Michael Gough, '70s British horror films and you're a *Doctor Who* fan who is intrigued to see Olaf Pooley in something other than "Inferno" (the 1970 Jon Pertwee story, for the uninitiated), then this should be your sort of film. It's also interesting because it's obscure and not your average Amicus/Hammer/Tigon fare. And how many other films feature someone in a Michael Gough mask hanging upside down? It's worth purchasing for that alone! The only real downside is that the disc looks terrible, but the good news is that a (presumably) spruced-up version has been released on Blu-ray, so hopefully the dreadful DVD release can now be shoved into a crate and thrown into the sea...

Yvonne Mitchell in The Corpse *(1971)*

DEATH LIVES
IN THE VAULT OF HORROR!
"TALES FROM THE CRYPT"
Metromedia Producers Corporation presents An Amicus Production
"Tales From the Crypt"
starring Joan Collins · Peter Cushing · Roy Dotrice · Richard Greene · Ian Hendry
Patrick Magee · Barbara Murray · Nigel Patrick · Robin Phillips and Sir Ralph Richardson
Screenplay by Milton Subotsky · Produced by Max J. Rosenberg and Milton Subotsky
Executive Producer Charles Fries · Directed by Freddie Francis
PG
CINERAMA RELEASING

CHAPTER 39

TALES FROM THE CRYPT (1972)

"Tales from the Crypt" by Randy Broecker

Directed by: Freddie Francis.

Written by: Milton Subotsky (screenplay), Al Feldstein (stories), Johnny Craig (stories), William M. Gaines (stories), Graham Ingels (uncredited) and George Evans (uncredited).

Starring: Joan Collins, Peter Cushing, Roy Dotrice, Richard Greene, Ian Hendry, Patrick Magee and more.

Studio: Amicus Productions.

A VERY EC FILM TO ADMIRE

THE AMICUS ANTHOLOGY films rolled on, but this one tried a different tact. Instead of the works of Robert Bloch, comic strip stories that appeared in EC comics in the 1950s (*Tales from the Crypt, The Vault of Horror, The Haunt of Fear*) were used as the source.

I always regretted missing this film, when it was shown in the usual Friday night 11.05 film slot on Tyne Tees because, apart from anything else, I had to endure listening to my schoolmates going on about what a great film it was and how awful it was that I'd missed it! I did finally catch up with it when it was shown again on Tyne Tees in 1982, this time at 10.30pm and, as expected, I loved it.

The film has a nice framing sequence involving a group of people exploring some ancient catacombs and getting trapped in a stone chamber with no way out, before a sinister monk-like figure enters – forget the silly animatronic puppet from the 1990s TV series, Ralph Richardson's Crypt Keeper is properly scary and sinister – and demands to know where they were all going before they were compelled to visit here.

First in the dock, so to speak, is Joanne Clayton (Joan Collins), an evil bitch who callously bashes her husband's head in on Christmas Eve while he reads the evening paper. This is to cash in his insurance policy, and to hell with the emotional effect on her young daughter!

While mopping up her husband's distinctly pink blood, Collins hears a newsflash on the radio about a nutter having escaped from a local asylum (I like to think it's the same one from Amicus' 1972 *Asylum*) dressed as Santa Claus. Needless to say (but I'll say it anyway), said nutter makes a beeline for the Clayton residence and after unsuccessfully attempting to get in through gates and windows, he is finally let in by the young daughter (Chloe Franks).

This first segment really catches a Christmassy atmosphere despite all the blood, screaming and corpses being thrown into cellars.

There's a constant medley of Christmas carols being played on the radio which acts as a nice, and slightly eerie (Christmas carols are slightly eerie, aren't they?!), aural backdrop to the action. I never really rated Joan Collins as an actress but she's very good here. After murdering her loving hubby (Martin Boddey, who *Doctor Who* fans will recognise from the 1972 story "The Sea Devils"), Collins contemptuously reads the loving tag attached to his present, before chucking it on the fire, although she does don the fancy ring he bought her – what a bitch!

Oliver MacGreevy is excellent as the insane Santa – when he first appears, walking up to the door of the house in the snow, just the simple act of tinkling a little bell he's carrying is enough to show that he's not the possessor of a full sack! There's a definite "jump" moment when Collins goes out to check the gate is locked and he tries to grab her, and similarly creepy parts when he's looking through the window, trying to catch a glimpse of Collins who is ducking down under the it, with her husband's fresh corpse lying nearby! Unfortunately, the climactic murder of Collins at the nutter's dirty hands looks like he's giving her a neck and shoulder massage rather than a brutal throttling.

Oliver MacGreevy and Joan Collins in Tales from the Crypt *(1972)*

The second tale is equally excellent, with Ian Hendry playing a man called Maitland (Amicus head Milton Subotsky had a thing about that name and there are quite a few characters in Amicus films called it) who deserts his very attractive wife and kids for a less fanciable woman and, while driving off with her at night, crashes the car.

This crash sequence is very well directed and leads to Hendry waking up with no sign of his girlfriend and wandering about in the dark, frightening a driver and a tramp, before deciding to return to his old house – where his wife suddenly has a new feller (she must have a thing for balding, middle-aged men!) – and then, after scaring the sherbert out of his wife, goes to his girlfriend's flat to find her blinded by the crash, which happened two years ago! This shock prompts Hendry to look at his reflection and we – and he – catch a quick glimpse of a zombie-like visage before Hendry wakes up back in the car with Angie – just before it crashes again (and presumably, again and again and again...).

Funnily enough, those school kids back in the late '70s could never remember this one, even though they remembered everything that happened in the other yarns. Anyway, this segment is short, sharp and to the point.

The third segment is the most popular amongst film buffs and stars the ubiquitous Peter Cushing – I always felt the reason *Vault of Horror* (1973) flopped was because it's the only Amicus anthology film he isn't in – as Grimsdyke, a kindly old chap who is friends with the local kids. Unfortunately, his nasty neighbours (the snobbish Elliot and son) want him out of the way and conspire to get his beloved dogs taken away, his retirement pension lost and to give him the reputation of a paedophile!

The final straw comes when they send him some Valentine's cards filled with rather witty, if cruel, verses ("A tree is beautiful if its owner prunes it, but our town isn't, as your presence ruins it") and he hangs himself. But a year later, he returns from the grave to exact a bloody, and equally poetic, revenge.

This segment is thoroughly excellent as well, with a great performance from Cushing – at times kindly and funny (when playing with the local kids and showing them his handmade puppets), at others sad (when his dogs are taken away, and his unhappiness and confusion as to why people have stopped being kind), while the scene where he uses an ouija board to contact his late wife shows him in a totally different light – I'm surprised he went ahead and filmed this sequence. Isn't dabbling with things like this meant to be very dangerous? – and his appearance as a living corpse at the end is downright scary. Another nice bit of character material comes with a scene near the end which shows his "murderers" feeling guilty as to the consequences of their actions, but it's far too late for that!

Peter Cushing in Tales from the Crypt *(1972)*

The main character in the fourth tale was first offered to Cushing apparently, but he turned it down, thinking it "sick". Instead ex-TV Robin Hood Richard Greene gets the plum role of an antiques dealer who is on the verge of bankruptcy, but who gets a second chance when his wife discovers a small statuette that grants three wishes to a person.

In typical "Monkey's Paw" fashion (the famous short story by W.W. Jacobs that I remember reading as a kid in 1977 and which gets mentioned in the segment itself) the wishes all go wrong and Greene ends up in eternal agony, his veins filled with embalming fluid and his stomach sliced open by his stupid wife who is to blame for his wretched condition. This ending is what turned Peter Cushing off the segment, but it isn't actually as deadly downbeat as it first appears – Greene's wife Enid (Barbara Murray) has totally messed up her three wishes but there's nothing to stop family friend Roy Dotrice from having a go and putting everything right... having said that, it seems these sort of things have a habit of going wrong no matter what – if you wished for a beautiful mate, you'd end up turned into a crab and your mate would be beautiful only to a crab (ie. another crab!), or if you wished for nine hundred pounds, it would be nine hundred pounds of frozen carrots tied up in a sack that would drop on your head, killing you!

This is another beautifully crafted segment anyway, with some nice creepy touches – for instance, after Greene has been killed in a car crash, Enid wishes he was returned as he was immediately before the crash. There's a knock at the door, and a bunch of sinister undertakers carry a coffin in, bearing Greene's corps – he had died of a heart attack prior to crashing!

Richard Greene and Barbara Murray in
Tales from the Crypt *(1972)*

The final segment is very good too, set in a home for the blind where a right callous ex-Army character takes charge, rationing the best food for himself and serving slop to the inmates. When one inmate dies of pneumonia on a freezing cold night, as a result of the heating being turned off and blankets rationed, the rest vow revenge...

This story was hyped up no end by my schoolmates back in 1977 – apparently when the director (played by Nigel Patrick) and his hunger-crazed dog are shredded by razor blades (part of a series of tunnels constructed by the inmates), every bit of blood and grue is seen in exquisite detail! Ironically, for a story about the blind, my schoolmates' eyes must have been playing tricks as there's not a drop of blood to be seen anywhere at the climax. In fact, there's nothing to be seen literally, as the inmates turn out the lights and what happens to Patrick and his mutt has to be imagined.

The film ends with the group of five being consigned to Hell by the Crypt Keeper who then turns to the audience and wonders if they will be next!

This is generally considered to be the overall best Amicus horror and I'd be inclined to agree – it's certainly far superior to the disappointing *Vault of Horror* which followed it and is equalled only by *The House That Dripped Blood* and *From Beyond the Grave*. Well worth checking out, as indeed are the EC comics the stories are based on – if you can find them!

Peter Cushing in Tales from the Crypt *(1972)*

WHY ARE THE GOOD PEOPLE DYING ?
LEE HESSEL Presents
THE CRAZIES
Starring LANE CARROLL · W. G. McMILLAN
with HAROLD WAYNE JONES · LOYD HOLLAR · LYNN LOWRY · RICHARD LIBERTY
Produced by A. C. CROFT · Directed by GEORGE A. ROMERO
Theme Song "HEAVEN HELP US" Sung by BEVERLY BREMERS · A Scepter Record
Musical Director STEPHEN METZ · A CAMBIST FILM ·

CHAPTER 40

THE CRAZIES (1973)

The Crazies *(1973)*

Directed by: George A. Romero.

Written by: Paul McCollough (based on a script by) and George A. Romero (screenplay).

Starring: Lane Carroll, Will MacMillan, Harold Wayne Jones, Lloyd Hollar, Lynn Lowry, Richard Liberty and more.

Studio: Pittsburgh Films.

DON'T DRINK THE WATER

I HAVE TO admit from the off, I'm not a fan of George Romero. *Night of the Living Dead* (1968) is a great film but the rest, in the words of Shania Twain, don't impress me much. Romero seemed to enjoy cheap and tacky-looking stuff, and everything from the original *...Dead* to his downright naff TV series *Tales from the Darkside* sports this awful look. In fact, most films of the '80 have the same sort of look which is why it's far from a favourite decade, horror film-wise, of mine.

The Crazies though is different. The Blu-ray picture has improved the tacky look of the film no end, and without that to distract you, you can concentrate on what's actually happening in the film. *The Crazies* had the dubious honour of being shown twice, as part of the BBC's perennial horror double bill seasons of the '70s/'80s: it's first screening on British TV came as part of the 1978 "Monster Double Bill", paired with *The Quatermass Xperiment* (1955) in week three. Cricket coverage separated the two films and I was pleased really, as the film sounded a bit disturbing to me and after my experience with *X: The Man with the X-Ray Eyes* the previous week (see separate chapter) I was a little wary of watching any SF-themed film that appeared unsettling. So, I went to bed (I still wonder why the film was included in a season of monster movies though).

The film was shown again in 1981 as part of that year's "Horror Double Bill" season – week four, paired with *Isle of the Dead* (1945) and I saw it this time. I wasn't really impressed though and it was a good decade or two before I caught up with it again. This time round, it was shown as part of the ITV "Night Time" service which meant you had to simultaneously watch it and try to ignore the presence of a desperately sign language-ing guy in the bottom right corner! Which ruined the film, not surprisingly.

So, it fell to the Arrow Blu-ray release to properly sell this film's merits to me, and I remember trudging home from a few hours' fast walking at about 18.00 hours on New Year's Eve 2019, and popping the disc in the player at about 20.15. Little did I know, settling down in my cosy reclining chair to sample the film's delights, that the world would soon be in the grip of a terrible man-made (?) virus which, at the time of writing in early April 2020, shows no signs of abating. Will this true-life horror/SF story have a happy ending? That remains to be seen, but this film certainly doesn't…

The movie gets off to a rollicking start, with a farmer insanely smashing his house while his two kids cower in fear, prior to the place being set alight. This is only the start though, as we soon learn that an Army plane crashing in the river has polluted the town Evans City's water supply and whoever drinks the water goes mad, either in an OTT "hack the wife and kids to death and stab someone with a knitting needle" way, or a more subtle, quiet insanity. Not everyone goes mad though – some are lucky enough to die.

The main trio of characters are fireman David (W.G. McMillan), nurse Judy (Lane Carroll) and another fireman, Clank (Harold Wayne Jones). David and Judy are a couple, and the situation is made worse by the fact Judy is expecting. All hell breaks loose when the Army arrive on the scene, clad in radiation suits and gas masks, and quarantine the town, herding the residents into the gym of the local school. Evans City was actually a small town in Pennsylvania, thirty miles from Pittsburgh and the locals were happy to co-operate with the shooting (in both senses of the word!) – in fact, they were perhaps a bit too happy, as you can plainly see that the extras are really enjoying it all, and perhaps the camera shouldn't have lingered on them so much. There's also a bit of confusion about the timeline – we see residents raving it up in a disco, but the film gives the impression this is all taking place in the early morning before midday.

Harold Wayne Jones in The Crazies *(1973)*

The scenes of mayhem are extensive and well-staged. Among the delights on offer here are the afore-mentioned "soldier getting stabbed with knitting needle" scene but we also see a priest dousing himself with petrol before setting himself alight, the local sheriff getting shot, and a crazy young woman sweeping the grass after a bloody confrontation between residents and soldiers. Before long, our trio of heroes are on the run and join up with teenage Kathy (Lynn

Lowry) and her dad Artie (the aptly-named Richard Liberty, as Artie takes a few liberties with his dick later when he tries to rape her!). This all ends in blood and tears, with the rape of Kathy being followed by her crazy dad hanging himself and Kathy's subsequent shooting by the military... ah, what a fun film!

Lynn Lowry in The Crazies *(1973)*

The film has one scene that always makes me laugh – Army scientist Dr. Watts (Richard France) thinks he might have found a cure for the virus (or, is he just infected by it and insanely *thinking* he's found a cure?) but in his haste to report his good news, he is mistaken for a nutter by the shoot-first-and-keep-on-shooting Army bods and bustled away with a crowd of crazies, desperately protesting until he tumbles down some stairs and his possible cure is smashed. I don't know if this scene is all that funny really, or is it just my sick sense of humour – answers in a test-tube please...

The action is underscored at times by an aptly titled track titled "Heaven Help Us", and the film reaches its disturbing and downbeat climax after Clank gets messily shot in the head, Judy is killed and David (who might be immune to the virus) surrenders. Colonel Peckem (Lloyd Hollar) is informed the virus has spread to another town and is taken out of the area in a helicopter – depressing stuff, though how nice it is that this sort of thing could never happen, eh?...

Overall, a great example of SF/horror. The film was a box office flop but time has treated it kindly and it's now a popular culty item which led to it being remade in 2010. Both versions are very good but the original is the best.

Lane Carroll in The Crazies *(1973)*

VINCENT PRICE
HAS RESERVED A SEAT FOR YOU
IN THE "THEATRE OF BLOOD"
"THEATRE OF BLOOD"
VINCENT PRICE ✕ DIANA RIGG
Starring IAN HENDRY
With Guest Victims HARRY ANDREWS + CORAL BROWNE
ROBERT COOTE + JACK HAWKINS + MICHAEL HORDERN
ARTHUR LOWE + ROBERT MORLEY + DENNIS PRICE
Executive Producers GUSTAVE BERNE And SAM JAFFE Produced By JOHN KOHN And STANLEY MANN
Screenplay By ANTHONY GREVILLE BELL Directed By DOUGLAS HICKOX Music By MICHAEL J. LEWIS
R
United Artists

CHAPTER 41

THEATRE OF BLOOD (1973)

Vincent Price (right) in Theatre of Blood *(1973)*

Directed by: Douglas Hickox.

Written by: Anthony Greville-Bell (screenplay), Stanley Mann (idea), John Kohn (idea) and William Shakespeare (plays, uncredited).

Starring: Vincent Price, Diana Rigg, Ian Hendry, Harry Andrews, Coral Browne, Robert Coote and more.

Studio: Harbour Productions Limited/Cineman Productions.

A HAM SANDWICH AND POODLE PIE

I FIRST SAW this superlative British horror film in 1981, shown as the final entry in BBC2's horror double bill season that year. This movie (and *The Body Snatcher* [1945], which it was paired with) helped to make up for what had been, up to that point, a disappointingly bland bunch of films.

Released in 1973, *Theatre of Blood* stars Vincent Price as Vincent

Price... sort of. A hammy star playing a hammy star, it couldn't fail. And it doesn't. The film is a masterpiece, with plenty of gruesome detail in the various killings mixed with a sense of black humour. This is a horror film that could very easily be described as being "for kids": such scenes as overweight critic Robert Morley being forced to eat his own beloved pet poodles in a pie, to the point where he chokes would perfectly suit a kid's sick and morbid tastes!

Price plays Edward Lionheart, a Shakespearian actor who is such a bighead that, on awards night, he stands up in anticipation of his name being read out for the accolade of Best Actor – only to be disappointed when another actor wins! Deciding to top himself, he is saved from death by a bunch of derelicts but decides to keep it quiet – the better to kill the critics who panned his performances and get away with it.

There's an all-star cast here, with actors who wouldn't normally be seen in a horror film, such as Michael Hordern, Arthur Lowe and Coral Browne (every horror fan must know that Price and Browne met and fell in love during the making of the film, so I won't mention it) taking their turn in the spotlight to die horribly. It's a pity Hordern's character gets wasted first – Hordern is one of those actors who can be hilarious without even trying (I find it impossible to watch 1968's "Whistle and I'll Come to You" without creasing up into gales of mirth), and he's good fun here. Genuinely believing that the police would ask a theatre critic to help move some disorderly tramps along, he pompously struts his stick at them only to be bloodily stabbed to death. The scene is hilarious though, despite the gore – I love it when Hordern asks Price (disguised as a policeman), "Officer – a little help here!".

The murders are all based on deaths from various Shakespeare plays, and after Hordern has been Julius Caesar-ed, it's time for a critic called Hector Snipe (Dennis Price) to be impaled with a spear and then dragged through the countryside by a horse, in a murder inspired by *Troilus and Cressida*. Arthur Lowe's Horace Sprout literally loses his head next, in a very funny *Cymbeline*-inspired sequence in which his wife complains about his noisy snoring in bed, when it's actually the sound of the saw cutting his head off!

Harry Andrews plays Trevor Dickman who gets his heart cut out *Merchant of Venice*-style after a hilarious exchange in which an eerily made up and garbed Price reminds Dickman of one of his reviews in which he compared Lionheart to a ham sandwich! The fifth murder has Oliver Larding (love these names!), played by Robert Coote, being drowned in a barrel of wine, as in *Tower of London* (1939)... Or should that be the play *Richard III*? The sixth murder isn't really a murder and is relatively dull, not befitting a man rejoicing in the name of Solomon Psaltery (Jack Hawkins). It's a case of Psaltery and battery as Lionheart arranges to have him taken into custody after he kills his wife in a jealous rage. This is based on *Othello*, apparently... not the board game!

Chloe Moon (Coral Browne) gets electrocuted by a hair dryer, a sequence which has a memorably camp turn from Price as a fey hairdresser. *Henry VI, Part 1* is the inspiration for this apparently. The best is saved for almost last, with Robert Morley's Meredith Merridew being force-fed his "babies" in a poodle pie in a scene inspired by *Titus Andronicus* – I might have to get into Shakespeare – his plays sound a lot more fun than I thought! Ian Hendry's Peregrine Devlin manages to escape death twice and the film ends with Lionheart's daughter Edwina (Diana Rigg) who had been helping him in the murders, being clobbered and killed, shortly before her dad joins her as the theatre is set alight and he presumably burns to death.

Bearing similarities to AIP's first Dr. Phibes film, this is the superior movie. A horror comedy that never fails to entertain and amuse, it was subsequently adapted for the stage, appearing in 2005 and had Diana Rigg's daughter Rachael Stirling in the Edwina part her mother had previously played.

Diana Rigg (left) in Theatre of Blood *(1973)*

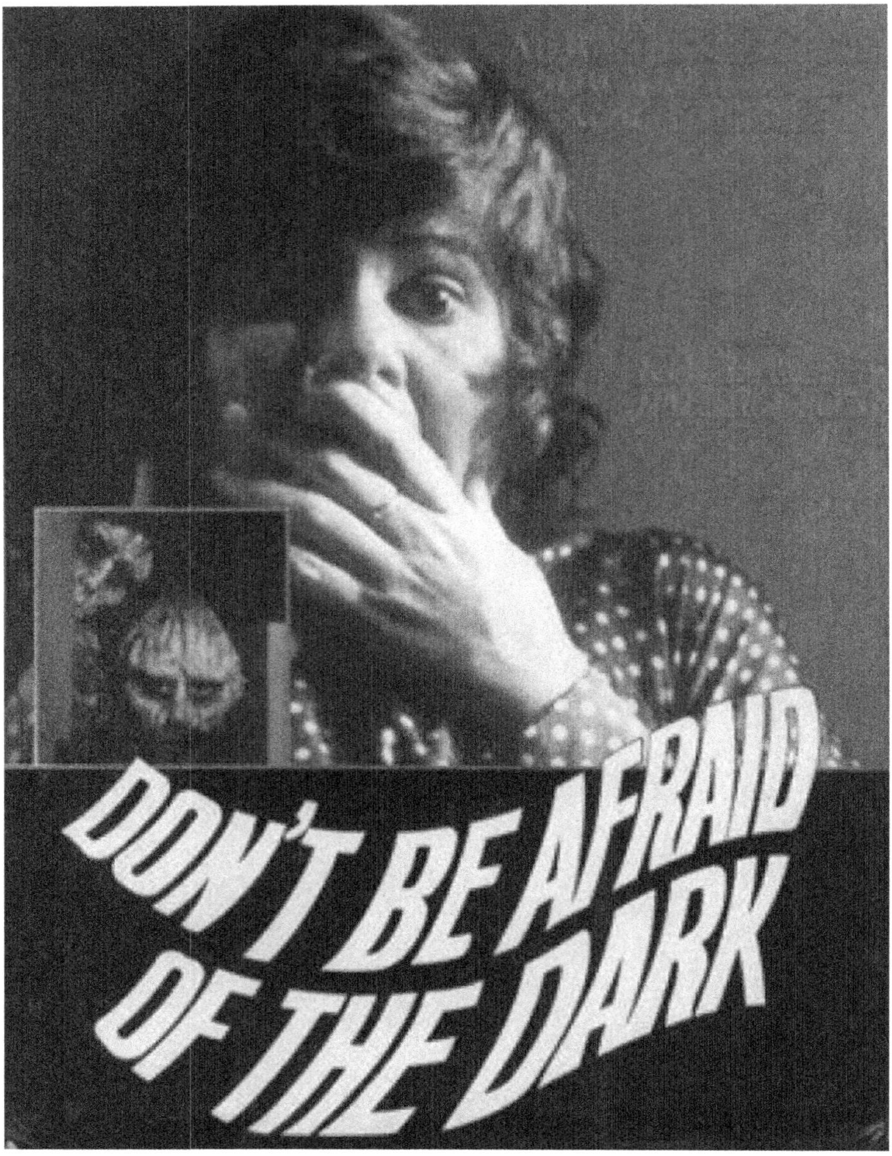
DON'T BE AFRAID
OF THE DARK

CHAPTER 42

DON'T BE AFRAID OF THE DARK (1973)

Don't Be Afraid of the Dark *(1973)*

Directed by: John Newland.

Written by: Nigel McKeand.

Starring: Kim Darby, Jim Hutton, Barbara Anderson, William Demarest, Pedro Armendáriz Jr., Lesley Woods, Robert Cleaves and more.

Studio: Lorimar Productions.

AN APPOINTMENT WITH THE LIGHTS OUT
FOR TV TERROR

EVERYONE RAVES ABOUT *Trilogy of Terror*, the 1975 TV movie that features Karen Black being terrorised by a weird African doll but, as fine as that film is, this one is my favourite.

Directed by John Newland (who created the bland and boring *One Step Beyond* late '50s/early '60s anthology series), the film stars

Kim Darby (who telefantasy fans will remember from the classic "Miri", one of the best episodes of the original *Star Trek*, and therefore, one of the most disliked – fans are a weird lot!) and Jim Hutton as a couple, Sally and Alex Farnham, who move into a plush, but still spooky, Victorian-type house on the outskirts of LA, and get more than they bargained for when Darby disregards creepy caretaker Harris's (William Demarest) advice and opens a fireplace door in the basement that unleashes three little demons!

The creepy mood begins straight away and watching this film in 1978 in the beloved Friday night film 11.05pm slot, I was bloody terrified! Over a shot of the house at night, we hear the very scary voices of the demons, plotting to turn Darby into one of them – enough to freeze the blood in your veins to ice!

The demons are fully seen fairly late into the film but we hear them quite a bit before then – after Sally has opened the fireplace door in the basement and allowing them to escape, we hear them excitedly proclaiming that "She set us free!". Once seen, they are no disappointment. Using midget actors in oversized sets works a treat and the demons are both scary and cute. Back in 1978, I was only able to steel my nerves and stay for the first twenty minutes or so but my cousin watched the whole thing and filled me in on what I'd missed – I couldn't imagine the sight of three little demons dragging a woman along the floor by rope and was gutted that I'd missed it.

The demons try to cut Sally with a razor while she's showering, spook her out by pushing an ashtray off a bedside drawer, and during a party held at the house, she simply freaks out after seeing one of the creatures under the table. It's not explained how none of the guests can see it, but it's implied that the creatures can move very quickly and it simply shot off in the ensuing melee – this scene is unintentionally hilarious, as Darby overacts somewhat. Sally's friend Joan (Barbara Anderson, who appeared in the Star Trek ep "The Conscience of the King", which was made directly after Darby's appearance in "Miri") tries to help out but the demons manage to get Sally all to themselves and, during a suspenseful sequence which is only marred by some obvious day-for-night filming, they drag her off to the basement fireplace where it all began, and it's goodbye Sally.

Apart from the demons, the film has a lot to offer, with a nice creepy location and good casting – William Demarest is the type of actor who was made for US horror TV movies, and his caretaker character is a treat, with his dire warnings about opening the fireplace door in the cellar, and his subsequent panic as the vengeful creatures trap him in the cellar to give him a good fright for grassing on them! It's a pity they didn't make a sequel to this, as Sally becomes one of the demonic creatures and is plotting with the other three to ensnare the next poor sod who ventures into the house – I wonder if Sally's demon looked like the others, or had a look of the woman she used to be? This TV movie became a cult success, being released theatrically and attracting the attention of the young Guillermo del Toro who, as a kid watching it on its initial broadcast, was so impressed and affected by it that he remade it as a director in 2010. As enjoyable as the remake is, the original remains the best.

Demonic fun in Don't Be Afraid of the Dark *(1973)*

Flesh to touch...
Flesh to burn!
Don't keep the Wicker Man waiting!
A TOTALLY CORRUPT SHOCKER FROM THE AUTHOR OF "SLEUTH" AND "FRENZY"!
ANTHONY SHAFFER'S
THE WICKER MAN
Starring
"THE WICKER MAN" · EDWARD WOODWARD · BRITT EKLAND · DIANE CILENTO · INGRID PITT
and CHRISTOPHER LEE as Lord Summerisle
Produced by PETER SNELL · Directed by ROBIN HARDY · Screenplay by ANTHONY SHAFFER
From Warner Bros. A Warner Communications Company
R RESTRICTED
74/185
"THE WICKER MAN"

CHAPTER 43

THE WICKER MAN (1973)

Christopher Lee as Lord Summerisle in The Wicker Man *(1973)*

Directed by: Robin Hardy.

Written by: Anthony Shaffer (screenplay) and David Pinner (novel, uncredited).

Starring: Edward Woodward, Christopher Lee, Britt Ekland, Ingrid Pitt, Diane Cilento, Lindsay Kemp and more.

Studio: British Lion Film Corporation.

BASKET CASE

THIS FILM IS a masterpiece, and has deservedly become a cult classic being one of the few horror films of the 1930s/'40s/'50s/'60s/'70s to gain its own (now long defunct) fan club. Reportedly Christopher Lee's favourite film of his own works, *The Wicker Man* has a *Prisoner*-esque vibe as an ordinary person encounters an isolated village that, at first sight, seems normal but which turns out to be anything but.

Edward Woodward plays Sergeant Neil Howie of the Scottish West Highland Constabulary. Howie is as stiff and straight-laced as four-week-old haggis, which makes his encounters with the inhabitants of Summerisle all the funnier, Summerisle being a remote Scottish island with its own rules and "King" in the form of Chris Lee's Lord Summerisle. Howie has been sent to the island to investigate the disappearance of a "young gurrl", one Rowan Morrison and what appears at first to be a straight-forward case takes a more bizarre turn.

Edward Woodward in The Wicker Man *(1973)*

It doesn't take long for Howie to discover the inhabitants of Summerisle are barking mad, and like all barking mad inhabitants of isolated villages and islands (apologies, dear reader, if you inhabit such a place yourself), they don't realise it and think that the interloper is the fool: When Howie arrives by seaplane, he is greeted by a bunch of skitty locals who evade his questions with downright lies and stand, laughingly taking the piss with hands in pockets, after he walks off. It's when Woodward books into the local pub that we realise how... err... "unusual" the place really is. The patrons subtly mock Howie's obvious straight-lacedness by singing a bawdy song filled with entendres about the landlord's daughter (Britt Ekland) who obviously enjoys being painted in the manner of such rude folk songs! Shortly after, Woodward exits the pub and finds a bevy of passionate couples having sex right in view outdoors! It's not on a par with the orgy scenes that litter *Caligula* but it gets the point across and is funny because of the rigid main character's frosty and angered response.

Edward Woodward and Britt Ekland in The Wicker Man *(1973)*

One of the many pleasures of this excellent film is the soundtrack – the film has quite a few musical numbers in it and without exception they are all memorable in one way or another, whether it's the music itself or the accompaniment – the famous scene where the landlord's daughter dances naked around her bedroom which adjoins Howie's to a rather catchy bit of music is a good example. The main character goes from one bizarre moment to another – seeing the school mistress giving a talk to a class full of kids about how men's penises are venerated throughout history as symbols of fruitfulness and symbolised by the maypole, just before Howie gets the willies put up him by encounters with creepy beetle-baiting kids and navel-stream obsessed gravediggers!

The film holds back Howie's encounter with the master of the island and their meeting positively sparks. Christopher Lee is on top form here, aided by a magnificent script. Lord Summerisle describes the origins of the heathen island and puts the case for their way of life quite effectively. But Howie isn't convinced, leading to some classic lines: "He (Jesus) had his chance and, in modern parlance, blew it", and when skittily saying farewell to Howie that it's "been a great pleasure, meeting a Christian copper!".

Of course, the islanders piss-taking attitude to Howie is down to the fact that the whole thing has been planned in advance, and Howie is due to be sacrificed for the sake of some apples. The missing girl was designed to lure the virginal copper to Summerisle, and his sacrifice to various heathen gods is intended to ensure a bountiful harvest of fruit come summer. It's clear to the viewer though that Howie's death will not make the slightest difference and the fruit will still wither and die on the branches, but there's nothing he can do, as he is dragged to the giant wicker man and locked in with various sheep and goats, as it is then set afire.

The Wicker Man *(1973)*

These scenes are genuinely disturbing and make one angrily question why, if there is a God, He doesn't do a thing to help Howie. Howie's final screams of agony are accompanied by the villagers all joining in a rousing sing-song – to them, it's a fun day out, a celebration they have grown up with and enjoy, as natural to them as Bonfire Night or Easter is to us. I would love to have seen a sequel to this film, set one year on and showing what happened when Howie's sacrifice failed to make any difference to the apples and pears – Lord Summerisle wouldn't have been amused, as his head would have been next on the block..

I first saw this film on a Saturday night on my local ITV station and though I enjoyed it, it didn't make that much of an impression. Seeing it several times since – I later realised, in cut form – I appreciated it more and we have the opportunity now to see this classic in full uncut mode, thanks to various DVD and Blu-ray releases. A compelling mix of horror, thriller, musical and sex, *The Wicker Man* is a classic. Doubly so, after the terrible 2006 remake.

Christopher Lee as Lord Summerisle in The Wicker Man *(1973)*

WILLIAM PETER BLATTY'S
THE EXORCIST
Directed by WILLIAM FRIEDKIN
Something almost beyond comprehension is happening to a girl on this street, in this house
...and a man has been sent for as a last resort. This man is The Exorcist.
ELLEN BURSTYN · MAX VON SYDOW · LEE J. COBB
KITTY WINN · JACK MacGOWRAN JASON MILLER as Father Karras
LINDA BLAIR as Regan · Produced by WILLIAM PETER BLATTY
Executive Producer NOEL MARSHALL · Screenplay by WILLIAM PETER BLATTY based on his novel
From Warner Bros. A Warner Communications Company
R RESTRICTED

CHAPTER 44
THE EXORCIST (1973)

The Exorcist *artwork by Allen Koszowski*

Directed by: William Friedkin.

Written by: William Peter Blatty (screenplay, based on his novel).

Starring: Ellen Burstyn, Max von Sydow, Lee J. Cobb, Jason Miller, Linda Blair, William O'Malley and more.

Studio: Warner Bros./Hoya Productions.

HEAD-TURNER

667 1780
669 6037
229 3475
554 1269
669 3632
441 3888

WHAT DO THE numbers above all have in common? Answer: they're all UK telephone helpline numbers which cinema patrons could call if they'd seen William Friedkin's 1973 film *The Exorcist*, and been so disturbed and horrified by the experience, that they had to seek counselling and help! It's unrecorded how many people actually rang any of these numbers, but it's a mark of the film's unique power to terrify and affect, that they had to be given out at all. The film made it's debut in UK cinemas on March 16th, 1974, and the furore that followed echoed what had happened in America, when the film's Boxing Day 1973 première had seen mass walkouts, audience members fainting, vomiting, and, in one instance, a member of the audience apparently jumping at the screen in order to kill the demon!

I was blissfully unaware of this at the time, as I was only six when the film was first released here in the UK, and only saw a few stills in articles on the film in various publications. I absolutely loved comics, both British and American, and horror/SF film mags. I would be met, at the infant school gates, by my mother who would then take me to the local paper shop – Finn's – and then on to the Post Office. In each of these, I would buy piles of comics, and occasionally, horror mags. My mother was a little wary about these for a time, after the sight of Chris Lee's Creature on a huge poster in *Monster Mag* had traumatised me, but I did get a few later, including the fondly-remembered *Movie Monsters*, and later, *Quasimodo's Monster Magazine*. Both of these mags contained articles on *The Exorcist*, and I did pick up on the fact that it was a very scary and controversial film.

Back then though, I was more into reading about the classic Universal, Hammer etc films which were relatively harmless in comparison.

Years passed, and I never really thought much about the film. Odd references would intrigue me – *Starburst* magazine had a news item in issue 22 (May, 1980) about the film being shown on US TV during the Winter Olympics and, though edited, it had caused a furore. TV stations were picketed and call lines were jammed, as viewers rang in to loudly complain. If I'd had a beard back then, I would have stroked it, but I was intrigued nonetheless. After this, *Starburst* kept promising an article on the film but it never appeared – pity. Funnily enough, I'd assumed it was a British film when I'd first read about it, and that it began with a priest being called out in the middle of the night to attend to a girl who has been possessed! Kitchen sink-type realistic drama. As it turned out, I wasn't that far wrong.

I didn't really think about the film again until late 1991. A friend of mine who was also heavily into horror films had acquired a copy on pirate video some years prior. We got chatting about the film, and he said that it was genuinely frightening, especially some parts where you see a really horrible white face for a few seconds. This intrigued me, and we planned a night at his house where we'd watch the film together. This came about in early 1992 – my mate's family had trundled off to bed, it was a quarter to midnight, the tape was pushed into the machine, and we were off. My friend's copy had a good picture but the opening Warner Bros. logo was cut off, and it started with the film's title and that terrifying chanting. Straight away, I felt a little queasy and knew this was going to be no ordinary viewing experience.

Max von Sydow in an iconic scene from The Exorcist *(1973)*

After a creepy prologue, the setting changed from Iraq to Washington, USA but the eerie atmosphere persisted. An actress, Chris MacNeil (Ellen Burstyn), was staying in a rented property with her twelve-year-old daughter Regan (Linda Blair) who mentioned she'd been playing with an Ouija board (don't try this at home, folks!), and been chatting to someone called Captain Howdy. Strange noises came from the attic shortly after, and Regan urinates on the floor during a swish party held by her mother – which turns out to be the start of lots of bad behaviour (and language). The dreaded "F" word had been heard before in films, but not the even more offensive "C" word, and it was the inclusion of these that helped to shock the film's original audience. Funnily enough, I didn't find the operating scenes particularly gruelling (but I was glad when they were over!), and the crucifix scene made no impression on me when I first saw it – it was only upon acquiring my own copy of the film, that I really became aware of it, and when I did, it made me go cold.

As the film continued, I felt distinctly uneasy. There wasn't any specific scene that affected me – it was the film as a whole. It had a definite atmosphere of evil about it which just seemed to ooze out of the screen! My mate was completely unaffected, and I wondered if similar viewers were either completely non-religious disbelievers, or just thick! I have an open mind about the existence of God, I wasn't (and still am not) a church-goer, and the last time I'd read the Bible was when I was ten, so the film shouldn't really have bothered me as much as it did. Just to digress for a moment, I have a creepy story to tell about something that happened when I was in my early twenties, in 1987, and this is as good a place as any to unload it! I didn't have a VHS player of my own, but I'd started to purchase video tapes and I had a large collection. I used to pester friends and family to watch my tapes on their machines, and a family (father, mother, three kids aged between seven and ten) that we knew had to regularly put up with me begging them to let me go round and watch my tapes on their video player. During the late summer of '87, they'd gone away for a couple of weeks and kindly left me the key to go round and watch videos whenever I wanted. I would get there for about 8pm, and stay until around one in the morning. One such night, it was getting to around 12.30 in the morning, and I was sat on the floor as usual glued to the TV screen. I suddenly heard a scratching sound at the door. The family didn't have any pets, and I was irritated that my viewing had been interrupted (I was always a stickler for completely uninterrupted viewing experiences even then). The scratching continued, so I felt obliged to get up and see what it was. Nothing there. This happened a second, and then a third time. Each time, there was nothing there. I began to feel a bit scared. When the scratching came again, I went outside and stood trying to identify the cause. The side of the house was painted completely white, there was a full Moon – and I suddenly noticed the shadow of a man, in profile, on the side of the house! I was puzzled, as there was no one in sight, and nowhere anyone could stand without being seen. So where was that shadow coming from?? As I stood pondering, the shadow vanished suddenly! Then I was frightened! I went shaking back into the house, watched a few more minutes of the film, and then, as you do when you are shit-scared, I began chatting to myself about how I was a bit tired!

Anyway, returning to 1992 (consider my story this chapter's equivalent of that chalk-white face popping up throughout the film, for no readily discernible reason!). The atmosphere in my friend's house was indeed spine-chilling. I tried to pretend I wasn't being seriously spooked by what was happening on screen, and made a half-hearted comment along the lines of the film being exciting but not frightening. By the time of the actual exorcism, I began to wonder if I'd ever watch another horror film again. Comparing *The Exorcist* to the average Amicus or Hammer horror was like comparing a PlayStation to an old Atari game! When the demon Pazuzu appears briefly in Regan's bedroom, it seemed as if the director had actually managed to catch on camera a genuinely supernatural and malign entity. By the time the younger priest Karras had taken a swan dive down those steps, I was glad my ordeal was over. Actually though, it was just beginning! After we chatted for a bit, the lights were turned off and we settled down to sleep (ha!), my friend on the chair, me on the settee.

I knew I had no chance at all of going to sleep that night. The film had seriously disturbed and unsettled me, and I wondered how anyone could watch it for a first time and not suffer any negative effects afterwards. It's difficult to describe, but there was a really horrible atmosphere in that house that night – it was as if something was in the room there with us, watching and lurking. It almost felt as though someone had just been murdered in the house and their corpse placed outside the door! Time passed, and it was getting on for about 3.30am, when something really frightening happened – the living room had a large window looking onto the garden, the curtains were drawn, but pulled along so that the edge of the window could be seen. And then, it happened! I saw, very briefly but unmistakeably, the demon Pazuzu! Lurking just outside the house! Obviously, it couldn't really be the creature I'd seen in a film, just two hours earlier, but who cares about logic and reason when it's 3.30 in the morning and you're scared out of your wits?! Had some sinister spirit or entity been drawn to my friend's house that night and was using the image that had so unnerved me? Or had the film's terrifying images burned themselves onto my eyes, so I was seeing Pazuzu everywhere?? I kept quiet, tried to calm myself down with logic, and thought about a barmaid I fancied to keep my mind off what had happened. I didn't tell my mate about this for a good few years – he's moved now – but it all conspired to make me wary of watching the film again, and of watching any horror films at all! As time passed, my fears subsided, I didn't see any more Pazuzus, and I bought a copy of the film myself which I watched a few times (always in the summer!), but always timed it carefully so that it would finish before three in the afternoon so that its chilling effect might begin to wear off by the time night rolled around. It still had a creepy effect on me every time I watched it – my fourth viewing of it was at a neighbour's house. She wanted to watch it, and as I inserted the tape into the machine, I was shivering and shaking like a leaf!

The Exorcist *artwork by Allen Koszowski*

I stopped watching the film after a bit, as the year took a really bad turn and I blamed the film for that. One curious effect it left me with was that I got a crush on the grown up Linda Blair. I'd had many crushes on women in film/TV over the years, a noble line that began with *Scooby Doo*'s Daphne when I was seven and had even included a chimpanzee at one point (*Planet of the Apes*' Zira)! I was curious to see how *The Exorcist*'s child star had matured over the years (she was thirty-one in 1992), and once I caught a few current photos and videos of chubby-cheeked Linda, I was smitten. That crush wore off in 1994, and was replaced by one on B'Elanna Torres from *Star Trek: Voyager*.

I managed to see the film on the big screen in 1995, when it was reissued (at midnight!), at the now, sadly, defunct main street cinema in Durham. Having been used to seeing the film on a cheap and nasty pirate VHS, I was naturally interested to see how it would look on a large cinema screen. I was also interested to observe the reactions of my fellow patrons, and I felt rather big-headed, wondering how many of them had seen the film before. The film began, and the eerie sound of the Islamic Call to Prayer seemed to spook most of the audience. As the Iraq-set prologue came to an end, I was delighted to see someone get up and leave their seat – obviously, I thought, the sight of that demonic statue followed by a vicious dogfight had proved too much for them! Unfortunately, I was wrong, as they returned a couple of minutes later laden down with bags of crisps and popcorn! As the film got into its stride, I was quite disturbed. Not by anything on the screen, but by the reactions of the audience – how they hooted and laughed at the sight of a pre-adolescent girl urinating on the carpet, and at the obscenities and swear words that came later (I actually wondered if my fellow audience members had something wrong with them, or that I'd wandered into a specially-organised screening of the film for members of a home for the seriously disturbed – bad language isn't that funny), but the crucifix scene shut them all up. There was actually a collective gasp at that point, and from then on, the hooting and laughter stopped. Friedkin had them all in his power! The audience was quiet for the rest of the film's running time. All those teen lads trying to impress their girlfriends must have wished they'd gone into screen two instead, as I detected some distinctly shocked and queasy faces as the lights came up. I was gratified to see that someone actually had a soaking wet crotch! I think maybe they'd spilled some ice cream or Tizer onto their lap, but I prefer to regard it as an indication of the film's effectiveness.

The film was finally passed uncut by the British Board of Film Censors in 1997, and released on video and DVD in several versions, the most interesting of which features unused footage from 1973 in which we see Regan crawl downstairs like a human spider, as well as extra bits of the demon's face appearing on walls and ovens!

Well, it took many years since that 1995 cinema screening, but I have actually seen it again now (twenty times, as of writing this – ten times for the original cinema release, ten for the *Director's Cut*!) on the fortieth anniversary Blu-ray release. I've also caught up with the 1977 sequel *Exorcist ll: The Heretic*, and so, the time seemed right for a reassessment of what I make of the film(s) now, over twenty years since I first saw them.

What made me decide to buy *The Exorcist*, and watch it again? No idea, just an impulse really – I'm a regular visitor to Amazon and eBay, and I think I'd maybe browsed the "other items you might be interested in" part when *The Exorcist* popped up. As soon as I saw the fortieth anniversary Blu-ray's marvellous cover art showing those famous steps down which Father Karras goes head first, I knew I had to have it, even if I didn't actually end up watching it! So, before I knew what I was doing, I'd clicked on "Add to Basket" and "Pay Now", and the film was mine! Or, almost. It arrived a few days after, and I put it, unopened, with the stack of 280 or so parcels I had saved up for Christmas 2014!

The Exorcist *artwork by Allen Koszowski*

Once Christmas rolled around and I'd opened all the stuff I'd saved up (which took until after seven at night), I scanned the box a few times, but put off watching the film, intending to view it during the summer. I eventually did, in August 2015, on a cheery Saturday afternoon. I returned from visiting friends, and at the "safe" time of 15.25 (I can imagine people reading this and thinking 'bah, what a softy!'), I took out the disc and prepared to insert it into the machine – and then promptly stopped myself, when I realised I'd taken out the *Director's Cut* instead! D'oh! Okay, a few seconds later and the right disc was in the machine, the phone was off, the door locked, curtains drawn, three separate trips to the toilet made (just to make sure I wouldn't get the urge to go while the film was on)... and I was really excited, and a bit nervous, at the thought of seeing the film still regarded as "The Most Frightening Film Ever Made!" again, for the first time in twenty years! I pressed "Play" – and was confronted with an intro by William Friedkin. Once I realised this intro was trying to spoil the fun, and include clips from the film (a practice I hate, by the way – what's the point of spoiling the surprise of what you're going to see by showing out of context clips of the best bits?!), I averted my eyes and listened to it. Very interesting stuff from Friedkin though, it got me hyped up to watch the actual film.

Jason Miller in The Exorcist *(1973)*

So, jumping ahead for a moment to the end of that viewing experience – did I find *The Exorcist* as disturbing and unpleasant as I did when I first saw it, back in the '90s? Sadly (or should that be happily?), no. Time, and the world, had moved on, and I personally think it's next to impossible for any film to genuinely terrify anyone over the age of twenty these days, especially with the obsession with over-the-top CGI. I'm a different person too – when I first saw the film I was twenty-four. I was forty-eight in 2015, so my response was bound to be different. Also, back in 1992, when I first saw it, there was no Internet, and I knew nothing about Linda Blair, Ellen Burstyn et al. Now, being a fully-fledged expert of the horror scene (he said modestly), I'm familiar with them and with a lot of the background of the film itself, which made it more familiar and thus, less frightening. In 1992, I spent a terrifying few hours after watching it (remember, I saw Pazuzu lurking outside my friend's house!) trying to get to sleep – on a bloody uncomfortable settee! Now however, we have the Internet – say I'd watched *The Exorcist* for the first time now, and felt a little creeped out by it, I need just go online and check out numerous interviews with the stars and director on YouTube, send a friend request to Linda Blair on Facebook, or follow her, or other members of the cast and crew, on Twitter, or check out the dozens of sites that no doubt exist and are devoted to this classic – all of which would help to make the film, or any film, more accessible and thus less frightening.

So, *The Exorcist* isn't frightening to me any more – but it's still a brilliant and powerful piece of filmmaking. Certain people's ears must have burnt right off, as I kept thinking about detractors' opinions of it, and I have nothing but sneering contempt now for any ridiculous views that *The Omen* (1976) is far better, and that the 1973 film's effects don't hold up well now, and that it looks tacky. Absolute rubbish on toast! *The Omen* is the film that is often compared to Friedkin's spine-chiller, but personally, I've never really rated it very highly – it's a good film, but not even remotely scary or disturbing. When it was first released, one critic described it as a "very undisturbing film" and more like a thriller than a horror movie, sentiments I agree with. The fact that some relatives of mine, who aren't exactly aficionados of the horror genre have always loved it says it all about Richard Donner's effort – it appeals to middle class fifty-somethings who wouldn't normally bother with something as "coarse" as a horror film, but might appreciate a gentle chill over their tea and cucumber sandwiches. One factor that definitely works against *The Omen* being a terrifying experience is that there are far too many familiar faces in it – in horror movies, familiarity breeds, not contempt (unless you're watching a Jess Franco, or Paul Naschy film) but cosiness. As much as we all love our fixes of petrifying Peter and creepy Christopher, I doubt that many of us would ever be on the phone asking a relative to come and spend the night with us after watching one of their films! Once you've seen a handful of horrors with Cushing and Lee in the cast, or Price or Karloff, or Lugosi or Chaney, and cottoned on to the fact that they are horror stars, then they become the friendly uncles of the genre and we know nothing harmful or horrible will happen to us while watching their movies, or afterwards. Similarly, with *The Omen*, the average TV/film viewer will spot people like Patrick (*Doctor Who*) Troughton, David (too many films to mention but none of them are disturbing, not even *Straw Dogs*, so we know we're safe) Warner, Billie (*The Krays*) Whitelaw and John (*Wilde Alliance*) Stride, and feel comfortable as a result. With *The Exorcist*, most of the cast are largely unknown to the average viewer, even today. Film buffs like us will be able to reel off Max von Sydow's screen credits, and what he likes to eat for lunch, but his face and name would mean nothing to many, so that helps to make the film more unsettling, as there are no familiar cosy faces or names for the average non-horror film fan to latch onto. So, no, *The Exorcist* didn't terrify me on this more recent re-watch, but it's definitely more effective as an unsettling horror experience than *The Omen*.

The views that many people express about the effects looking tacky are just... well, completely wrong. Actually, I can't spot a single moment where the effects don't work – everything from the life-size Linda Blair dummy, to the vomiting, to the head-turning, to the appearance of Pazuzu (in Regan's bedroom, not my friend's garden this time, thankfully!) work perfectly, and I couldn't spot any wires in the levitation scenes either. The effects work because they are all physical effects, not cartoony and unrealistic CGI as is often the case now. Also, of course, they were achieved with hard work, blood, sweat, tears, sprained backs and sore feet, and plenty of cursing aimed at William Friedkin, unlike most films now where the effects come courtesy of a fat, beer-swilling guy in a vest sat on his arse at a computer.

It was a fascinating experience watching it again after all those years. The Blu-ray picture is stunning (not something that always happens with older movies), and I was intrigued to see so many little parts I'd forgotten about but remembered as soon as I saw them – Max von Sydow giving a master class in acting quietly terrified and worried at the café, then almost being run over by a sinister toothless crone in a coach, for example. The whole intro in Iraq is like a brilliant mini-movie in itself, and knocks seventeen shades of sherbert off the whole running times combined of overrated rubbish like the *Saw/Hostel/Underworld/Twilight* etc etc films, and no other horror film can compare.

Watching the film again has made it clear that a large part of the reason *The Exorcist* is so popular, and cultish, is down to the six main characters, and the interactions between them: Chris, Regan, Merrin, Karras, Kinderman, and, of course, Pazuzu. All interesting, and all working well together, even though some don't actually meet. *Doctor*

Who, *Star Trek*, *The Prisoner*, *Star Wars*, *Buffy* etc etc all have vast fan networks, with lots of fan fiction being written, and some published professionally. I bet that there are fans of this film out there who have been toiling away, writing their own stories about the further adventures of Regan, Chris, Kinderman etc, and if there aren't, then there should be. Personally, I'd like to see a story which takes place in a parallel universe, where Karras wasn't killed, just badly injured, and upon his discharge from hospital finds Chris and Regan waiting for him, so he now has a ready-made family! Ahhhh... Or, how about a tale in which Pazuzu returns, but ends up needing the help of the human characters, as another entity has appeared on the scene, one even more powerful and evil than the big "P"? The possibilities are endless.

Linda Blair in The Exorcist *(1973)*

One thing I've never properly understood is, just who does that ghastly white face belong to? It's clearly not Pazuzu, as it looks nothing like the winged monster with the huge todger which we see as a statue, and then the real thing later on, so who and what is it? My theory is that it's an evil spirit, one that thrives on the abuse and torture of children (someone who was a paedophile when they were alive perhaps?), so when Regan is possessed, this spirit is attracted to that and joins in the "fun", so to speak ("Where is Regan?", "In here, with us"). Watching it again though has also made a few things I'd previously overlooked clearer – when the possessed Regan says to her terrified mother, "Do you know what she did, your cunting

Daughter!!?", I hadn't previously realised it was Burke Denning's voice (The "C" word must have been a favourite epithet of his, as he uses it in reference to the housekeeper Karl earlier on), and that the demon was deliberately trying to taunt/upset Chris by using his voice, and referring to the fact that Regan had killed him. In fact, until watching the disc, I hadn't realised that Burke Dennings was the rat-faced, rat-arsed director of the film-within-the-film. I assumed he was the guy in the grey suit who Regan tells "You're gonna die up there". I assumed "up there" meant Regan's bedroom. Instead, the guy in the grey suit is an astronaut, and "up there" is outer space!

Re-watching it has been an epiphany of sorts for me – when I first saw the movie, I came to regard it as an evil, wholly negative affair. Now, my view is the opposite. I regard it as a strangely optimistic, life-affirming piece, where a malevolent force gets its nose soundly wiped by the forces of good. The film actually got me hyped up at certain points in a wave of near-religious fervour! This is what William Friedkin and William Peter Blatty wanted the audience to think and feel all along, and I'm finally mature enough to get their message. Watching it again has also reinforced to me how much I love the film (despite being terrified to watch it for so many years, I always respected it as the grand-daddy of all horror movies) – not just my all-time favourite horror now, but the greatest horror film, full-stop (bah, I'll see you *Dracula* 1958, and raise you *Bride of Frankenstein*!) Maybe it's not terrifying any more but at least it was once, and that's something not many films can boast. Rather than being frightened this time around, I thoroughly enjoyed it, and as I mentioned earlier, have watched it numerous times since – even late at night, something I thought I would never dare do! It's a masterpiece, and anyone who disagrees deserves to be puked on and thrown head first out of a window, and down a flight of eighty steps on a dark night. Blindfolded. It's a 10/10 from me.

Now, *Exorcist ll: The Heretic* (1977) is a film that I often forget exists (I bet William Peter Blatty did the same, or tried to!), and I even forgot that I saw this sequel back in January, 1993. I was still suffering from my crush on Linda Blair at the time, and bought every video I could find with her in, which led to me watching a lot of irredeemable rubbish which shall remain nameless. Even though (*Roller Boogie*) I watched this on a dark evening, I wasn't disturbed or horrified by it, and I knew in advance that the film was generally (*Savage Island*) thought of as being a worm in the apple of the horror genre (*Wild Horse Hank*), so I didn't expect to suffer any adverse effects after watching it (*Up Your Alley*). Well, I was basically bored by everything in it, bar lovely Linda – all I could remember a week after watching it was that we see Regan running around New York in a nightie, and something about Richard Burton flying to Africa on a giant grasshopper! I was curious to see the film again, and bought it on its own disc – I'd bought the fortieth anniversary *Exorcist* Blu-ray, rather than the anthology set because a) it had a few more extras, and, b) more importantly, it had a better cover – now come on, we've all done it...

So I settled back to watch *Exorcist ll: The Heretic*. Apparently, Burton and Blair got on very well together, despite the former's habit of turning up for work regularly sauced-up, then having the nerve to berate Blair when she was late, and he would regale her with a string of filthy Welsh rhymes. You would expect Blair and Burton to go together like cheese and banana on toast, but they make an unexpectedly good team. Shockingly, I'd completely forgotten that Max von Sydow was in it, looking very young (not surprising, as he played Merrin in the first film with make-up to look about thirty years older). The scenes from the events of the first film, re-shot with von Sydow and a different actress playing Regan in possessed mode, are okay, but lack any of the power or impact of the original. Part of the reason for the sequel's low regard among fans of the first film are the fact that at times, it comes across as quite unintentionally funny – the part where Burton is chased out of Africa is a scream, not to mention the section on the bus en route to Georgetown where he berates the driver who is trying to enjoy a large sandwich, telling him that "the girl (Regan) has to get home!". The funniest part is where Regan goes gaga during a top hat and tails stage performance – if the cast and director didn't collapse with hysterical laughter when this was shot, they have a very impressive humour threshold! The film isn't scary at all either – once you've seen those stills from *The Exorcist* at the beginning of the video-released version, you've seen the scariest part of it – but it doesn't seem to be trying to be. It's a totally different type of film, and a colossal disappointment to those audiences in 1977 who went to the cinema expecting to be grossed-out and terrified, as they had been in 1973/4, and instead were confronted with, let's face it, a load of pretentious nonsense – but very entertaining pretentious nonsense, with a great cast, nice direction and shooting etc. I must say, I also like the ending and had forgotten about all that stuff with the house caving in and Blair and Burton walking away holding hands

To finish, a few brief words on *Exorcist III* which followed in 1990 and the only disappointment with this film is that Regan MacNeil isn't in it – I would have liked to have seen what happened to the character in the intervening years – maybe married to Richard Burton's character from *Exorcist II*, then divorced after getting sick of both his drinking, and his endlessly forcing her to listen to his Welsh limericks?! Apart from that, it's an excellent slow-burning horror film, not as good as the original though, but better than the second. It was also good to see Jason Miller back again, and that scene in the hospital corridor is the single most effective moment in any '90s horror film, at least until *The Blair Witch Project* came along.

Note: A version of this chapter first appeared in *We Belong Dead* magazine.

The Exorcist *(1973)*

Terror
to delight
worshippers
of the
Macabre.
From Beyond The Grave
IAN BANNEN, IAN CARMICHAEL, PETER CUSHING, DIANA DORS, MARGARET LEIGHTON, DONALD PLEASENCE
NYREE DAWN PORTER, DAVID WARNER IAN OGILVY LESLEY-ANNE DOWN · Associate Producer JOHN DARK
AN AMICUS PRODUCTION · Screenplay by ROBIN CLARKE and RAYMOND CHRISTODOULOU · Produced by MAX J. ROSENBERG and MILTON SUBOTSKY
Directed by KEVIN CONNOR · TECHNICOLOR

CHAPTER 45

FROM BEYOND THE GRAVE (1974)

Peter Cushing in From Beyond the Grave *(1974)*

Directed by: Kevin Connor.

Written by: Robin Clarke (screenplay), Raymond Christodoulou (screenplay) and R. Chetwynd-Hayes (based on stories by).

Starring: Peter Cushing, Donald Pleasence, Ian Carmichael, David Warner, Ian Bannen, Diana Dors and more.

Studio: Amicus Productions.

SNUFF MOVIE

THE LAST OF the seven Amicus anthology horrors – seven Hammer Dracula films, seven Hammer Frankenstein films... funny, that – is one of the best, and one of the best '70s horrors in general. Amicus went out on a high here, with a neat number in which the stories are based on works by R. Chetwynd-Hayes, an author whose work I've never read but always intended, although haven't got around to yet.

Peter Cushing, an actor whose presence was essential to the

success of these anthology films – the only one he wasn't in, 1973's *The Vault of Horror*, was a flop – gives one of his best turns as a Yorkshireman who is the Proprietor of Temptations Limited, a scruffy antique shop hidden away in a London backstreet. Cushing's character must be the unluckiest shopkeeper in England, as all of his customers try to diddle him! They get paid back though, by various supernatural means.

David Warner plays the first diddling customer, who pays a cheap amount for a very expensive antique mirror and, on reflection, wishes he hadn't! The mirror contains an evil character played by Marcel Steiner who ends up controlling Warner and forcing him to kill innocent young women and feed their blood to the man in the mirror, eventually giving him the strength to swap places with Warner and enter the real world.

David Warner in From Beyond the Grave *(1974)*

Warner is quite the hit with the ladies and pulls more birds than Bill Oddie, inviting them back to the flat for a cosy spot of kissing and cavorting that always ends with Warner being covered in blood, his lady friends dead, and the landlord complaining about the drops of blood dripping down from his ceiling! This opening segment is great fun, very atmospheric and well-acted, with some really eerie moments, such as when Warner finds himself briefly within the mirror, in a moonlit, very creepy wood... shortly before he is confronted by the Steiner character who stabs him. The end of the story is predictable after a bit, with Warner ending up in the twilight world of the mirror, but the story is great fun.

The second story is a bit bizarre. Ian Bannen plays an odd clerk who not only has the strangest voice ever committed to film, but gets excited at the thought of spending a pleasant summer evening in the company of an impoverished street salesman and his moon-faced daughter, played by the real-life father/daughter pairing of Donald and Angela Pleasence. These two become acquainted with Bannen after the latter buys a couple of shoelaces, and then gets chatting, which leads to Bannen pinching a medal he doesn't deserve from our old friend the Proprietor's shop, and then things turn nasty. From just friendly small talk and chatter, as soon as Bannen steals that medal, Pleasense invites him to his squalid flat and we know that Bannen's goose is cooked.

Like father, like daughter. Donald and Angela Pleasence in *From Beyond the Grave* (1974)

Voodoo and witchcraft are the main themes here, with Bannen getting in with Pleasense's daughter and sampling her meat pie, before getting a nice head massage. His shrewish wife (Diana Dors) ends up dead, and so does Bannen: after a bizarre finale in which he and Angela get married and Bannen's son cuts the cake... We discover that apparently, Bannen's son, so peed off with his parents' continual arguments, has prayed for their deaths and his prayers have been answered.

I think this is an example of a story adapted from book form for the screen requiring a reading of the original short story in order to make complete sense – for a start, it might explain why the kid is tired of his parents, when in fact, their arguments are comedy gold – Bannen's weird delivery of the line, "Matches and laces don't run Rolls Royces... never heard 'a such nonsense" has me in stitches every time!

The third segment has a funny side too, with Ian Carmichael playing a posh city gent who discovers he has an invisible demon called an elemental sitting on his shoulder. Silly (but strangely sexy) old clairvoyant Madame Orloff (Margaret Leighton) offers to exorcise it from him, for a fee. The result is devastation, and lots of feathers blowing about in his living room, until the spooky ending in which we learn that Madame Orloff's exorcism has not quite worked – the demon has simply hopped from Carmichael's shoulder to possess his wife. I bet Madame Orloff never saw that coming...

Ian Carmichael and Margaret Leighton
in From Beyond the Grave *(1974)*

The prelude to this tale is equally amusing, with Carmichael sneakily swapping the price tags on a couple of snuff boxes, leading to the classic line in which Cushing sardonically informs Carmichael that he hopes he enjoys snuffing it.

As one metaphorical door closes, another literal door opens – though the final customer of the day, William Seaton (played by yet another Ian – Ogilvy, this time – what is it with casting actors called Ian in this film?), who soon wishes it didn't. Seaton is the only customer who doesn't cheat Cushing and as a result, he cheats death in this yarn. Purchasing an antique door for his study, Seaton finds it leads to a sinister house from the past inhabited by a scary-looking cove named Sir Michael Sinclair (Jack Watson) who found that men averted their eyes rather meet his gaze, as he "wore my knowledge about me like a cloak!", the knowledge in question being of the black arts and all sorts of demonic dabblings. These dabblings have enabled the sinful Sinclair to survive through the centuries, along with his house, via the door. The story is similar to the first tale involving the mirror, but here the hero comes up trumps by the simple expedient of hacking the door to pieces with an axe.

Lesley Anne-Down makes for a good heroine, and is saved from being carried off just in time. Nice effects as the room disintegrates, along with the villain. The film isn't quite over, as there's a nice little coda in which an opportunistic character, who has been hanging around outside the shop throughout the film, tries his luck at robbery but gets done in, when the heavy metal he throws at the Proprietor (a couple of guns) leads to his death in an iron maiden! The film ends in characteristic style, with Cushing addressing the viewer directly. This would have made a rather fine TV series, actually.

A superb film.

Peter Cushing in From Beyond the Grave *(1974)*

Who will survive
and what
will be
left of
them?
America's most
bizarre and
brutal crimes!...
"THE
TEXAS
CHAINSAW MASSACRE"
What happened is true. Now the motion picture that's just as real.
THE TEXAS CHAIN SAW MASSACRE · A Film by TOBE HOOPER · Starring MARILYN BURNS, PAUL A. PARTAIN, EDWIN NEAL, JIM SIEDOW and GUNNAR HANSEN as "Leatherface"
Production Manager, RONALD BOZMAN · Music Score by TOBE HOOPER and WAYNE BELL · Music Performed by ARKEY BLUE, ROGER BARTLETT & FRIENDS, TIMBERLINE ROSE,
LOS CYCLONES · Story & Screenplay by KIM HENKEL and TOBE HOOPER · Producer/Director, TOBE HOOPER · COLOR · A BRYANSTON PICTURES RELEASE
R RESTRICTED

CHAPTER 46

THE TEXAS CHAIN SAW MASSACRE (1974)

Gunnar Hansen in The Texas Chain Saw Massacre *(1974)*

Directed by: Tobe Hooper.

Written by: Kim Henkel (screenplay and story by) and Tobe Hooper (screenplay by).

Starring: Marilyn Burns, Allen Danziger, Paul A. Partain, William Vail, Teri McMinn, Edwin Neal and more.

Studio: Vortex.

HELL FOR LEATHERFACE

I FIRST SAW this iconic shocker on DVD, in February 2001. I chose to watch it, for some reason, before I went to work on night shift – and I wish in retrospect that I hadn't. It would have been far more fun if I'd saved this landmark chiller concerning persons of questionable intellect and taste till the next day, rather than watching it so that it finished about fifteen minutes before I was due to head off to spend the night with er... persons of questionable intellect and taste! If I'd saved it until the next night, when I was off, it would have given me something to look forward to – never mind, there's always the limited edition Blu-ray... And, bearing in mind my comment above, it was rather apt!

Based loosely on the real-life atrocities of Wisconsin farmer Ed Gein, who had an obsession with corpses and skin, flesh, blood and bone, the film is set in the hot summer of 1974 and involves a bunch of jovial teens who head off into the hot Texas countryside for a few hours and end up butchered.

The group comprises of Sally, Kirk, Pam, Jerry and Sally's wheelchair-bound pain in the ass brother Franklin (apparently, the actor himself, Paul Partain was a similar pain on set), and they decide to visit Sally's old family home, a decision they'll soon regret.

Franklin is quite a hoot, and tests the audience's political correctness to the limit, as anyone with any sense of humour will find themselves in creases, laughing at the misfortunes which befall a fat guy in a wheelchair! Whether first urinating into an empty can (and looking for all the world like he's tossing himself off!), then shrieking as his wheelchair slips and he's sent hurtling down the hill, or doing an impression of a slaughterhouse device, Franklin is hilarious.

The others are fairly bland, but it doesn't matter as they are simply set up as chainsaw fodder, to be dispatched in a variety of ways, most of which aren't particularly gory, and the film is a good example of how audiences can be made to think they've seen the most horrific stuff when it was actually all in their minds. We get a chilling warning of what's ahead for our band, as they come across the remains of a tent, with various items scattered about including a compass nailed to a tree. Prior to that, they pick up a crazy hitchhiker (Edwin Neal), who cuts the luckless Franklin's arm before being chucked out of the truck, and whom they'll meet up with again later...

The farmhouse-dwelling family of meat-obsessives – all either ex-slaughterhouse employees or with an unhealthy obsession with said slaughterhouse – are headed by Jim Siedow's garage proprietor, who seems sane initially but is soon revealed to be as barking as the rest of his crazy clan. The hitcher (Edwin Neal) is excitably crazy, but gets his comeuppance at the end when he is messily run over by a truck. Serve the sick bastard right! Leatherface (Gunnar Hansen) is the most frightening by far – this overweight oaf wears a mask of human skin, taken from various victims and when we first see him, bursting out of his slaughtering and preparing kitchen area to land a heavy metal mallet on the head of Kirk, we can tell that the relatively cosy period of Hammer and AIP horrors is over – this is genuine violence, perpetrated by a genuine monster and it genuinely unnerves its audience.

Some nice touches in the direction here; after Leatherface has killed Kirk and Pam – she is dragged screaming into the kitchen, then hung up on a hook and stuffed in the freezer later – we see him become visibly confused, by the arrival of these strangers, and is probably wondering if there are going to be any more! Not a bad performance, considering the actor is more or less completely hidden behind a grotesque mask.

The scene where Franklin is killed not long after makes us stop laughing at the character for once, as he is messily killed by the chainsaw-wielding Leatherface, who then pursues the screaming Sally through a genuinely nightmarish wood. This has to be one of the most effective scenes in horror film history – the direction is perfect, cutting in for a closer view of the terrifying Leatherface as he runs after Sally, his chainsaw buzzing and combined with the eerie score to create a perfect effect. Sally actually makes it to the farmhouse, just has enough time to take in the bizarre surroundings, then runs back the way she came, through the wood with the ever-buzzing Leatherface close behind her – too close, as it turns out. Marilyn Burns (Sally) was running so slowly, it would have been easy for Gunnar Hansen to catch up, so he had to deliberately try to run slower. It never becomes noticeable on screen, though.

Sally ends up trapped in the house for a while, before making an escape in the early hours of daytime. The end of the film surprised me, as I mistakenly assumed Burns would get killed in the closing moments – it's certainly a cheer-worthy result when the hitchhiker gets run over and Leatherface cuts his own leg on his chainsaw. The end of the film makes you want to see what these characters get up to next, as a new day dawns – they would indeed return for the OTT sequel in 1986... say no more! It's an '80s film, so it was bound to be a bit naff. There have been quite a few other sequels and rehashes of the story, but the original film remains not only the best, but the only good one.

LA EUROPEAN INCORPORATION PRESENTA
VIOLENZA!
L'ULTIMO TRENO DELLA NOTTE
FLAVIO BUCCI • MACHA MERIL • GIANFRANCO DE GRASSI
MARINA BERTI • FRANCO FABRIZI
REGIA DI ALDO LADO
E CON ENRICO MARIA SALERNO
ENNIO MORRICONE
GABOR POGANY
GIUSEPPE BURICCHI E PAOLO INFASCELLI
P.A.C.
DISTRIBUZIONE

CHAPTER 47

NIGHT TRAIN MURDERS (1975)

Night Train Murders *(1975) aka* Last Stop on the Night Train *aka* L'ultimo treno della notte *(original title)*

Directed by: Aldo Lado.

Written by: Roberto Infascelli (story), Renato Izzo (screenplay), Aldo Lado (screenplay) and Ettore Sanzò (story).

Starring: Flavio Bucci, Macha Méril, Gianfranco De Grassi, Irene Miracle, Laura D'Angelo, Franco Fabrizi and more.

Studio: European Incorporation/Rewind Film.

LAST CARRIAGE ON THE LEFT

IF ANY FILM would put you off travelling on a late night train, it's this one. I came to this '70s Italian film quite late but it was one I always wanted to see, after reading a write-up about it in *The Darkside* magazine (issue 37, December 1993, to be precise).

Directed by Aldo Lado, the film features two young girls called Margaret (Irene Miracle) and Lisa (Laura D'Angelo) travelling by train through Germany to Italy, to meet the family of Lisa for Christmas Day. Unfortunately, they don't manage to get there, having fallen foul of two unsavoury yobs (Blackie and Curly) and an equally-depraved posh woman who remains nameless and shameless.

Blackie (Flavio Bucci) and Curly (Gianfranco De Grassi) establish their unpleasant credentials from the start – the film is set over Christmas Eve and Christmas Day, and we see their holiday spirit is in short supply, as they beat up a street Santa and grab his takings. Shortly after, they ruin a woman's fancy coat, before boarding a train and causing some bother. The two heroines are also on this train, and catch the eyes of the nutters, who get the girls to hide them from the ticket inspector, before encountering the demented woman (Macha Méril) who is the main villain of the piece.

This superficially well-bred woman is a dirty so-and-so from the word go – enticing Blackie to touch her up in the train's toilet, we get some provocative flashes of her stockings and suspenders. Shortly after, a fracas breaks out and the girls realise the yobs aren't playing with a full box of matches and try to get away. The girls end up on a different, somewhat dilapidated and deserted, train after a bomb scare forces everyone off the other one, but their pleasure is short-lived, as the sinister sounds of Curly's harmonica tip them off that the three nutters are on board with them.

This is one of those films where you can imagine yourself in the place of the poor sod/s who are the victim/s – there are plenty of nutcases about in the world and I'm betting that something similar to what happens here must have befallen some poor souls at some point. It starts fairly innocuously, with the blonde woman and Blackie taunting the virginal and sexually-shy girls and touching each other up in front of them. Soon though, the gruesome threesome are spurred on to sicker and more depraved thrills, with forced masturbation and a good beating on the menu – the "highlight" of which is when a startled passer-by sees Blackie getting his tool tickled, does a hilarious double-take, and is subsequently seen and roped in to sexually assault Margaret by the loathsome blonde.

With Margaret subsequently knocked sparko, Curly is free to try his luck with Lisa. Egged on by blondbitch, he pulls down Lisa's knickers and tights but finds she is as stiff as "a frightened asshole" and he can't get it up! So, he uses a knife instead, resulting in Lisa dying a slow and unpleasant death. Margaret follows not long after, and there is a hint the men feel some remorse for their crimes.

The film is a rip-off of *The Last House on the Left* (1972) but it's very effective and one of my favourite Italian/giallo horror/thrillers of the decade. Things get very *Last House*, when the three evil swines end up staying at the house of Lisa's parents, and predictably get found out. I would have preferred the threesome's comeuppance to be bloodier – when Blackie is shot, it's disappointingly quick. I would have liked to see the bastard suffer! Curly's death is the most satisfying, as Lisa's doctor dad finds him injecting heroin into his arm, then plunges the needle right in and beats him to the verge of death with various equipment. The blonde psycho completes the job, as Curly crawls outside and grabs her before she shows how well-heeled she is when she kicks him into the afterlife.

The one aspect of the film guaranteed to get anyone's dander up is the fact that the well-heeled cow gets away scot-free with her crimes. The police might eventually have caught up with her, off-screen, but that's not enough – justice should have been seen to be done! Apart from that, this is a very good example of an Italian horror/thriller and one that ended up on the infamous "Banned List" in the early '80s.

Irene Miracle in Night Train Murders *(1975)*

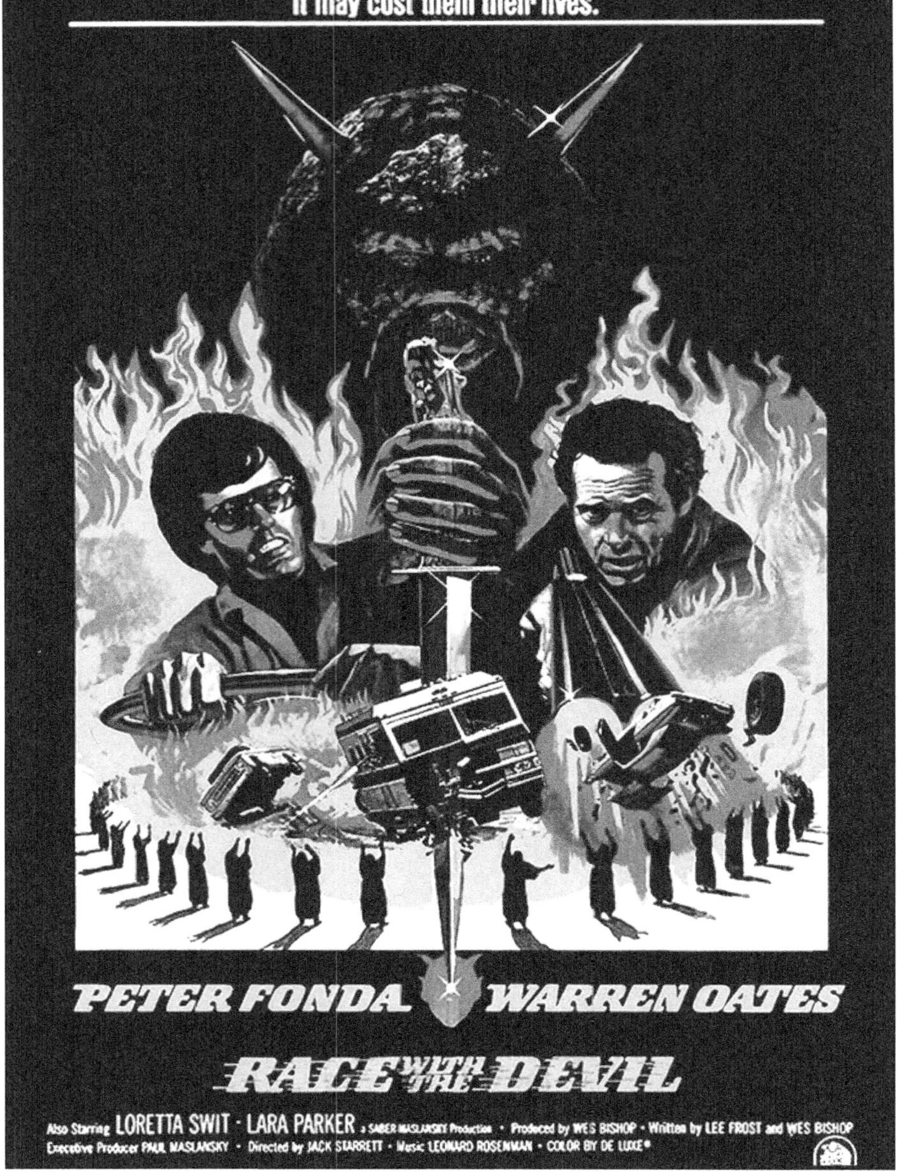
THEY WITNESSED AN UNSPEAKABLE ACT!
It may cost them their lives.
PETER FONDA
WARREN OATES
RACE WITH THE DEVIL
Also Starring LORETTA SWIT · LARA PARKER a SABER MASLANSKY Production · Produced by WES BISHOP · Written by LEE FROST and WES BISHOP
Executive Producer PAUL MASLANSKY · Directed by JACK STARRETT · Music LEONARD ROSENMAN · COLOR BY DE LUXE®

CHAPTER 48

RACE WITH THE DEVIL (1975)

Peter Fonda in Race with the Devil *(1975)*

Directed by: Jack Starrett.

Written by: Lee Frost and Wes Bishop.

Starring: Peter Fonda, Warren Oates, Loretta Swit, Lara Parker, R.G. Armstrong, Clay Tanner and more.

Studio: Saber Productions/Twentieth Century Fox.

HELL OF A CAMPING TRIP

IF THIS 1975 SHOCKER doesn't put you off holidaying in Texas, nothing will...

Once past a very effective opening intro, with a soundtrack that mixes the macabre with motor-racing, *Race with the Devil* involves two couples Roger and Kelly (Peter Fonda, Lara Parker) and Frank and Alice (Warren Oates, Loretta Swit) heading off into the rural wilds of Texas to enjoy a getaway in their fancy, all mod-cons mobile home.

Unfortunately, it all goes wrong on the first night – parked up in a secluded spot, they hear sounds across the river and the two men set off to investigate... just in time to see a Satanic ceremony that ends with a girl getting a knife plunged into her. The two women come to join their partners and make such a racket that the Satanists are alerted and the race/chase is on – with our four heroes (and cute dog!) driving across America (or so it seems), with the Devil worshippers hot on their heels and determined to destroy them...

This was actually Peter Fonda's second car chase film, having starred in *Dirty Mary Crazy Larry* a year earlier. He and Warren Oates (remember him as the big-eyed mutant from an episode of *The Outer Limits*?) had also previously starred together in *The Hired Hand* in 1971 and would star again in 1975's *92 in the Shade*.

Not to be quibbling about such a brilliant and well-crafted action/horror film, a few questions nevertheless come to mind. Firstly, why is everyone in Texas a Devil worshipper? As the film goes on, it seems that everyone our desperate quartet bump into, from the crustiest sheriff and his deputy, to the most innocuous gas station attendant (actually a cameo from director Jack Starrett) and seemingly innocent bus-load of school kids is either one of the Satanists or is in league with them. As mentioned elsewhere, I can never understand why anyone would worship the Devil – that bastard would do you no favours! And since everyone in Texas is apparently in love with Old Nick, why are the Satanists so spooked/enraged/desperate to see who has been spying on them, and then catch them?

Anyway, the initial pursuit is bloody excellent as the tension is ramped up when the vehicle gets stuck in some mud. The excitement continues throughout the film, culminating in a lengthy chase along the highway in which the Satanists are twatted at every opportunity by our resourceful heroes in scenes that will have you cheering. Aside from all the action stuff, the film does well with the more subtle scenes too – when the foursome stay overnight at a recreation park, they get sinister vibes from the other residents, even down to Kelly being gawped at menacingly by one of the band musicians (shortly before the place erupts in a lively brawl!). The scenes at the park culminate in a nasty shock for the characters and the viewer, as Kelly's cute dog is found hanged by the murdering, horned-beast arse-lickers who have also been kind enough to put some rattlesnakes in our heroes' cupboards!

Good vs. Evil is always a popular theme in most (all?) horror films and this is a fantastic, pulse-pounding example. Frank and Roger manage to divert all attempts to do them in and even manage to get in one or two memorable lines ("Maybe they ran out of cats" is a gem, after the Satanic sheriff has tried to convince them it was actually a moggy being slaughtered by stoned hippies that they saw), while the useless women spend all their time cowering and screaming (they do manage to steal some occult books from a library, however).

It's a huge shame that, after all their struggles, evil has to win – or does it? Yes, the mobile home and its occupants are surrounded by a ring of fire set up by the chanting Satanists at the conclusion, but they could still have survived. Maybe, they took a chance and drove through the flames, hopefully killing some of the Satanists as they did so. Or, if the Satanists had tried to break into the van, Frank and Roger would have put up more than a token struggle...

Anyway, I like to think that – in a parallel universe somewhere where the events in films are real – our heroes managed to get away after the conclusion of the film.

A remake of this masterpiece was slated for production in 2005, but ultimately came to nothing. Maybe there'll be a stage show?...

Some of the cast of Race with the Devil *(1975)*

SALVATORE ARGENTO presenta
UN FILM DI
DARIO ARGENTO
JESSICA HARPER
STEFANIA CASINI
Suspiria
FLAVIO BUCCI MIGUEL BOSE'
BARBARA MAGNOLFI SUSANNA JAVICOLI EVA AXEN
con ALIDA VALLI nel ruolo di 'Tanner' e con JOAN BENNETT
direttore della fotografia LUCIANO TOVOLI
musiche dei GOBLIN con la collaborazione di DARIO ARGENTO
edizioni musicali BIXIO - CEMSA (Milano)
un film prodotto da CLAUDIO ARGENTO per la SEDA Spettacoli S.p.A. (Roma)
distribuzione P.A.C. PRODUZIONI ATLAS CONSORZIATE
regia di DARIO ARGENTO
TECNOVISION-TECHNICOLOR

CHAPTER 49

SUSPIRIA (1977)

Jessica Harper in Suspiria *(1977)*

Directed by: Dario Argento.

Written by: Dario Argento (screenplay), Daria Nicolodi (screenplay) and Thomas De Quincey (book, uncredited).

Starring: Jessica Harper, Stefania Casini, Flavio Bucci, Miguel Bosé, Barbara Magnolfi, Susanna Javicoli and more.

Studio: Seda Spettacoli.

DANCES WITH WITCHES

I'M NOT A huge fan of Italian horrors – I always thought as a younger fan that those who were very *into* them had a purple streak of pretentiousness running through them: "Oh, British and American horror films are so old-hat... I much prefer the offerings of Mario Bava and Giannetto De Rossi these days!", said he, twirling a champagne glass in his hand...

I'm a bit older and wiser now, and while there's nothing, in my opinion, that particularly makes Italian horrors stand out above their British and US counterparts, they are at their very best, at least equal to the best of them.

Dario Argento was a name I encountered quite a lot in print, back in the '80s/'90s. I read how his films such as *Inferno*, *Tenebrae* and *Deep Red* were masterpieces, and anyone who considered themselves a horror fan should be familiar with Argento's oeuvre. One of the very best of the "Pasta Master of Cinematic Sadism's" offerings was his 1977 witchcraft chiller *Suspiria*, apparently.

I finally got to see the film, at a mate's house sometime in 2009 – a few of us were staying over and the general view was that the next film on our all-nighter of DVD terrors should be a serial-killer thriller. However, I argued long and hard that a supernatural film should be next on the bill, and *Suspiria* seemed the ideal choice...

Jessica Harper in Suspiria *(1977)*

The film stars Jessica Harper as Suzy, a young girl who has gone to stay at a swish dance school in Germany. Straight away, I noticed the rich colours that critics had raved about, with the opening scenes of Suzy leaving the train station being illuminated with the most vivid reds, greens and blues I've ever seen on screen. This visual treat is accompanied by an equally impressive and bombastic score, which gives an almost subliminal warning/hint of what we are about to face later in the film, with the word "witch" being repeated on the soundtrack.

Jessica Harper was chosen to play the lead role by Argento after he'd seen her in Brian De Palma's 1974 *Phantom of the Paradise*, and she had the good sense and taste to turn down a role in *Annie Hall* (1977) in order to appear in Argento's macabre masterpiece.

Unfortunately, Harper was seen but not heard when *Suspiria* premièred in its native country, as she was dubbed by an Italian actress.

It soon becomes clear something strange is happening at the dance academy, as one of the students is horribly murdered within fifteen minutes of the film opening. This scene is one that Argento's fame and reputation as a brilliant director has been based upon – we see the character of Pat being attacked by something with very scary monstrous hands, which leads to a great shot in which poor Pat is hung with a noose and her bloodied corpse comes crashing through a skylight, with the shards of glass and debris killing her friend below. The framing, music and technical expertise is masterful and it makes me wonder how Argento's newer films come across, as many fans have complained that he has well and truly lost his touch now – or, is it just that he's older, and that his fans are so used to his style of filmmaking that everything he does seems blasé and old hat now?

Suspiria *(1977)*

This film is the first of a projected trilogy of films that has taken rather longer than anticipated to complete – *Inferno* was released in 1980 and the final film *Mother of Tears* came out in 2007 to a barrage of criticism, laughter and abuse! The idea is that there are three witches – the Mothers – and they unleash evil every so often from different parts of the world, this particular film revolving around the Mother of Sighs, with Mother of Darkness and Mother of Tears (for the audience?) in the sequels.

The dance academy here was set up by the witch, Helena Markos, and she and the instructors are plotting to take the lives and souls of the students. One eerie moment occurs when we see and hear the hoarse breathing of the witch behind the flimsy curtains in the dance hall, as the students have to spend the night there, the dormitory being out of bounds due to a torrent of maggots. There's something about witches that strikes a primal chord of fear in us, in a way that vampires, werewolves and the like don't, and scenes like this one play on that.

Stefania Casini in Suspiria *(1977)*

Daniel (Flavio Bucci, who was in *Night Train Murders*) is the school's blind pianist and his death occurs when he has his throat ripped out by his apparently possessed German Shepherd in another great sequence – he'd been fired from his job earlier that day so he wasn't having a very good time of it. In the spine-chilling finale, Suzy overhears the instructors at the academy talking about her, and plotting her demise. When the reanimated witch appears, her appearance and creepy voice, revealed by flashes of lightning, are no disappointment – she sounds like she smokes a hundred fags a day, and her skin is like a desiccated coconut! The effect is terrifying and even more so when she reanimates Suzy's friend Sara (who had been earlier killed by barbed wire in another stand-out sequence) to kill her. When watching this film for the first time, I knew I'd seen the creepy Sara zombie before from a still in a magazine or book, and it's a memorable image. The film ends shortly after, and ends as it began – loudly, with the piercing shriek of the band Goblin's music echoing on the soundtrack and in the viewer's ears.

The film had apparently been inspired by a story related to screenplay writer Daria Nicolodi by her grandmother. Apparently, the grandmother had gone to piano lessons at an unnamed academy and had encountered some form of black magic, a terrifying encounter that prompted her to flee, and her granddaughter to write this film (along with Argento). Argento was a fervent believer in witchcraft and the supernatural, and another inspiration for the film was Disney's *Snow White and the Seven Dwarfs* (1937), not just in it's theme of a young girl menaced by an evil witch, but also its colour.

Suspiria is a masterpiece and I only hope the two sequels are as good, not to mention the 2018 remake... I look forward to finding out.

Going back to that merry night at my mate's house all those years ago, I'm so pleased I argued for this film to be shown as it gave me my first look at the films of Dario Argento and the chance to see a much-respected example of Italian horror cinema, and it also meant that, luckily, I didn't get to suffer through the steaming pile of cinematic crap my mate wanted to put on – *Sleepaway Camp*, anyone?

Jessica Harper in Suspiria *(1977)*

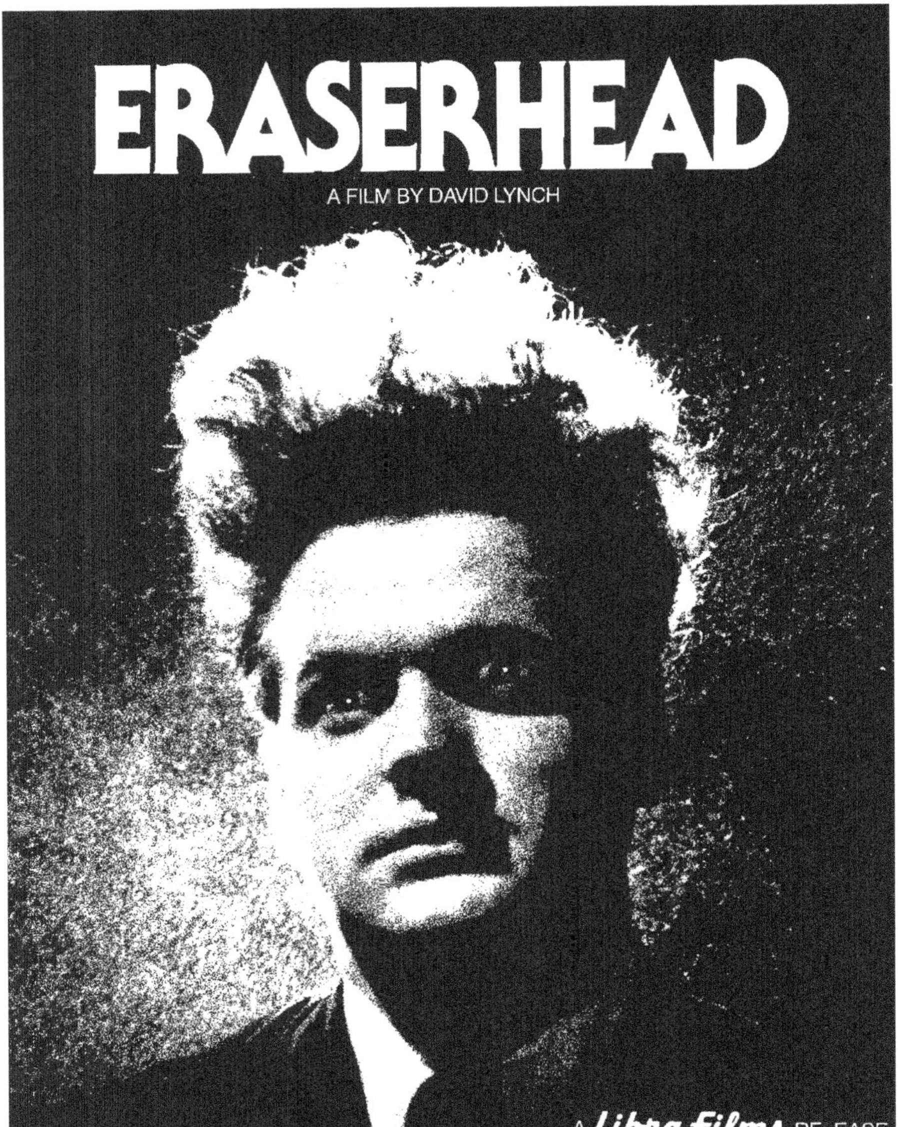
ERASERHEAD
A FILM BY DAVID LYNCH
A Libra Films RE_EASE

CHAPTER 50

ERASERHEAD (1977)

Laurel Near in Eraserhead *(1977)*

Directed by: David Lynch.

Written by: David Lynch.

Starring: Jack Nance, Charlotte Stewart, Allen Joseph, Jeanne Bates, Judith Roberts, Laurel Near and more.

Studio: American Film Institute (AFI)/Libra Films.

SWEET DREAMS

I'M NOT A fan of David Lynch and his work generally but this black and white mid-'70s spooker is a masterpiece, and one that made me very nervous when I first saw it back on Channel 4 in 1989, as part of the "It's Later Than You Think" series of horror/SF double bills.

You see, the worrying thing about this one is that, upon first viewing, you don't know what to expect – the film throws potentially anything at the viewer so your worst nightmare or the one thing that really freaks you out could pop up on screen at any time, and that results in a fairly unsettling experience. Many film critics have tried to "explain" and analyse the film over the years, but it's actually quite easy to do so. The film is a literal dream/nightmare basically – anything can happen, however illogical or far out and it makes perfect sense to the participants. Presumably, the person having the dream is Henry (Jack Nance), who is the main character.

Henry lives in a grotty apartment block in a bleak wasteland, where the sound of machinery clanking and groaning is ever-present. The apartment block is very dark and Henry spends his time in his room looking at strange characters outside his window (a seemingly deformed/scarred guy sat by some railway levers and pulling them is surprisingly chilling) and behind the radiator! Henry's girlfriend Mary (Charlotte Stewart) has apparently given birth – without Henry's knowledge that she was even expecting! – so he goes to her parents' house to see his offspring.

The parents and daughter are a weird bunch who make the Addams Family look like the Waltons – when they all sit down to dinner, weird little man-made chickens are brought out and when cut, begin to bleed copiously, which cause the mother to go psycho! The baby looks like a little skinned lamb, and when Mary and baby go to stay at Henry's, the film becomes even more bizarre.

Henry and Mary seem to spend the rest of the film lying in bed, trying to get to sleep over the constant crying of their baby. There's a particular shock moment at one point, where the baby is covered in horrible sores, its eyes rolling. Apparently Lynch was inspired to make the film due to his own fears of fatherhood, and the region in Philadelphia where he grew up, which influenced the look of the industrial dump where the film is mainly set.

One element of the film that I found particularly "gross-outing", so to speak was that blonde-haired lady who dances between the bars of the radiator in Henry's permanently dark flat. She looks normal at first, until we go closer and see she has two grotesque lumps on either side of her face which we earlier took to be curls in her hair! She looks at the camera and tentatively starts to dance, until foetuses start to plop on stage at her feet and she stamps on them, all the time giving a winsome smile to camera. This is accompanied by some strangely disturbing music and a song about Heaven...

David Lynch appears to be a genius when it comes to the strange and the bizarre, on the evidence of this film. Even minor little touches – Henry's girlfriend trying to get her suitcase from underneath the bed – have a bizarre slant to them, and when it comes to Henry cutting open his baby, to release tons of what looks like either scrambled egg or rice pudding which eventually cover and suffocate it, Lynch goes for broke.

Overall, a weird film that mixes body horror, sexual imagery and themes, and black comedy. It's like an experimental, not intended to be seen short film expanded to feature length and released in cinemas. There's no other film like it in evoking a feeling of the weird and the strange – the feeling of a dream, in fact, as that's what the film is presenting. So, settle back in your chair and watch this one late at night for maximum effect.

Just try getting to sleep afterwards...

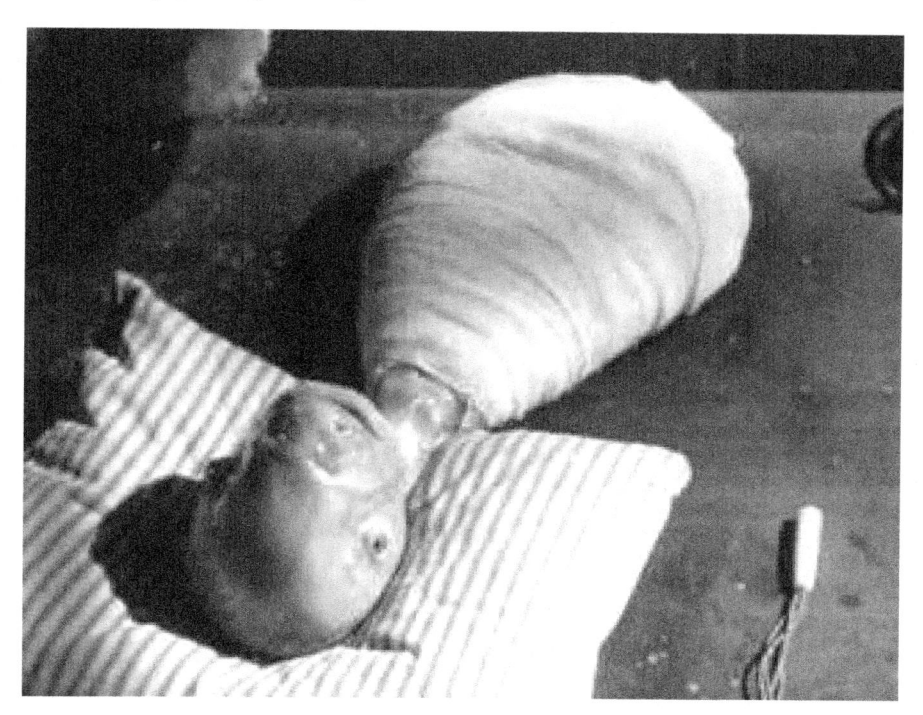

Eraserhead *(1977)*

THIS WOMAN HAS JUST
CUT, CHOPPED, BROKEN, and BURNED
FIVE MEN BEYOND RECOGNITION...
BUT NO JURY
IN AMERICA
WOULD EVER
CONVICT HER!
I SPIT ON YOUR GRAVE
...AN ACT OF
REVENGE!
JERRY GROSS presents "I SPIT ON YOUR GRAVE"
A CINEMAGIC PICTURES PRODUCTION
A MEIR ZARCHI FILM
starring
CAMILLE KEATON · ERON TABOR · RICHARD PACE · ANTHONY NICHOLS
produced by JOSEPH ZBEDA · written & directed by MEIR ZARCHI
DISTRIBUTED BY THE JERRY GROSS ORGANIZATION Color By METROCOLOR
R RESTRICTED
UNDER 17 REQUIRES ACCOMPANYING
PARENT OR ADULT GUARDIAN

CHAPTER 51

I SPIT ON YOUR GRAVE (1978)

Camille Keaton in I Spit on Your Grave *(1978)*

Directed by: Meir Zarchi.

Written by: Meir Zarchi.

Starring: Camille Keaton, Eron Tabor, Richard Pace, Anthony Nichols, Gunter Kleemann, Alexis Magnotti and more.

Studio: Barquel Creations.

ENTERING AND BREAKING

IF EVER A TV news report in the '80s/'90s centred on the subject of banned horror films, or "Video Nasties" as they were known, then a VHS of *I Spit on Your Grave* would usually be seen on top of the pile of offending videos that an urgent-voiced journalist with more scoops than sense would be excitedly pontificating about.

    I Spit on Your Grave was released in 1978 under the equally emotive title, *Day of the Woman,* and features silent film comedian

Buster Keaton's granddaughter Camille Keaton as Jennifer, a writer who moves from happ'nin Manhattan to a small and quiet town in Connecticut to write her first novel. Renting a small cottage near a lake, she soon attracts the unwelcome attention of a group of dirty-minded yobs, who end up raping her not once, not twice, but three times, leaving her for dead in the process.

Once she recovers, Jennifer decides to pay these bastards back and she does so in spades. First to perish is the simpleton Matthew (Richard Pace), who exhibited some slight sympathy for his victim but after being encouraged to lose his virginity by the other three men, got stuck in anyway. Matthew proves to be well-hung, and so he ends up – swinging from a rope tied to a tree.

The most satisfying of the revenge murders comes next, as Jennifer seduces Johnny (Eron Tabor) and pretends to accept that the rapes were all her fault for wearing revealing clothing! Johnny ends up getting his manhood sliced off in a bath, a scene that might make male viewers wince but is quite funny due to the fact the dozy swine doesn't immediately realise what's happened and is sat moaning in sexual ecstasy after having his tool tickled by Jennifer – before he suddenly realises what he's missing!

Next to go is Andy (Gunter Kleemann), whose end is quite swift compared to the others, as Jennifer plants an axe in his back. Shortly after, Stanley (Anthony Nichols) gets chopped up by a speedboat propeller, before our heroine speeds away, her mission complete...

Directed by Meir Zarchi, Keaton's husband, *I Spit on Your Grave* is a very powerful film experience but oddly, not as disturbing as I expected it to be. The film was almost unanimously panned by critics when first released, and the first I heard of it was when it was reissued in 1982 and simultaneously reviewed in *Starburst* magazine (issue 46) by Alan Jones who described it as an "unutterable piece of trash" and a film that placed a strong onus on audiences as to whether they should be watching it under the guise of entertainment.

Did I find it entertaining when I finally saw the film on Blu-ray in 2015? Yes, I did. I watched it at a mate's house late on a Friday night (when else?), fuelled by some alcohol and we spent a merry night laughing at the inept performance of Richard Pace as the moronic Matthew – or is it actually a great performance, bearing in mind the character is a few beads short of a rosary? – and cheering as the evil bastards get their just desserts. The rape scenes didn't produce any laughter – these scenes are genuinely uncomfortable, especially the second (anal) rape and it's only the realisation that this is a film that makes them palatable at all. Director Zarchi applauded Keaton for accepting the role, and she delivers a great performance, winning the role after over 4,000 actresses auditioned.

Reviled in it's day, subsequently banned when released on video and only in later years getting any modicum amount of praise, the film is strong stuff for sure, but I'd rather watch it any day than something like *A Serbian Film*, or any of the *Saw* or *Hostel* films.

Camille Keaton and Eron Tabor in I Spit on Your Grave *(1978)*

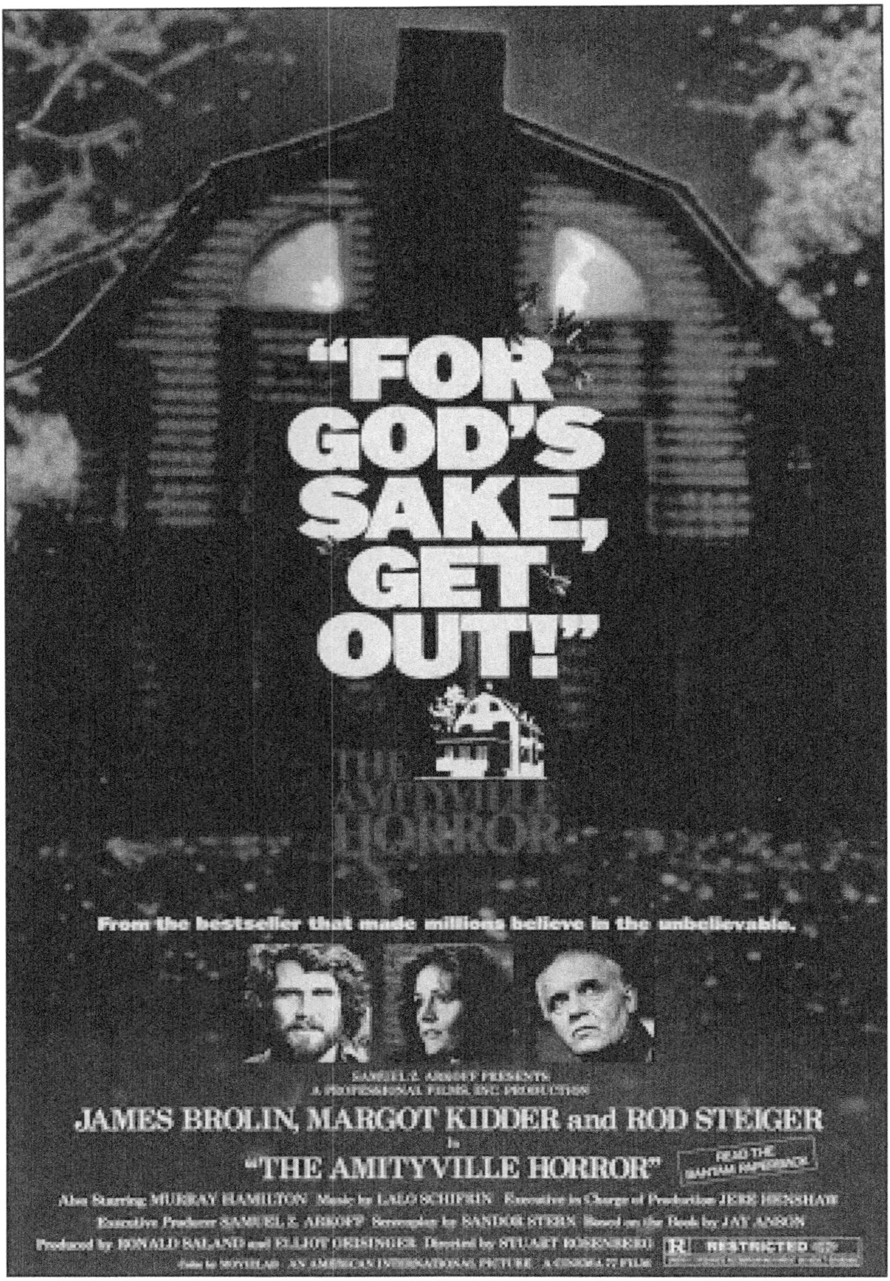
"FOR GOD'S SAKE, GET OUT!"
THE AMITYVILLE HORROR
From the bestseller that made millions believe in the unbelievable.
JAMES BROLIN, MARGOT KIDDER and ROD STEIGER
in
"THE AMITYVILLE HORROR"
READ THE BANTAM PAPERBACK
R RESTRICTED

CHAPTER 52

THE AMITYVILLE HORROR (1979)

Margot Kidder and James Brolin in The Amityville Horror *(1979)*

Directed by: Stuart Rosenberg.

Written by: Sandor Stern (screenplay), Jay Anson (based on the book by), George Lutz (story, uncredited) and Kathy Lutz (story, uncredited).

Starring: James Brolin, Margot Kidder, Rod Steiger, Don Stroud, Murray Hamilton, John Larch and more.

Studio: American International Pictures (AIP)/Cinema 77/Professional Films.

PARANORMAL PIG

I FIRST ENCOUNTERED the tale of the Lutz family and their freakish stay at the creepy-looking Long Island residence in 1977/8, in either *Woman's Own* or *Woman* weekly publications, though I can't recall which. My mother regularly bought these, and the story of the Lutz family and their supernatural experience was serialised in the mag, with a colour photo of the family smiling and laughing to accompany a brief interview to kick things off. The story of what happened to them then unfolded, like an actual story and punctuated by artwork, spread over several issues. I recall vaguely glancing at the artwork, some of which showed what was meant to be a huge pig sat at the window of a little girl's bedroom, looking out. But the significance of the piece was lost on me, a strapping ten-year-old who didn't wish to be seen perusing women's weeklies!

A few weeks, maybe a month after, and it was the last few minutes before the bell rang to signify the end of the school day. It was that magical period, where for ten minutes or so, anything goes. Cue two girls who asked the teacher if they could stand up in front of the class and regale everyone with the story they'd recently read in *Woman/Woman's Own* concerning an American family who'd stayed in a haunted house for a while – their stumbling, and inaccurate account ("The story is called 'The Anvil Horror'!") nevertheless intrigued me enough to seek out those precious issues, to properly read them and discover the story for myself. Cue a ten-year-old boy desperately trying to find back issues of his mother's magazines!

I did in fact manage to find one of the issues, and subsequent write-ups in magazines of the time clued me in a bit more about the real-life case which led to the film I'm chatting about here. *The Amityville Horror* was released in 1979, and was a smash success for AIP – not surprisingly, after all the publicity the book by Jay Anson, and the apparent case it was based on, had attracted.

George and Kathy Lutz, with their three kids and a dog, had moved into the house in December 1975, and managed to stay for twenty-eight days before deciding to get the heck out of the place. The house had been the scene of a mass murder thirteen months earlier, when twenty-three-year-old Ronald Joseph DeFeo Jr. (also known as Butch) had blasted the rest of his family in their beds with a rifle, and was subsequently sentenced to several terms of life imprisonment. DeFeo Jr. just passed away on 12th March 2021, aged sixty-nine, and his terrible crime resulted in one of the most famous haunted house stories ever. One that was apparently corroborated when the Lutzs took a lie detector test, and the result indicated they were telling the truth!

The number of spine-chilling occurrences that happened to the family once they moved in could fill a book... and it did, of course. A room that attracted unseasonal flies; strange unholy stinks wafting around the place from an unknown source; episodes of the family levitating at night; strange green slime rolling down the cellar steps; the terrifying appearance of a pig at a bedroom window at night, looking down at George as he went outside to investigate strange noises, are just some of the eerie events the Lutzs had to endure. It all came to a head in January 1976, with a night the family refused to talk about afterwards, claiming it was too frightening...

Scary stuff indeed, and just waiting for a film to be made based on it...

Margot Kidder and James Brolin in The Amityville Horror *(1979)*

James Brolin and Margot Kidder play George and Kathy Lutz, and the film was dismissed several years later by *Starburst* critic Alan Jones as being the usual brand of "low-grade exploitation" from AIP. However, while I was mildly disappointed by the film when I first saw it – with Jones' words rolling around in my mind throughout the viewing (it was shown on ITV in the mid-'80s), my subsequent TV-based viewings endeared the film to me. My favourite part of the whole story is the fact that an evil, unholy "pig" featured prominently and for some reason, I completely missed that in the film. Later viewings showed that the terrifying Jodie *is* included and so the film went up in my estimation as a result.

Lots of memorable moments are featured, some of which are quite unintentionally funny – the bilious nun, for example, and one part that always makes me laugh is the scene where the £1,500 owed to the caterers after Kathy's brother's engagement party goes missing, and the subsequent brouhaha. Some chilling moments too, such as the babysitter getting locked in a cupboard and the resultant screaming when the lights go out. The priest (Rod Steiger) famously being ordered to "Get out!" by an unseen presence when he attempts to perform a blessing on the house is another chilling moment, and his later blindness.

The Amityville Horror *(1979)*

Sadly, the story was effectively debunked in later years – simply made up by the Lutzs, in collaboration with DeFeo Jr.'s lawyer William Weber over "many bottles of wine" according to the latter. But the many paranormal investigators who entered the house later (including Ed and Lorraine Warren [versions of which appear in *The Conjuring* film series]) claimed they felt something and there's at least one photo showing a ghostly child to back up their claims. George and Kathy Lutz are both dead now, having split in 1988, but they both maintained the truth of their account. Also, George's stepson has revealed that his stepfather dabbled in the occult, in which case he may then have deserved everything he got...

The film doesn't quite reach the scary heights of more recent shockers like *The Conjuring* (2013) and *Annabelle* (2014), but because the "true" story it's based on is so bloody terrifying, the film will always have that added scare factor reflected back at it. One question though, is why – if the events are all true – did the family remain there for nearly a month? I'd have been out the door after a week.

James Brolin and Margot Kidder star in The Amityville Horror *(1979)*

Vincent Price
Donald Pleasence
John Carradine
MONSTER
CLUB
A tongue-in-cheek
trilogy of terror!
JACK GILL PRESENTS FOR CHIPS PRODUCTIONS A SWORD AND SORCERY PRODUCTION THE MONSTER CLUB STARRING VINCENT PRICE
DONALD PLEASENCE JOHN CARRADINE STUART WHITMAN RICHARD JOHNSON BARBARA KELLERMAN
BRITT EKLAND SIMON WARD ANTHONY VALENTINE PATRICK MAGEE PLUS SONGS BY B.A. ROBERTSON
(NIGHT THE PRETTY THINGS THE VIEWERS) SOUNDTRACK MUSIC BY JOHN WILLIAMS UB40 EXPRESSOS
SCREENPLAY BY EDWARD AND VALERIE ABRAHAM FROM THE NOVEL BY RONALD CHETWYND-HAYES
EXECUTIVE PRODUCER BERNARD J. KINGHAM PRODUCED BY MILTON SUBOTSKY DIRECTED BY ROY WARD BAKER

CHAPTER 53

THE MONSTER CLUB (1981)

Vincent Price (main focus) and friends in The Monster Club *(1981)*

Directed by: Roy Ward Baker.

Written by: R. Chetwynd-Hayes (from the novel by), Edward Abraham (screenplay by) and Valerie Abraham (screenplay by).

Starring: Vincent Price, John Carradine, Donald Pleasence, Britt Ekland, Anthony Steel, Simon Ward and more.

Studio: Chips Productions/Sword & Sorcery.

SCREAM INN

THE MONSTER CLUB is an Amicus anthology film in all but name – it was made by "Sword & Sorcery" productions (and with a name like that, it's no surprise they didn't last!), and can be seen as the last gasp of the sort of cosy British horror films churned out by Hammer and Amicus in the '60s and '70s. The film was laughed and jeered off the screen when it debuted in the early '80s, as the audiences who were expecting a *Shining*-type shock-fest were instead presented with a fairly mild and inoffensive children's horror film in which the monsters are extras wearing tacky rubber masks, and where their own eyes are clearly visible behind the eye holes! Take the film in the spirit it was intended – as a bit of enjoyable fluff for the teens – and you'll love it.

The film is based on stories by R(onald). Chetwynd-Hayes, an excellent writer of horror fiction. Allegedly. I have to admit, I've never read a single story by RCH. Not by intention, just down to the fact I never happened to come across any of his stories in the various horror anthologies I would buy in the '70s and '80s. RCH is a writer I've always wanted to become familiar with and have a few saved up on various Amazon and eBay lists, including one that has a complete collection of his vampire stories. I will definitely get around to buying these – I'm just waiting for the prices to come down a bit.

Anyway, this film is not just based on stories by Chetwynd-Hayes but features the writer himself, played by ageing "almost but never quite made it as a horror film star" John Carradine. As the film opens, Chetwynd-Hayes has just finished perusing a selection of his works through a bookshop window, then he's attacked by a vampire – Eramus, played by Vincent Price. Eramus is quite polite, all things considered, and after taking just enough blood to prop himself up, he invites Chetwynd-Hayes to a club hidden in the foggy backstreets of London, which is frequented entirely by monsters. As mentioned before, the monsters are just extras in tacky masks but once over that initial disappointment, the film is quite fun. Sitting down at a coffin-shaped table, Eramus begins to instruct Chetwynd-Hayes on the various types of monsters, with the help of a very nicely illustrated genealogical tree on the wall. This leads into the first of the three stories...

The first tale involves a shadmock, a creature which kills by whistling. A greedy young woman (Barbara Kellerman) and her partner (Simon Ward) hit on a get rich quick scheme, involving a reclusive millionaire who wants a personal assistant to help him in his country mansion. This guy is the shadmock, and when Kellerman first meets him, she is so horrified by his appearance that she quickly makes her excuses and leaves. The shadmock is well played by James Laurenson, but the make-up doesn't go far enough – it was meant to look like Chaney's Phantom of the Opera, a horrific skull-like face, but instead Laurenson is simply a normal-looking guy with a tragic hairstyle and pale skin. This segment is great fun though, as Kellerman returns, through her greed for her employer's fortune, to his mansion, and ends up agreeing to marry him.

There are some nice scenes where Kellerman meets her fiancé's relatives, who are wearing transparent masks but their strange features can still be seen underneath. Unfortunately, it all goes wrong as Kellerman gets caught robbing her husband-to-be blind, and is subjected to his whistling, which results in her becoming a gooey, but ambulatory, mess (unlike the cat earlier on, which was fried to the ground after the shadmock killed it because it had stiffed one of his beloved feathered friends). I quite like the final scene of the shadmock sat on the dance floor, tears brimming from his eyes, while his relatives all stand in a circle around him, shaking their heads in sympathy.

This segment is followed by a musical act, as BA Robertson and his band launch into a quite catchy number called "Sucker for Your Love", which is followed by the second tale.

John Carradine and Vincent Price in The Monster Club *(1981)*

This yarn is introduced by a Lintom Busotsky, which is an easy to spot anagram of Milton Subotsky, the guy behind this film, and the great Amicus films that came before it. This segment is my least favourite in the film. It's basically a comedy, and a distinctly childish and unfunny one at that, which is also unnecessary, as the tone of the framing sequence in the club is rather silly enough in itself. The story stars Richard Johnson as a vampire who lives with his wife (Britt Ekland) and wimpy son, and who is being hunted by The Bleeny, basically a bunch of vampire hunters dressed as civil servants, complete with bowler hats, and played by familiar faces such as Donald Pleasence, Anthony Valentine and Neil McCarthy.

The story has a nice musical score, as indeed does the whole film, but the jokes are silly and the ending, with Johnson getting up out of his coffin after being "staked", to reveal he was wearing a "stake-proof vest, with tomato ketchup" had audiences groaning in their seats.

Donald Pleasence (right) in The Monster Club *(1981)*

After this, comes another quite nice musical number, called "Stripper". This involves an actual stripper on stage stripping off down to her bones while the band belts out the song. The effect was described in a review at the time as being "accomplished with remarkable ingenuity" but in fact, it's obvious how it's done, with the real stripper being substituted for a cartoon. It's still a fun effect though, and leads into the final (and best) story.

Stuart Whitman plays a film director who scouts out a suitably eerie location for his next film, and finds the creepy Loughville which, despite being only a few minutes from a busy, sunshine-strewn motorway, is perpetually gloomy and overcast. It's populated by shambling, scruffy, flesh-eating ghouls and Whitman finds he's next on the menu. Again, the monsters aren't very monstrous but this is a nicely atmospheric piece, and it has the benefit of some great art from John Bolton (remember his comic strips in the great *House of Hammer* mag of the 1970s?), as Whitman reads about the origin of the place in a derelict church. Just as Whitman appears to have gotten away at the end, things take a downbeat turn and he's right back where he started from... Strangely enough, the two actors playing the policemen at the end aren't credited, which is a bit strange as they are given dialogue, and regular TV watchers will recognise Prentis

Hancock, perhaps best known for playing Paul Morrow in the first season of *Space: 1999*.

The film ends with Eramus giving a speech about how humans are the worst monsters of the lot, as Chetwynd-Hayes is inducted into the club, and everyone starts dancing to a cheesy song – "Monsters Rule O.K." – or, in the cases of Carradine and Price, trying to! This song is quite catchy and brings the film to a satisfactory conclusion. Chetwynd-Hayes fans will probably enjoy it, and those of us who haven't yet sampled the author's stuff will either dismiss it as childish nonsense, or as a fun film which is a nice addendum to *Tales from the Crypt, From Beyond the Grave* and their ilk. Unfortunately, the film was a box-office disaster and plans for a follow up disintegrated as quickly as the victim of a shadmock's whistle. *The Monster Club* gets a solid 9/10 from me, and I can't help but think how nice it would be if some enterprising soul was to open a real-life establishment based on the one in this film!

Party time in The Monster Club *(1981)*

DANIEL RADCLIFFE
WHAT DID THEY SEE?
THE WOMAN IN BLACK
HAMMER
FEBRUARY 2012

CHAPTER 54

THE WOMAN IN BLACK
(1989 and 2012 versions)

"The Woman in Black" by Randy Broecker

THE WOMAN IN BLACK (1989):

Directed by: Herbert Wise.

Written by: Susan Hill (based on the book by) and Nigel Kneale (screenplay).

Starring: Adrian Rawlins, Bernard Hepton, David Daker, Pauline Moran, David Ryall, Clare Holman and more.

Studio: Central Films/Granada Television.

THE WOMAN IN BLACK (2012):

Directed by: James Watkins.

Written by: Susan Hill (novel) and Jane Goldman (screenplay).

Starring: Daniel Radcliffe, Ciarán Hinds, Janet McTeer, Liz White, Jessica Raine, Shaun Dooley and more.

Studio: CBS Films/Cross Creek Pictures/Hammer Films/Talisman Productions/Filmgate Films/Film i Väst/Alliance Films/British Film Institute (BFI)/Vertigo Entertainment.

IF YOU TOLERATE THIS, THEN YOUR CHILDREN WILL BE NEXT

I WAS NEVER a particular fan of the 1989 TV movie *The Woman in Black*, based on a 1983 novel of the same name by Susan Hill. I've never read the novel to this day, but it proved such a spine-chilling success that it lead not only to the 1989 TV movie version but a long-running stage show, as well as a radio adaptation, and the film I'll be more amiably chatting about here, the 2012 Hammer film (how good/weird it is to type/say that!) starring Daniel Radcliffe.

Firstly though, the 1989 film: I remember seeing it when it was shown on ITV on Christmas Eve, 1989, a Sunday in which it absolutely poured down all day. I don't really recall much of watching it then but I rented the video of it a few years later and viewed it a couple of times. With a screenplay by the creator of *Quatermass*, Nigel Kneale, *The Woman in Black* stars Adrian Rawlins and Pauline Moran in the ghostly tale of solicitor Arthur Kidd who travels "oop" North, to settle the estate of the reclusive Alice Drablow and finds himself spending a terrifying night at the isolated Eel Marsh House, which is haunted by the malevolent ghost of Mrs. Drablow.

Poster for the 1989 version of The Woman in Black

The atmosphere is superbly spine-chilling, with the terrified Kidd trying to keep the house's generator going, lest he be left in darkness (and what a prospect that would be!). Pauline Moran looks very creepy as the titular character and the film has a downbeat ending which is even more grim than that of the novel – in the book, Kipps' (not Kidd) wife and child come a cropper when the malevolent spirit appears near the end, but in this TV version Kidd dies too, a moment presaged by the eerily floating on water spectre. The TV movie has a few "jump" moments but nothing compared to the 2012 film...

The return of Hammer films was a great landmark moment in cinema history, but after a mere handful of films, they seem to have vanished again. Out of that handful of films, *The Woman in Black* is by far the best. Daniel Radcliffe casts off the shadow of Harry Potter and enters whole-heartedly into a "Hogwarts and all" spooker that gets my vote as the single most frightening film concerning ghosts ever put on the big screen. I remember seeing this at the cinema when it came out, and the audience had plenty of loud and raucous teenage twonks in it but even they had cause to put down their smartphones for a few minutes and get invested in the decidedly creepy events going on onscreen.

Funnily enough, for all the effective moments where we see the Woman, or her shadow, the part that made the teenage audience (and myself!) jump the most was the section where we suddenly hear a noisily leaking tap! The film begins with several deaths, as three children in the nineteenth century suddenly lose interest in their little tea party and jump out of a window. Forwarding to the early part of the twentieth century and Arthur Kipps (Radcliffe)'s wife dies in childbirth. The bulk of the film takes place several years later, with Kipps travelling to the isolated and terrifying Eel Marsh House and getting caught up in all the supernatural activity you could ever wish to see in a film – no sooner has darkness fallen, than Kipps hears the sounds of a carriage crashing and a screeching kid on the marshes outside, but he inexplicably decides to stay put.

This film has so much to offer – it's almost an embarrassment of riches. Apart from the chilling moments where the Woman's presence leads children to kill themselves, Janet McTeer gives good support as the wife of local landowner Sam Daily (Ciarán Hinds), driven to occasional bursts of hysterical madness over the death of her young son and using her fine poodle collection to help fill the gap in her life. Scenes such as the dead child of the title character crawling out of the mud and advancing on the house at night, or Radcliffe looking out of the window during the day and the camera showing the spectral woman, who unbeknownst to him, is standing right behind him would be effective enough shocks by themselves to support a film, but *The*

Woman in Black delivers these and keeps on delivering.

Daniel Radcliffe in The Woman in Black *(2012)*

    The film ends with Kipps, having found out via correspondence what went on between Jennet (the Woman) and her sister Alice which led to Jennet hanging herself in the nursery, assuming that all is well and Jennet's spirit has been laid to rest. No such luck! There's a final shock for the audience, one which confused me slightly at the cinema until I realised what had happened, which leads Kipps to a conclusion that is both tragic and happy. I enjoyed the manner in which the Woman stares wistfully after the departing souls of Kipps, his wife and son, then looks malevolently straight at the camera...

    With a screenplay by Jonathan Ross's wife Jane Goldman, and excellent direction from James Watkins, the film turned out to be a huge success – which makes Hammer's apparent departure from the scene not too long after all the more puzzling and disappointing. If they'd continued to turn out gems like this, the company might well have lasted for another three decades.

    The film lead to a sequel a couple of years later, and though *The Woman in Black 2: Angel of Death* (2014) is a solid effort, it suffers from following this film which is basically unbeatable.

jodie foster / anthony hopkins / scott glenn
the silence of the lambs
from the terrifying best seller
a jonathan demme picture / jodie foster / anthony hopkins / scott glenn / "the silence of the lambs" / ted levine / music by howard shore / production designer kristi zea /
director of photography tak fujimoto / edited by craig mckay, a.c.e. / executive producer gary goetzman / based upon the novel by thomas harris / screenplay by ted tally /
R RESTRICTED
produced by kenneth utt edward saxon and ron bozman / directed by jonathan demme
prints by DeLuxe
ORION

CHAPTER 55

THE SILENCE OF THE LAMBS (1991)

Jodie Foster and Anthony Hopkins in
The Silence of the Lambs *(1991)*

Directed by: Jonathan Demme.

Written by: Thomas Harris (based on the novel by) and Ted Tally (screenplay by).

Starring: Jodie Foster, Anthony Hopkins, Scott Glenn, Ted Levine, Brooke Smith, Anthony Heald and more.

Studio: Strong Heart/Demme Production/Orion Pictures.

READ THIS CHAPTER WITH A NICE CHIANTI

NOT EVERY HORROR film made in the '90s was... er, how can I put it? Rubbish is as good a word as any. This is one of the handful of good/great ones, and a film I'd recommend to anyone, but probably not while you're eating.

More of a macabre thriller than a horror film, Anthony Hopkins plays Dr. Hannibal Lecter, a cannibalistic nutcase and securer of Academy Awards for Best Actor! I was wary of Hopkins' performance after reading John Brosnan's preview of the film in *Starburst*, where he described the parts he'd seen of Hopkins as Lecter as being "all baleful stares" and looking "like a wicked witch out of a pantomime". But when I saw the film, taped from its late night Saturday screening on ITV in the '90s, I was quite impressed. I didn't bother to watch the tape again, or seek out the film until 2019, so it obviously made a huge impression on me! But I really enjoyed it this time around, watching the film as part of the Hannibal Lecter Blu-ray boxset (with *Hannibal* [average] and *Red Dragon* [very good]) so felt I should include it – if only to boost this book's coverage of '90s horror cinema! Don't worry though, if this book is a success, I intend to write a follow-up which will concentrate fully on every decade from the 1910s to the 2010s, and the 1990s will get its just due there (and no, it won't be a blank page...).

Jodie Foster plays FBI Agent Clarice Starling and is okay in the role, as are the rest of the cast. The highlights though are the scenes with Lecter and when he isn't on screen the film suffers slightly. Starling is sent to talk with Lecter in an attempt to get one psychotic maniac's perspective on another, as a killer called Buffalo Bill is out and about skinning his victims, and Clarice's boss thinks Lecter may be able to provide an insight into barmy Bill's mind and modus operandi.

The scenes with the smart-suited Starling sitting opposite Lecter in his medieval-type cell have a certain frisson, with Hopkins able to expertly put across the unsettling effect Lecter has on those around him – in addition to the fact he's a very dangerous man with a literal taste for human flesh, he's able to get under the skin of others (before he's cooked it!) by using his psychoanalysing abilities. Clarice has already had her flesh creep and her skin crawl, with the warden of the asylum showing her a nice photo of a nurse who got too close to Lecter (we don't see the photo, but we can imagine it's not pretty), and then walking past the other cells on her way to Lecter's, which are filled with semen-flicking unsavoury nutters of every shape and size!

One of these nutters, the semen-throwing Miggs, ends up killing himself after Lecter takes exception to this and talks him into his death – a good example of the creepy doctor's ability to influence others. As for Bill, we see him club his latest victim unconscious with a phoney cast on his arm, and put her on ice, keeping her for three days in his usual manner, before he plans to skin her and dump her corpse. Nice. Barmy Bill has a thing about death's-head moths too and stuffs one in the mouths of his victims, who are generally kept in a pit with a noisy white poodle to keep tabs on them.

We get a brief, but very effective look at how physically dangerous Lecter can be, as he ends up being transferred wearing a face muzzle, which is scary in itself: he uses a piece of a gold pen to unlock his handcuffs while he's being fed by two guards who both end up horribly dead, one of them literally losing face and Lecter uses his face as a disguise in his escape, and that's about it from him until the finale of the movie, and his famous line about having "an old friend for dinner" (Chilton, the asylum director), relayed by phone to the freshly-graduated FBI Agent-proper Clarice. Prior to this, the scenes in the maniac Bill's house in which the night-goggles-wearing nutter stalks Clarice before getting a body full of bullets, hit the spot. His poodle gets killed too.

The Silence of the Lambs was a huge success but was criticised by LGBT groups for its depiction of the (arguably) transvestite, women's skin-wearing Bill. The film was loved overall though and ended up being cited as one of the greatest films of all time, ranking 48th in *Empire* magazine's list of 500.

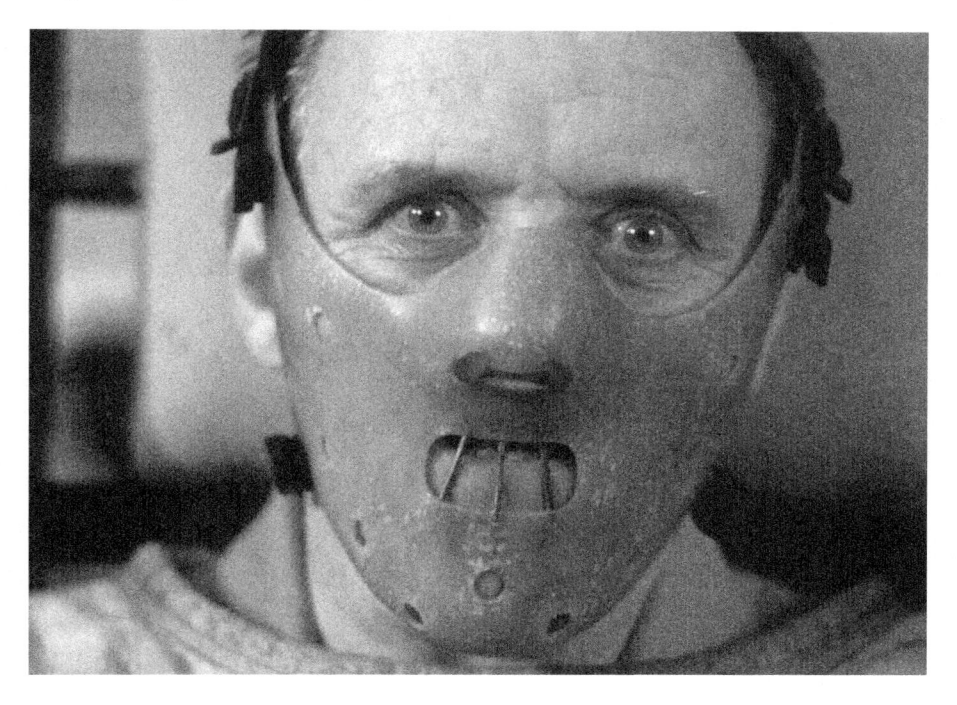

Anthony Hopkins as Dr. Hannibal Lecter in
The Silence of the Lambs *(1991)*

In October of 1994
three student filmmakers disappeared
in the woods near Burkittsville, Maryland
while shooting a documentary...
A year later their footage was found.
THE BLAIR WITCH PROJECT
ARTISAN

CHAPTER 56

THE BLAIR WITCH PROJECT (1999)

Michael C. Williams in The Blair Witch Project *(1999)*

Directed by: Daniel Myrick and Eduardo Sánchez.

Written by: Daniel Myrick and Eduardo Sánchez.

Starring: Heather Donahue, Joshua Leonard, Michael C. Williams, Bob Griffin, Jim King, Sandra Sánchez and more.

Studio: Haxan Films.

WOOD YOU BELIEVE IT?

I'M NOT A fan of 1990s horrors and that's putting it mildly. Comparing the poor remake of *The Haunting* (1999) to the (overrated-but-fun) 1963 original tells you all you need to know about the horror films made in the last decade of the twentieth century – it's a typical example: it's OTT, filled with endless CGI special effects and light shows, with cardboard characters and a reliance on jump scares that fail to make your eyes widen, never mind your backside jump. This is is a classic example of how *not* to make an effective and scary haunted house movie, and apart from Catherine Zeta-Jones' legs, the film has nothing at all of interest to offer. It's not alone, as most other horror films of the 1990s were similarly childish OTT-ness, showing everything and delivering nothing – until a no-budget film appeared from nowhere in the last year of that dreary (for films) decade and reversed the formula, showing us nothing, but delivering everything.

The Blair Witch Project is the perfect horror film, at least in concept: "Woods haunted by an evil old witch" is light-years away from stuff involving Freddy, Chucky, Cenobites, vampires etc etc and it's much more effective because it's much more plausible. There's not much chance of meeting Pinhead or Freddy Krueger on a dark post-pub night – they are OTT, more like comic book super-villains than genuinely disturbing and frightening creatures of the supernatural. A sinister old crone lurking in a wood, who delights in killing kids and adults alike, is much more terrifying because, in a strange way, you can imagine it actually happening (as many cinema-goers did, of course). *The Blair Witch Project* harkens back to the spine-chilling yarns of the great M.R. James, and even the film's most vocal detractors (mainly teenagers, who can only accept a horror film if it's drenched in blood, guts and CGI) might think twice about going camping after watching it!

The film is so good that it's a pity it only lasts for about ninety minutes – it is so enthralling it could have been twice the length, and still entertained.

Three likeable student filmmakers, the Shaggy-esque Josh, the laid-back Mike and the attractive Heather, who is the "leader" of the group, head into some large woods on the edge of the town of Burkittsville (formerly Blair) to spend several days camping and recording a documentary film about a sinister witch who is reputed by local legend to exist there.

Things start relatively slowly, but once Mike has kicked the map of the woods into the creek, the situation starts to unravel for the unlucky threesome. The first night leads to the following morning's realisation that they have been watched during the dark hours. This doesn't worry the three too much but after the second night in the woods, they wake up next morning to find some strange blue, jelly-like gunk smeared on the tent and equipment. They also find that they are lost, and no matter which direction they travel in, they come back to the same point where they started – some great acting here, and realistic reactions: you *would* start hurling abuse at God if you found yourself in such a situation, and that's exactly what happens here. All three stars deliver impressive performances, partly helped by the fact that they didn't actually have a script to help them and had to improvise, with only a rough idea of what the filmmakers were going to do. Low food supplies and lack of fags didn't help to ease tensions and by the third night, the audience's nerves are jangling as much as the cast's, especially with the characters' terrible realisation that they are in virtually the same area of the wood setting up camp as they were the previous night.

Heather Donahue in The Blair Witch Project *(1999)*

The third night gets rudely interrupted at about 3am. The previous night had seen the trio understandably shitting themselves upon hearing strange sounds in the woods – supposedly people moving around, though it doesn't sound that way to the viewer. This time is even more terrifying, with a perceptibly audible groan followed by sounds of giggling children! Then something tries to get into the tent, which causes its three occupants to lose it completely. It's a pity that we don't see anything at all. I'm all for more subtlety in a situation like that, but it's a shame the filmmakers didn't think to have the cast set up cameras around the tent during the night – imagine how scary it would be if the three of them examined the footage the next day and saw something bloody creepy! I actually hope that a Director's Cut of the film is made one day, reuniting the cast and adding extra parts such as that.

After another awful day spent getting nowhere fast, the next night sees the scare factor rammed up to one hundred, as Heather and Mike wake up to find Josh has gone missing. Detractors of the film simply don't get the point of the movie – it's scary because it's realistic banter and chat, and something that could conceivably happen. Heather and Mike's near-panic reaction upon discovering Josh has gone and the subsequent discovery of some of his guts wrapped up in a bundle of twigs the next morning packs more wallop than the entirety of most other horror films of the period.

Joshua Leonard in The Blair Witch Project *(1999)*

Towards the end, the pair seem to make some progress as they encounter a derelict old house, obviously the witch's base of operations. The utter horror and dread the characters must have felt at that point is enough to give you the chills just thinking about it. Unfortunately, the film has a slightly disappointing ending: if only we'd seen a quick glimpse of the witch's face. A terrifying old woman's face, seen leering at our heroes from the shadows for just a second would have made this film utterly perfect. Instead, we see nothing but can imagine what's going on. When I first saw the film at the cinema, it looked to me like Mike was taking a leak at the end, but the witch is actually forcing him to look away while she makes mincemeat out of Heather and will no doubt do the same to him afterwards. This downbeat ending, combined with the fact that many people believed the film's events were real lead to many viewers being seriously spooked and disturbed by it. It's a pity that the pretence couldn't be maintained, though in a way it's a good thing – the film would be unbearable if you genuinely did believe it was all true. Imagine watching it by yourself at night!

A masterpiece, the film has spawned a mini-industry of merchandise, as well as two sequels (the first, *Book of Shadows* [2000], is rubbish. I have yet to see the second) and for a while, it sparked a boom in found-footage horror shot on grainycam. Maybe its success and subtlety, not to mention the fact it's genuinely frightening, was what led to the genre being revitalised in the subsequent two decades, with more excellent horror films in one year than we saw in ten through the 1990s.

Michael C. Williams in The Blair Witch Project *(1999)*

"ONE OF THE MOST PROVOCATIVE AND TERRIFYING THRILLERS OF THE YEAR! ★★★★!"
KELLY REILLY MICHAEL FASSBENDER
THEY WANTED TO GET AWAY FROM IT ALL
INSTEAD THEY FOUND...
EDEN LAKE
Third Rail

CHAPTER 57

EDEN LAKE (2008)

Eden Lake *(2008)*

Directed by: James Watkins.

Written by: James Watkins.

Starring: Kelly Reilly, Michael Fassbender, Tara Ellis, Jack O'Connell, Finn Atkins, Jumayn Hunter and more.

Studio: Rollercoaster Films/Aramid Entertainment Fund.

SERPENTS IN EDEN

THIS FILM FALLS into a select group of films that will make you very angry – well, it certainly made me angry! Seen by some as a film that makes a blatant "them and us" statement of upper class snobs versus lower class yobs, *Eden Lake* made me angry, not because of that but because of various things that I'll get to in the course of this chapter. Oh, and the fact the two "heroes" are so bloody incompetent maybe didn't help either!

Michael Fassbender plays Steve Taylor (also the name of a companion from the B&W era of *Doctor Who*!), who goes on a quiet weekend with his girlfriend Jenny (Kelly Reilly), who he is planning to propose to, but they are disturbed by a bunch of teenage assholes who, with their pet Rottweiler, make a hell of a noise on the secluded beach they go to. This made me angry – the Rottweiler part: why do people think it makes them look "hard" to have a dog like this? If you were that "hard" you wouldn't need a bloody dog to protect you!

Anyway, Steve's request for some peace is met with insults and bravado ("You lookin' at my tits??") and things get worse when the yobs steal the couple's car keys and phone, and then the car. To be frank, it's stupid Steve's own fault – anyone with any sense would realise those teen tossers would return, and have gotten the hell out of there! The ensuing confrontation ends with a fracas that sees the Rottweiler Bonnie getting its throat cut (I was delighted, not because I hate dogs – exactly the opposite – but I hate cowardly scum of the sort seen here relying on a dog to protect them whilst simultaneously thinking they look tough) and the couple fleeing while they can but crashing their car into a tree.

The film is very skilful at making a bunch of teens seem very menacing, though as mentioned before, the inept hero and his lass don't help – when our "hero" confronts the teen tossers and asks for his car back, they respond with the usual piss-taking lies and insults, and Jenny tells Steve they should just leave – yeah right, and let the teen tossers keep their car, phone and wallet as well, eh? And after Bonnie the Rottweiler has been sliced, Steve, instead of saying something along the lines of, "It'll be your fucking throat next if you don't give me those fucking keys etc!", stands there like a wuss, stammering on about how it was an accident, and he didn't mean to kill the dog etc. Warra wimp!

The teen tossers end up tying Steve up with barbed wire, and taking turns to cut him with a knife while female teen tosser Paige (Finn Atkins) records it on her phone. Jenny watches this from a distance and, after luring the TTs away, doubles back and eventually meets up with Steve who, in a rare moment of competence, has managed to free himself! Steve dies from his wounds not long after, and is burnt to cinders by the gang anyway, but Jenny escapes. This made me angry too – instead of pouring petrol on the ground then setting light to it, why didn't she throw the petrol over Brett (Jack O'Connell), who is the ringleader of the TTs, and then chuck the burning wood at him?! At least three of the TTs get their comeuppance anyway – Paige is run over (Hooray!), psycho Brett beats another of the gang to death, and Cooper (Thomas Turgoose) gets glassed in the neck by Jenny – another sign of her incompetence, as he was actually attempting to help her at the time!

Some nice twists follow, but the film ends on a downbeat note, which is a shame in some ways. I liked it anyway, although it's a pity the main villain of the piece (Brett) doesn't get his comeuppance but does get a nice pair of sunglasses! After the, in my view, fairly rubbish years of the 1990s, the 2000s and 2010s are another Golden Age of great horror films, and *Eden Lake* is one to add to a lengthy list. See it and prepare to get angry!

Michael Fassbender in Eden Lake *(2008)*

Christine Brown has a good job,
a great boyfriend, and a bright future.
But in three days,
she's going to hell.
DRAG ME TO HELL
COMING SOON

CHAPTER 58

DRAG ME TO HELL (2009)

Lorna Raver in Drag Me to Hell *(2009)*

Directed by: Sam Raimi.

Written by: Sam Raimi and Ivan Raimi.

Starring: Alison Lohman, Justin Long, Lorna Raver, Dileep Rao, David Paymer, Adriana Barraza and more.

Studio: Universal Pictures/Ghost House Pictures/Buckaroo Entertainment/Curse Productions/Mandate Pictures/Wonderworks Films.

CHRISTINE'S CURSE

BASICALLY A BIG budget reinterpretation of 1957's *Night of the Demon*, *Drag Me to Hell* is a masterpiece.

Directed by Sam Raimi, best known for the overrated *Evil Dead* films, and the excellent *Spider-Man* films, he surpasses himself here. Keeping gore in its place, he concentrates instead on atmosphere and tension, with the escalating panic felt by the heroine as her moment of death approaches.

The central hero of this film is no rugged American who looks like he's wandered in from a John Wayne Western, as in *Night of the Demon*, but instead is an attractive young woman. Alison Lohman is nicely vulnerable in the role, which makes the downbeat ending even more shocking. Lohman plays Christine Brown, a nice young lady who works in a bank. She is advised by her boss to toughen up a little, and so, to flex her mortgage muscles, she refuses to grant another extension to a frankly terrifying old gypsy woman who, after grovelling in debasement, puts a curse on the younger woman – Christine is now fated to die in Hell after three days of being pursued by a sinister spirit called the Lamia!

Alison Lohman in Drag Me to Hell *(2009)*

Lots of gruesome and scary stuff ensues – stapled eyelids, Christine's nose pours with blood at work (her boss seems to take this in his stride, suggesting she takes some time off from work!), she sacrifices her pet kitten to appease the Lamia, and wakes to see the horrible face of the gypsy woman (who has since died) leering down at her before vomiting flies all over her...

Lorna Raver is brilliant as Mrs. Ganush, the unforgiving gypsy witch, and future *Grimm* star Reggie Lee plays Christine's conniving co-worker Stu. Justin Long plays Christine's long-suffering and sceptical boyfriend Clay (the scene where Clay takes Christine to meet his parents is a stand-out in the film and both funny and frightening), and there's a nice performance from a CGI goat during a hectic sequence where an attempt is made to exorcise the Lamia, by having it possess the creature.

Rather than the papers of the 1957 film, it's a button that the heroine here is desperate to return to her tormentor. A happy ending seems imminent, after our mud-caked banker manages to return the cursed object by ramming it in the mouth of the dead Ganush! But the film has one last surprise up it's sleeve...

As with most of the newer films here, I saw this one for the first time on disc, back in 2011, and loved it as I knew I would – there's something about more modern films where it's easy to tell if they are going to be great or not just based on the title and the DVD/Blu-ray case cover! I have a good track record of picking films to buy on disc that I've not seen or know much (if anything) about, and this one didn't let me down either.

Drag Me to Hell *(2009)*

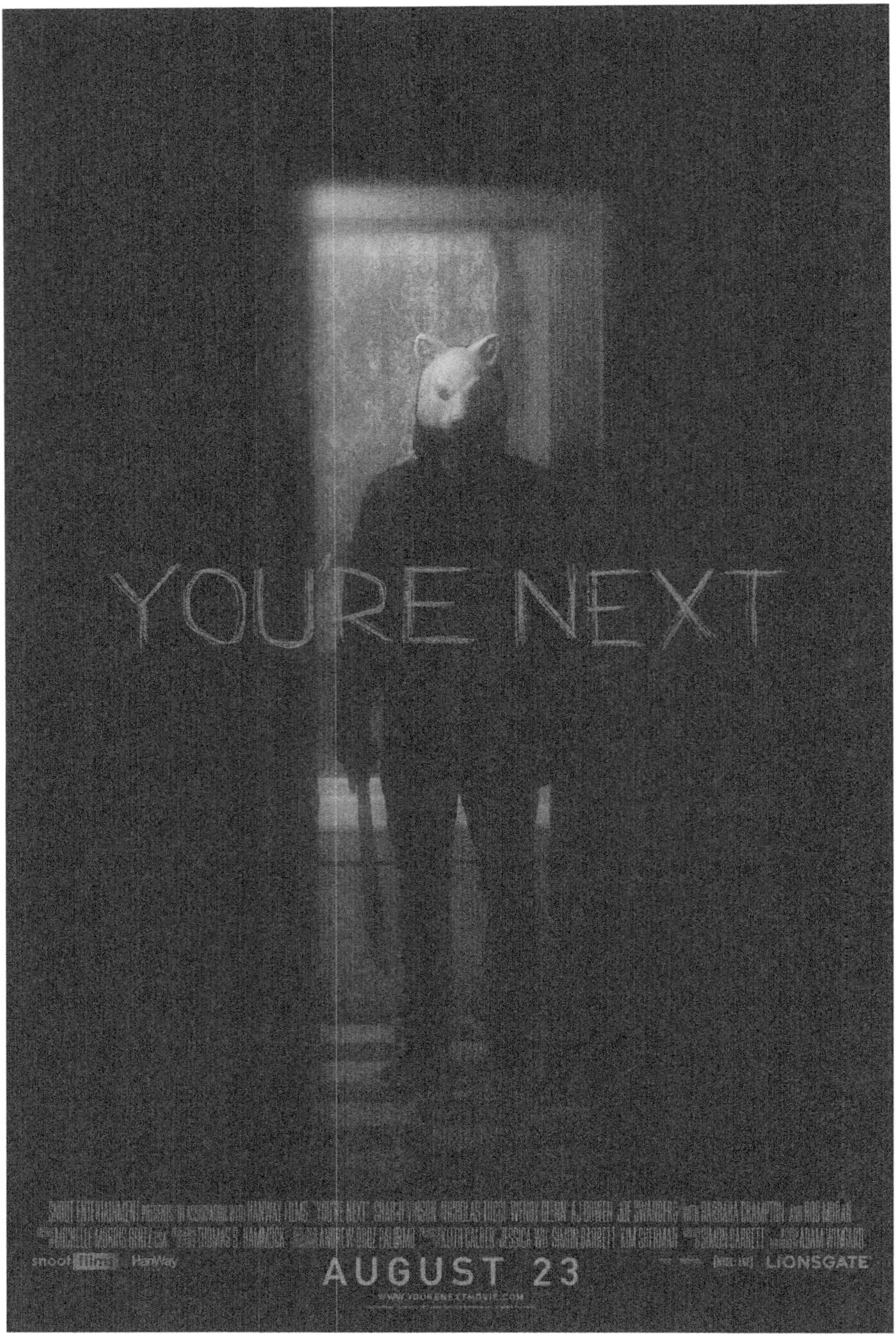
YOU'RE NEXT
AUGUST 23
LIONSGATE

CHAPTER 59

YOU'RE NEXT (2011)

You're Next *(2011)*

Directed by: Adam Wingard.

Written by: Simon Barrett.

Starring: Sharni Vinson, Nicholas Tucci, Wendy Glenn, AJ Bowen, Joe Swanberg, Margaret Laney and more.

Studio: Snoot Entertainment/HanWay Films.

ANIMALS BEHIND MASKS

I'D NEVER HEARD of this brilliant slasher, and so it sort of crept up and leapt at me, like a teenager coughing over people during the Covid crisis (Mr. Topical – that's me!). I was a bit perturbed to hear though, in one of the two accompanying commentary tracks on the Blu-ray disc, that the makers regard it as a black comedy. I certainly didn't think of it as being in any way a comedy when I saw it. Quite the opposite – it made my blood boil!

The film stars the Sharni Vinson (an Australian actress I'd never heard of) as Erin, the girlfriend of Crispian, who is coming to visit his rich parents in their isolated vacation home, along with the rest of the quite large family, and their girl/boyfriends. This wedding anniversary reunion is butt-clenchingly uncomfortable but things soon get worse when the occupants of the large and remote house are targeted by a gang of scumbags wearing animal (tiger, lamb, fox) masks, and who had earlier polished off the occupants of a nearby, similarly-remote dwelling.

Sharni Vinson in You're Next *(2011)*

The attack starts slowly, but it isn't long before we get the expected histrionics and bloodshed, with a spectacular and unexpected near-decapitation. Things go downhill for the assembled group from then on, but throughout, the capable Erin turns the tables on her attackers, ramming a large knife into the hand of one of the animal-masked murderers when he tries to grab her and, even more satisfyingly, kicking one in the gonads before whacking his head into a bloody pulp. I promise you'll be cheering at this point, as I was. One of the bad guys getting their comeuppance – love it! And there's lots more to come...

The film doesn't hold back on the gore but unlike many '80s and '90s films, the gore isn't the whole show. We are invested in the main character and cheering her on, as she dishes out justice with a gutsy killer instinct – stabbing one of the animal-gang with a screwdriver, setting up nail traps for the killers to unsuspectingly jump onto, and finally, sorting out the two lowlifes who were in on it from the start, Felix and his girlfriend Zee (I knew that Zee was a wrong 'un from the start!), and her own scheming boyfriend Crispian, who gives away his part in the murders when he phones Felix (who has been killed by Erin with a food blender to the bonce), and ends up chatting to Erin instead. Zee (who is played by Wendy Glenn, a friend of Vinson's) gets knifed (hooray!) and Crispian is killed by his blood-spattered girlfriend after he admits his part in the financially-motivated murders and tries to bribe her. The film ends shortly after, with one last effective shock...

You're Next is a brilliant example of the "home invasion" type of horror film, always a sub-genre that is guaranteed to get my blood boiling, as it's so easy to put oneself in the unfortunate victims' place! If ever this type of thing was to happen to me in real-life, I'd at least have plenty of ideas from films like this as to how to overpower the attackers and get my own/home back!

Sharni Vinson in You're Next *(2011)*

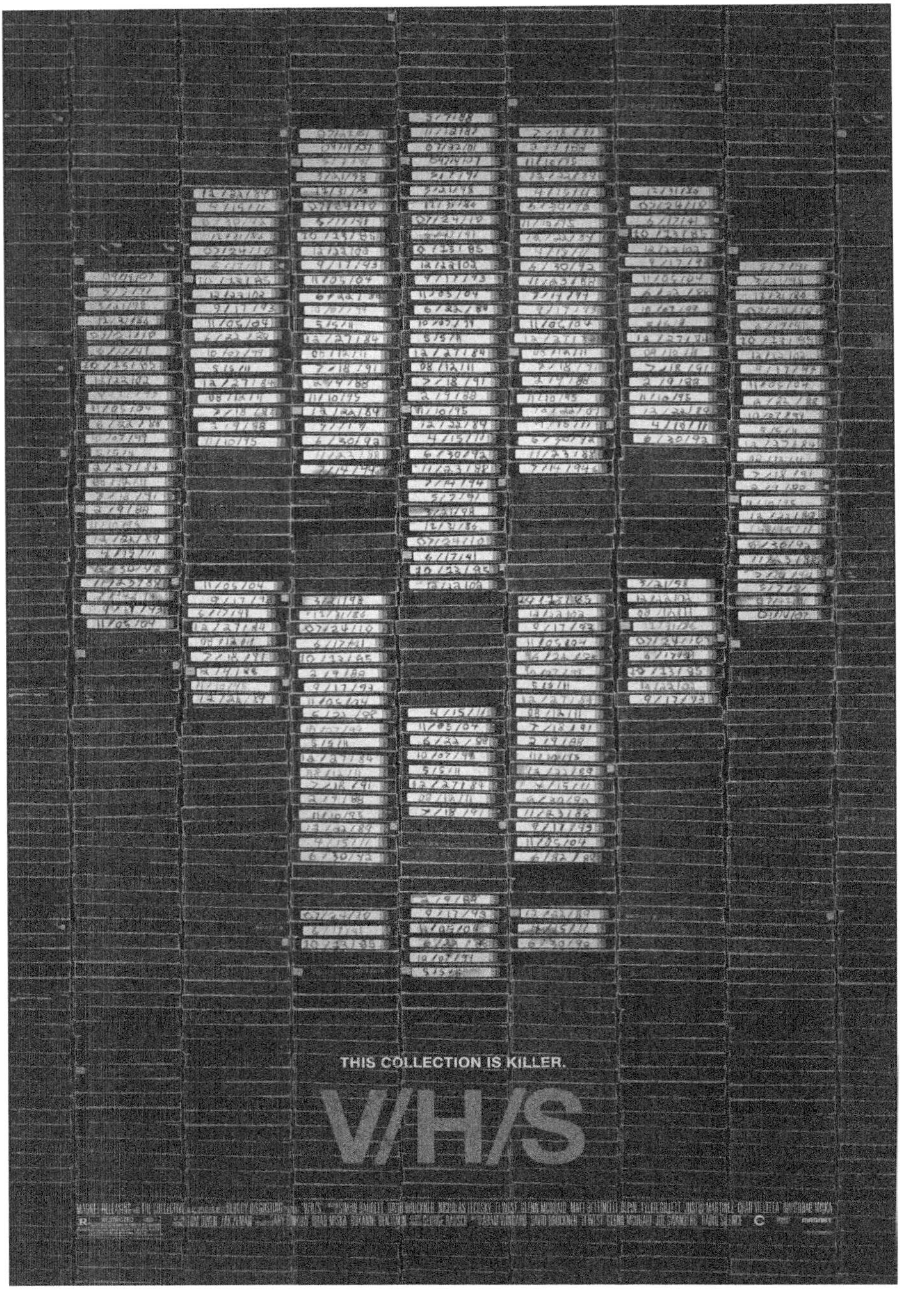
THIS COLLECTION IS KILLER.
V/H/S

CHAPTER 60

V/H/S (2012)

Hannah Fierman in V/H/S (2012)

Directed by: Matt Bettinelli-Olpin, David Bruckner, Tyler Gillett, Justin Martinez, Glenn McQuaid, Radio Silence, Joe Swanberg, Chad Villella, Ti West and Adam Wingard.

Written by: Brad Miska (concept), Simon Barrett, David Bruckner, Nicholas Tecosky, Ti West, Glenn McQuaid, Radio Silence, Matt Bettinelli-Olpin, Tyler Gillett, Justin Martinez and Chad Villella.

Starring: Calvin Reeder, Hannah Fierman, Joe Swanberg, Norma C. Quinones, Helen Rogers, Chad Villella and more.

Studio: 8383 Productions/Bloody Disgusting/Studio71/The Collective Studios.

TAPE PLEASURE

I FIRST ENCOUNTERED this one when someone posted about it on Facebook (I dabble on FB, but unlike many millennials who can't live without tags, pokes, Marketplace, events and pages, it's just the starter of my daily Internet experience and not the full banquet), and I was intrigued enough to seek out the film on Amazon – soon the Blu-ray disc was in my possession and saved up for Christmas 2018.

Watching it in early 2019, I enjoyed it so much I watched it again the night after. *V/H/S* is a weird film: the whole thing appears as a series of camcordered/recorded videos of varying quality. A gang of unsociable, window-breaking and girl-molesting yobs are given a job to do by an unknown client – he wants them to go to a house and bring back a particular videotape. Trouble is, when they get there, there's a mountain of videotapes! A TV set in an upstairs room is playing a fuzzy screen and white noise, while the corpse of an old man sits opposite. The TV is attached to a video recorder, and surrounded by piles of videos, and while the other yobs search the house, one remains in the TV room and watches a couple of the tapes. These contain recorded footage, and present the viewer with five separate stories which are, as I said earlier, all of varying picture quality.

I don't actually mind the camcordered look the film has, though as the stories progress, it gets slightly irritating as the picture breaks up like a genuine videotape would, with seemingly endless jumps, flashes and the screen struggling to realign itself (always at the best bits)! This film makes you feel faintly nostalgic for the old VCR days but it also shows up how utterly bad videos were – we just didn't realise it at the time!

Nice direction, as the watching yob sits with the creepy corpse of the old man behind him – a corpse which vanishes, then later returns! It's subtle moments like this that mark the film as a genuine class act, and not the piece of rubbish it would no doubt have ended up being if it had been made in the '90s. The first story involves a group of three horny young lads going for a night out, one of the group, a bespectacled nerd with little experience of women and also equipped with a hidden camera in his specs, with which he hopes to record any hopeful action.

The group gets involved with two girls one of whom is really weird and creepy-looking, and they all go back to the lads' place for a night of carnal pleasure... which goes spectacularly wrong, as the weird-looking girl is actually some sort of demon! Two of the lads are spectacularly torn apart – the film doesn't shy away from gore and, despite its low-budget feel, the effects are very impressive indeed. Speccy, who is a complete prat, manages to escape through the back door but falls down some stairs and breaks his arm. This first segment ends soon after and gets the film off to a great start – the female demon monster looks genuinely unnerving and horrible (just watch the part where she/it tries to initiate oral sex!) and the joy of seeing these overhyped-up and over-sexed assholes get their comeuppance gives the story its considerable entertainment.

The second story looks a lot better, and involves a couple going for a romantic break, but they end up being shadowed by a girl who – in the gory conclusion which involves the guy getting his throat realistically cut during the night – it turns out is having an affair with the wife and the whole thing was planned in advance. A good example of the depths some human beings will sink to, this has a creepy atmosphere and excellent direction. More of a slow burner than the first tale but worth it.

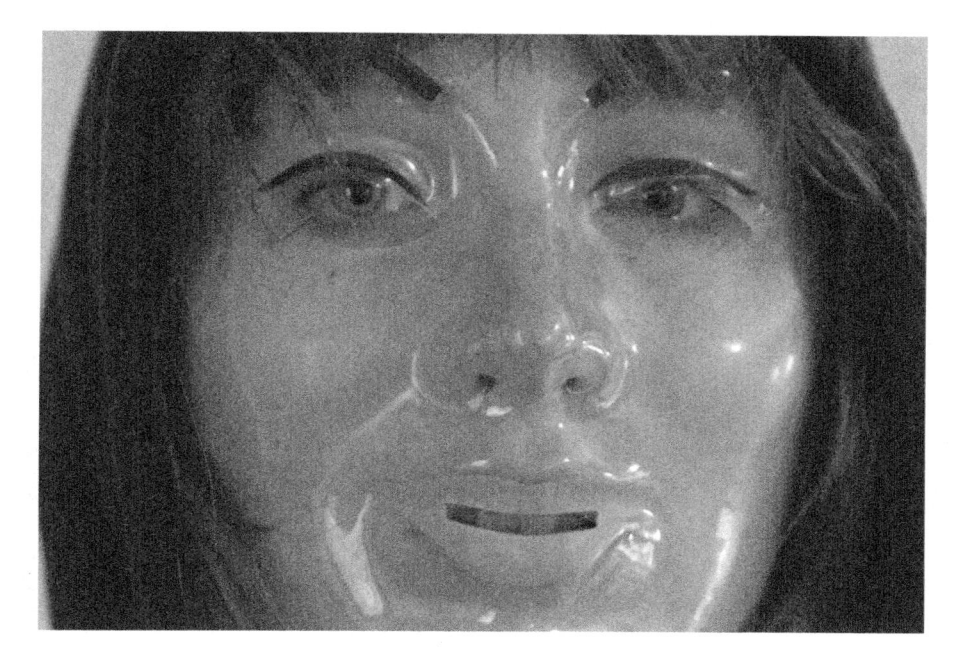

Kate Lyn Sheil in V/H/S *(2012)*

The third story is a weird yarn involving some horny teens (are there any other sort?) returning to the woods where a strange killer massacred some young people earlier. This mysterious character is referred to in the credits as "The Glitch" and is never properly witnessed on screen, as their features are obscured by a persistent tracking error effect! Gore lovers are not short-changed in this segment, which features an unexpected stabbing in which a girl is knifed through the face, followed by various impaling, throat slittings and evisceration!

The next story is my least favourite – a rather distasteful (and, in this film that's saying something!) tale of a man and woman chatting via video, which leads to the revelation that the woman's apartment is apparently haunted. The story takes a sick SF twist, as it turns out the man has been involved in using the woman as an incubator for alien/human hybrids. Ghastly scenes of the woman having the foetuses removed from her body ensue, and there's an earlier part where she digs at the unsightly lump on her arm with a knife!

Jeannine Elizabeth Yoder in V/H/S *(2012)*

The fifth story is excellent, and involves a group of young men who are invited to a Halloween party but end up at the wrong address. Encountering grabbing hands reaching out of the walls, the gang think it's a very realistic Halloween haunted house, but a group torturing a woman up in the attic soon convinces them otherwise, and it all ends in a desperate chase for freedom, which involves the woman who was being tortured suddenly disappearing from the men's car after they've escaped! The car suddenly stops, right in the path of a speeding train – and the doors won't open! This segment brilliantly mixes the horror with humour, which is unintentional but makes it all the funnier – try to watch the frenzied reaction of the guys at the end, as they try without success to get the car started, as the train bears down on them, without laughing!

The framing sequence of the film is no less successful, and ends with the gang being slaughtered by the old man, who has become a zombie!

V/H/S is a superb film, its innovative style and structure being repeated in two sequels, the first of which was rushed into production as a result of the success of the original film.

Settle down and enjoy this heady melange of murder, alien experiments, succubi, unstoppable killers and ghosts – the perfect antidote to all the lacklustre "found footage" films that followed in the wake of the excellent *Blair Witch Project*, and a potent mix of laughs and scares that will have you jumping as many times as the picture.

Hannah Fierman in V/H/S *(2012)*

FROM THE DIRECTOR OF SAW AND INSIDIOUS
THE CONJURING
BASED ON THE TRUE CASE FILES OF THE WARRENS
NEW LINE CINEMA PRESENTS A SAFRAN COMPANY/EVERGREEN MEDIA GROUP PRODUCTION
A JAMES WAN FILM "THE CONJURING" VERA FARMIGA PATRICK WILSON RON LIVINGSTON AND LILI TAYLOR
JOSEPH BISHARA KIRK MORRI JULIE BERGHOFF JOHN R. LEONETTI, ASC
WALTER HAMADA DAVE NEUSTADTER CHAD HAYES & CAREY W. HAYES
TONY DeROSA-GRUND PETER SAFRAN ROB COWAN JAMES WAN
JULY 19
NEW LINE CINEMA
#TheConjuring

CHAPTER 61

THE CONJURING (2013)

Vera Farmiga in The Conjuring *(2013)*

Directed by: James Wan.

Written by: Chad Hayes and Carey W. Hayes.

Starring: Vera Farmiga, Patrick Wilson, Lili Taylor, Ron Livingston, Shanley Caswell, Hayley McFarland and more.

Studio: New Line Cinema/The Safran Company/Evergreen Media Group.

OUIJA BROAD

THIS FILM IS bloody scary – or at least, the extras are! Watching the Blu-ray disc, I just about managed to get through the main feature itself with my goosebumps kept in check (having previously seen it at the cinema when it was released), but when it came to the accompanying documentaries about the apparent real-life case that inspired the film, and the real-life ghost-hunting couple who the characters in the film are based on, I was terrified! The extras make a good case for the existence of real demonic and evil forces and anyone who meddles with them does so at their own risk. Watching something like that at around midnight in the bleak midwinter is a seriously chilling experience!

The Conjuring stars Patrick Wilson and Vera Farmiga as a pair of real-life paranormal investigators, Ed and Lorraine Warren. This film is based on one of their cases, and the real family who were involved in the haunting depicted herein appear in photos over the closing credits. They also made a decision not to watch the film itself when it was released, as they wanted to distance themselves from the memory of the events that befell them, back in 1971 – and after watching this film, who can blame them?

Patrick Wilson and Vera Farmiga in The Conjuring *(2013)*

Set in Rhode Island, the film has the Perrons (dad Roger, mom Carolyn, and five daughters, Andrea, Christine, Nancy, Cindy and April) moving into a creepy and isolated house, where strange things start to happen. The family pooch is scared to enter the home (and later winds up dead), the clocks all stop at around 3 in the morning and birds fly into the house's windows. Seriously scary stuff ensues, when Christine claims to see a malevolent spirit, that wants the family dead!

It isn't long before the Warrens arrive, and discover the ghastly presence is a long-dead witch called Bathsheba. The rest of the film has a possession, appearances in the cellar by ghosts, and some very scary stuff involving a possessed (and bloody terrifying) doll named

Annabelle, which would later return for several films in this franchise. The sections involving the character that only a child can see, in the bedroom at night standing behind the door, the music box that shows in its mirror the spirit of a dead child, Ed Warren's tour and description of his room that contains all the occult objects from their various cases including the aforementioned Annabelle, are all great moments in a great film, and at last a horror film franchise worth watching!

What makes this film – and many other horror films of the 2010s – work so well is the fact it combines the best elements of 1960s/'70s horrors with the (relatively few) better elements of films from the '80s/'90s, but without any of the OTT, unscary and in-your-face rubbish of the latter decades. It also looks better – how can you enjoy watching a horror film that looks like an MTV video, which is the fate that befell a lot of films from that decade after the '70s? It is also, and again, unlike films from the '80s and '90s, genuinely frightening and unsettling, making me jump at least five times, and those on multiple viewings! Funnily enough, I first saw the film at the cinema, on a Sunday afternoon with some friends, and I wasn't that impressed – this film is one that needs to be viewed by yourself, at home, late at night, in order to get the full petrifying effect.

A masterpiece of the macabre, I can't wait to see the sequels!

Lili Taylor (right) in The Conjuring *(2013)*

The producer of PARANORMAL ACTIVITY and INSIDIOUS presents
OCULUS
You see what it wants you to see
#SEEYOUREVIL
IN THEATERS APRIL 11
RELATIVITY

CHAPTER 62

OCULUS (2013)

Karen Gillan in Oculus *(2013)*

Directed by: Mike Flanagan.

Written by: Mike Flanagan (screenplay), Jeff Howard (screenplay) and Jeff Seidman (based on a short screenplay by).

Starring: Karen Gillan, Brenton Thwaites, Katee Sackhoff, Rory Cochrane, Annalise Basso, Garrett Ryan and more.

Studio: Intrepid Pictures/MICA Entertainment/WWE Studios/Blumhouse Productions/Lasser Productions.

A BAD TIME TO REFLECT

DOES SPEAKING IN a different accent to your own for any length of time hurt your mouth? I've wondered that ever since David Tennant was the TV Doctor Who and forsook his natural Scottish accent for a "mockney" one. With *Oculus*, one-time *Doctor Who* companion Karen Gillan, who is also Scottish, plays an American and has to speak in an

American accent throughout the film, and I found myself wondering if it made her mouth hurt. Probably not, or not as much as it would hurt eating a glass light bulb – but I'm getting ahead of myself here.

I bought the Blu-ray of *Oculus* without knowing a thing about it, other than the fact Karen Gillan was in it. Such is my faith in 2010s horror films – as I mention elsewhere in the book, I think it's a golden age for the genre – I tend to buy lots of horrors on disc without knowing much/anything about them. I just get an instinct that, because it's a film from a great decade for films, it's going to be good. And I'm usually right.

Oculus concerns a cursed/haunted antique mirror and the film blows away the mirror segment of 1945's *Dead of Night*, and is also superior to the mirror story in 1974's *From Beyond the Grave*, as good as that is. The film unfolds in two strands, one present and the other consisting of flashbacks to the past. Gillan and Brenton Thwaites play siblings Kaylie and Tim, whose mom and dad met unpleasant ends eleven years earlier, thanks to the mirror and its ability to affect reality for those nearby. In flashbacks, we see how Marie (the mom) was haunted by visions of her decaying body in the mirror ("Grotesque cow!"), while Alan (the dad) was tormented by hallucinations of a sexy young woman who seduces him in his office, leading to the complete breakdown of the family – Marie ends up like a mad animal, chained up in her bedroom, cutting her mouth when she tries to eat a china plate and gradually becoming psychotic, and Alan ends up shooting her, plus gets his son Tim to shoot him.

As well as all the trouble with humans, the mirror also apparently eats dogs, as the family pooch disappears after being locked in a room with it. The many ghosts of its previous victims also appear, as Tim is dragged away by the police, protesting his innocence and blaming it all on the mirror – I don't think that will stand up in court, kid!

These flashbacks are continually interspersed with the present-day sequences and it all works very well, with the two storylines running in tandem. Kaylie has it all worked out, setting up surveillance cameras all around the room with the mirror, in order to be able to prove her brother's innocence (he's spent the last eleven years in a mirror-less padded cell) by exposing the mirror's supernatural powers. There is also a "kill switch" in the form of a heavy metal anchor/axe attached to the ceiling, in such a way that it can swing down and destroy the blasted mirror.

The fact that bloody evil mirror doesn't get smashed into smithereens is the only mildly disappointing aspect of this otherwise superb film – sometimes films where evil wins can work but here, when the evil force is a glass mirror, the audience is obviously primed for a literally smashing scene that never comes. Nevertheless, this is a great film. The mirror's history and a list of its fatalities is recounted by Kaylie, complete with photographic evidence, and we hear/see of poor sods who bit through live wires, were horribly castrated etc etc. The mirror has the power to wilt plants, and distort memories and God knows what else, and towards the end the two adults see each other as kids on the way to the downbeat conclusion – which appropriately mirrors what happened eleven years earlier.

    The film was expanded from a short devised by the same guy, Mike Flanagan, and the feature film is much better than the short. Flanagan believed it was better not to go too closely into the mirror's origins and what lay inside it, liking the idea of something so totally alien and evil it could bring insanity to anyone who even tried to understand it. A masterpiece of the macabre, watch this film late at night but preferably not with a large mirror in the room...

Karen Gillan in Oculus *(2013)*

NONSTOP ENTERTAINMENT PRESENTERAR
"ONE OF THE MOST INVENTIVE, EXCITING, AND TRULY FRIGHTENING HORROR FLICKS IN AGES"
REEL FILM REVIEWS
IT FOLLOWS
EN FILM AV DAVID ROBERT MITCHELL
IT DOESN'T THINK. IT DOESN'T FEEL. IT DOESN'T GIVE UP.
animal kingdom
visitfilms

CHAPTER 63

IT FOLLOWS (2014)

Jake Weary and Maika Monroe in It Follows *(2014)*

Directed by: David Robert Mitchell.

Written by: David Robert Mitchell.

Starring: Maika Monroe, Bailey Spry, Carollette Phillips, Loren Bass, Keir Gilchrist, Lili Sepe and more.

Studio: Northern Lights Films/Animal Kingdom/Two Flints.

SOLVING A NIGHTMARE

SEX EQUALS DEATH, or at least it does in this eerie chiller which was a big success in the mid-2010s, and finally entered my radar in 2018 when I got the Blu-ray (what else? – I'll never be a fan of streaming. I think most fans of film and TV would rather own a copy of a film/TV show and streaming doesn't allow you to own anything – instead it just gives you the chance to watch what other people own. Not for me. The picture quality is supposed to be sub-par too).

It Follows (the title doesn't appear on screen until the end which is slightly annoying but not disastrous) is sort of a sexual version of "Casting the Runes"/*Night of the Demon,* in which, instead of papers being passed from person to person, thus leading them to a nasty demise, it's sexual intercourse. Just how nasty a demise is revealed in the film's opening, in which a girl runs frantically to her car to get away from someone or something. She ends up at the beach, and foolishly decides to get out of the car and wander off – the next morning we see what's left of her and it isn't pretty...

The film stars Maika Monroe as Jay, an ordinary young girl who goes with her boyfriend for a night of passion (once you get older, you realise just how overrated sex is and how stupid teenagers look for being obsessed with it) and gets more than she bargained for when, after rendering her unconscious, her creepy boyfriend Hugh (Jake Weary) ties her to a wheelchair and leaves her to lie in wait for... what? What is actually behind the murders and how it has the power to change shape is never explained, and it could be just as much extraterrestrial as supernatural. The "thing" appears here as a naked woman and presents a really terrifying image, as it moves like a figure from a dream, getting closer and closer no matter how far or fast you run. The film is presented as a nightmare and has been subjected to a lot of scrutiny, with theories ranging from the idea the film is a metaphor for the horrors a rape victim has to endure afterwards to the notion that the pursuing figure represents a personalised STD (that's sexually transmitted disease, by the way, not *Star Trek: Discovery*!). These theories all seem valid but it's best not to dwell on them too much and just enjoy the unfolding suspense and excitement onscreen, as these hormone-fuelled teens are going to get shagged, right enough!

One scene takes place in Jay's university class, where she notices a sinister-looking old woman slowly walking towards her from outside. Jay should have stayed where she was but she quickly leaves and the horror spreads to her home, where she and her sister Kelly, and friends Paul and Yara, have a terrifying experience when Jay sees a bedraggled, half-naked woman, and then later a creepy guy with no eyes, enter the house. It's that sinister entity again, and it continues to pursue them after they flee and head to a house by the sea, actually attacking Jay at one point and impervious to being whacked over the head by a chair. This beach encounter ends up with Jay in hospital, having driven off in a panic and crashed.

Greg, Jay's gentlemanly neighbour, winds up taking on the curse himself by having sex with the hospital bed-bound Jay and he ends up dead, as the entity kills him after taking the form of his own mother, in a very disturbing sequence. Later, Paul actually offers, very nobly, of course, to have sex with Jay and thus take on the problem of being followed by the "thing" but it's just because he has a soft spot for her and he finally gets his wish, and his leg over. The film ends abruptly not long afterwards and I was a little disappointed first time round, but after re-watching it several times, it's an okay ending, just not what you expect. A bit like first-time sex itself.

Writer and director David Robert Mitchell came up with the idea for the film after recurring childhood dreams of being followed and later came up with the sex angle as a way of transferring the threat from person to person. The result is yet another masterpiece in a decade overflowing with them, and like many of the best horrors, is a film to make something ordinary and routine become frightening and strange. It's a film that should stick in many a fornicating couple's minds, so the next time you have a quick game of "Hide the Hot Dog" with your beloved, make sure you keep your eyes peeled and in the back of your head whenever you go out again!

It Follows *(2014)*

WINNER
sundance
THE
VVITCH
A New-England Folktale
EVIL TAKES MANY FORMS
2016

CHAPTER 64

THE WITCH (2015)

Anya Taylor-Joy in The Witch *(2015)*

Directed by: Robert Eggers.

Written by: Robert Eggers.

Starring: Anya Taylor-Joy, Ralph Ineson, Kate Dickie, Harvey Scrimshaw, Ellie Grainger, Lucas Dawson and more.

Studio: Parts and Labor/RT Features/Rooks Nest Entertainment/Code Red Productions/Scythia Films/A24/Maiden Voyage Pictures/Mott Street Pictures/Pulse Films/Very Special Projects.

FOREST FRUMP

I SPENT THE early part of watching this film wondering where I'd seen the lead actor, Ralph Ineson, before – I knew I'd definitely seen him in something, *Eastenders* being a strong possibility. As it turned out, after Googling him, I was close – Mr. Ineson was in *Coronation Street* for a while. It was quite a feat that I remembered him, as the last time I sat down and properly watched an episode of Britain's beloved soap opera was in the late '80s.

Anyway, from Weatherfield to witchcraft in seventeenth century New England, *The Witch* is a spine-chilling masterpiece, described somewhere – in a quote that stuck in my mind, even if the source didn't – as "a film so fucked-up, Satan would see it twice"! It's a grim fairytale indeed and works perfectly on that level. Filmed in Canada with a British cast, Ralph Ineson and Kate Dickie play William and Katherine, who with their daughter Thomasin, son Caleb and twins Mercy and Jonas, set up a farm on the outskirts of a massive, secluded forest. Katherine has also recently given birth to a baby son, Samuel.

The film wastes no time – no sooner has Samuel popped out, so to speak, than the sinister witch who inhabits the forest has popped off with him, killing him and using his bloody entrails to create a lotion that will enable her to fly! We don't see too much of the witch but what we do see is bloody terrifying.

The film deftly creates an atmosphere of pure evil working against good, God-fearing people. Before long, the family are at each other's throats, with dissent and discord leading to murder and death, all caused by the evil, largely unseen witch and a goat called Black Phillip which is owned by the family and turns out to be the Devil himself!

Now, I'm an animal lover, but there are moments during this film where I would have loved to give that bloody goat a good kicking! It's obviously a conduit of the witch's evil powers in some way and its presence leads to the death of the family's dog, Fowler, and later Caleb, who had been searching for Fowler in the woods, and after finding its mangled corpse, ends up in the witch's lair…

The death of Caleb is a stand-out sequence and involves him returning after his entrapment by the crone, naked and delirious, and vomiting an apple from his mouth. The memorably-named Harvey

Scrimshaw gives a solid performance here, with some frightening monologues which will cause you to quake. He dies shortly after, which unsettles the family no end and causes William to lock up the twins and Thomasin in an enclosure outside. At this point, things become really scary, with the kids seeing the terrifying leering witch drinking milk from the goats, Katherine being pecked by a crow and William waking up the next morning to find Mercy and Jonas gone, plus the goats (but not Black Philip) dead! It isn't long before he joins them, being attacked and gored by Black Philip in a shocking sequence. Katherine is killed by the blood-spattered Thomasin with a cleaver soon after.

The film doesn't hold back with the gore but it's the atmosphere that gives the story its impact, aided by the creepy dissonant score. This is a film that would lose some of that unique impact if seen with a popcorn-munching crowd of twenty-somethings, checking their smartphones for a Snapchat message every ten seconds (and always at a crucial moment in a film). By the way, I've never understood why (predominantly among teen and twenty-somethings) cinema audiences can't do without eating during a film – isn't it possible to spend two to three hours without stuffing their stupid millennial faces? The film works better, I would think, when viewed by oneself in the comfort of one's own home. It certainly did for me – watching the Blu-ray disc (sadly devoid of any extras at all) late one February 2019 night, continually looking around the room and over my shoulder!

The ending of the film is definitely worth the wait: as night closes in, Thomasin is left alone and surrounded by corpses – then, the Devil formerly known as Black Philip appears... forsaking goat form, and appearing as a handsome (?), shadowed stranger. This scene is spine chilling as he offers Thomasin the chance to "live deliciously" and to taste butter! Thomasin signs away her soul, and we see an incredibly spooky and chilling vision of the young woman and the goat walking into the woods before Thomasin strips off and levitates into the air with a group of other witches. The perfect end to a perfect film.

The Witch is another in a line of twenty-first century horrors to challenge *The Exorcist*'s long-held position as the most frightening horror film ever, and Robert Eggers (the director) certainly delivers the goods – if I had have seen this as a kid, I would have been traumatised!

The final moments linger in the memory, and like a lot of horror films from the 2010s this is a film to watch with the lights on.

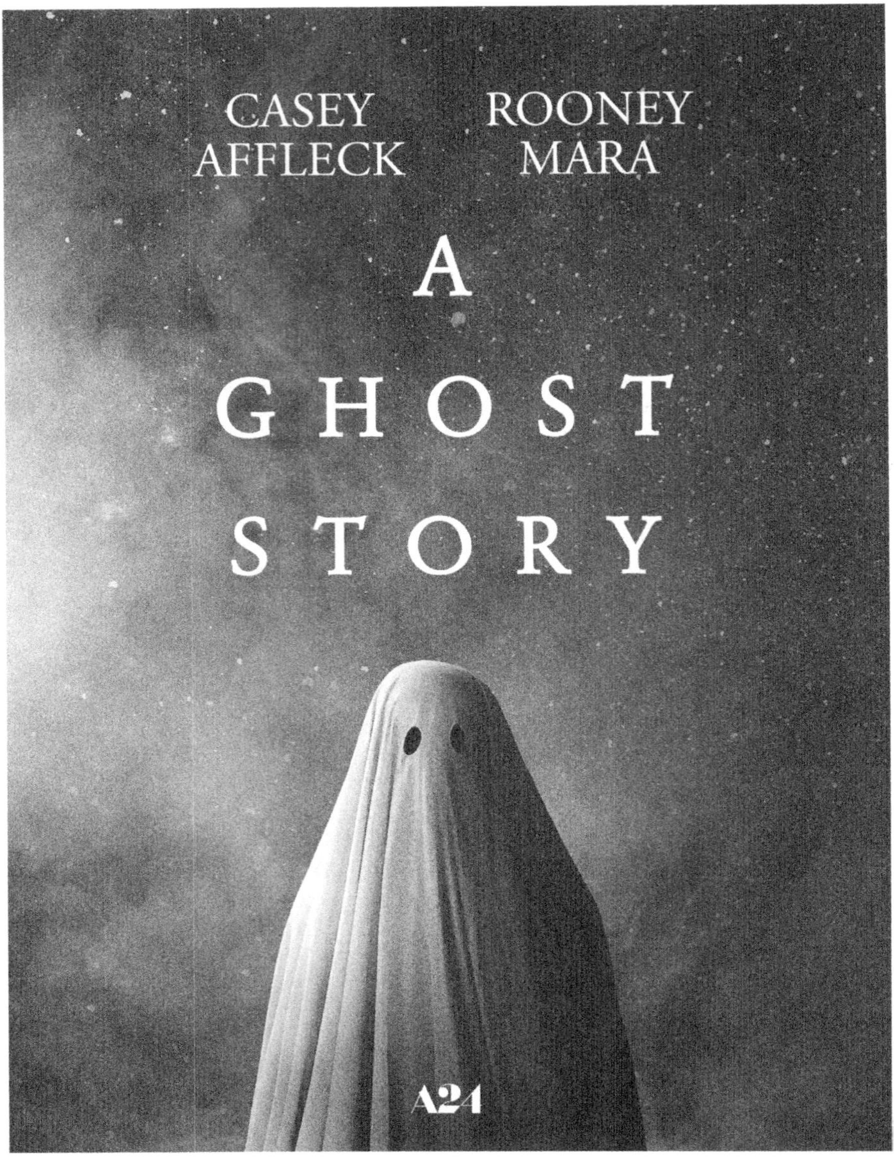
CASEY
AFFLECK
ROONEY
MARA
A
GHOST
STORY
A24

CHAPTER 65

A GHOST STORY (2017)

Casey Affleck in A Ghost Story *(2017)*

Directed by: David Lowery.

Written by: David Lowery.

Starring: Casey Affleck, Rooney Mara, McColm Cephas Jr.,

Kenneisha Thompson, Grover Coulson, Liz Cardenas and more.

Studio: Sailor Bear/Zero Trans Fat Productions/Ideaman Studios.

THE SPIRIT MOVES YOU

THIS IS ANOTHER example of the excellence of 2010s horror films, crossing the boundaries between being sad and scary and ending up being a masterpiece. The film involves a young couple (Casey Affleck and Rooney Mara), who live in a cute little house in an isolated spot in Dallas. He is a musician and her job, if any, isn't specified. Living an idyllic life, it's rudely shattered when he's killed in a car crash but returns as a vaguely-laughable looking ghost – basically a sheet with eye holes – who haunts his wife and the house, losing all concept of time as he observes events from the future and past and, finally from an alternate future.

For a film in which very little, relatively speaking, actually happens, it seems to move very quickly and is never boring. Even a lengthy scene of someone eating a chocolate cheesecake holds the interest! The ghostly sheet-covered figure could be viewed as funny but it never is, and the film has a remarkably poignant atmosphere especially when another ghostly figure appears in the window of the house opposite – apparently waiting for someone who never appears.

The clever tricks with time are effective, and basically show that linear time holds no meaning in the afterlife. Events which take place earlier in the film – the characters hearing a sound in the middle of the night and getting out of bed to investigate – are replayed later in the film from the ghost's point of view, and the forlorn spirit goes back to the nineteenth century at one point, witnessing a family setting up in the spot where the couple's house would one day be built, but being massacred by Indians.

One running little sub-plot throughout the film involves the deceased husband trying to extract a note left by his wife in a door jamb shortly before she moves – once the ghost finally succeeds and reads it, he disappears and the sheet drops to the floor.

Not much to say about the film because not much actually happens – it's a very effective mood piece more than anything, and a film that will haunt you long after the end credits. There's at least one other film out there called *Ghost Story*, but this is definitely the best, ranking very well in a decade of excellent supernatural chillers.

CHAPTER 66

JUST WHEN YOU THINK IT'S ALL OVER...

This Island Earth *artwork by Dave Carson*

THIS LAST CHAPTER is a quick look at some of the films that did not make the top 100, either because they didn't make the grade, or because I'd seen them too late to write about them in the book (the case with many of the more recent films – where once we would have a mere 140-odd horror films in the whole of the 1930s, in the single year of 2015 we had 1,224, far more than can be seen, never mind written about).

Looking at them randomly, a few Hammer films were edged out, none of them from the 1950s. I still think that a large part of the reason for the popularity among critics now of those late-'50s Hammer films is because they were such a stark contrast to the British chillers we'd had up until then. Prior to *The Curse of Frankenstein*, most British horror films consisted of men in grey suits standing talking to each other about the supernatural, interspersed with occasional moments of gore-free action, but the classic Cushing and Lee fright-flick changed all that by putting blood on the screen along with various gruesome details. These films were certainly revolutionary at the time, but for me, the Hammer films of the '60s and '70s surpass them. The '50s was mainly a SF-oriented decade for films anyway, with gems like *This Island Earth* (1955), *Forbidden Planet* (1956) and *Invasion of the Body Snatchers* (1956) from the US, and weird British items like *Fiend Without a Face* (1958), among the stand-outs. Back to Hammer, and *The Brides of Dracula* in 1960 isn't a Dracula film, despite it's title. Instead, Peter Cushing returns as Van Helsing to tackle the frighteningly camp Baron Meinster (David Peel, who reportedly turned up on set each day with his two fluffy poodles and caused a stir – good thing it wasn't the set of 1973's *Theatre of Blood*, or they might have been roped in as guest stars). The film is overrated and isn't *that* good, but it certainly has its moments and is actually a lot more entertaining than the 1958 film which audiences expected this to be a sequel to.

The Plague of the Zombies (1966) is one of the two Cornwall-based chillers made back-to-back in order to save money by using the same sets. It's a great film, with André Morell making an effective substitute for Cushing as a crusty old professor who goes to investigate strange deaths in a Cornish village, and finds the local Squire (John Carson) has been raising the dead. The zombies are very effective, especially in the celebrated dream sequence, in which the hero (Brook Williams) dreams the dead are rising from their graves and advancing on him in a creepy, fog-shrouded studio cemetery, all to the accompaniment of a creepy score by James Bernard. This scene appears in another great British film that didn't quite make the top 100, 1971's *Fright,* in which Susan George plays a babysitter in a creepy old house who tries to calm her nerves by watching this

Hammer film on the telly!

The Plague of the Zombies (1966)

Hammer's *Dr Jekyll & Sister Hyde* is a 1971 corker, with Ralph Bates as Jekyll and Martine Beswick as his evil female alter ego, whom Jekyll informs his nosey neighbours is his sister, Mrs Hyde! A great and clever screenplay by *Avengers* creator Brian Clemens ropes in body-snatching with Burke and Hare, Jack the Ripper, and an intriguing premise that involves Bates wanting to find a cure to all known diseases but realising he needs to find a way to live forever first, quaffing a formula that turns him into a female version of himself – when I first saw this in the late 1970s, I expected a campy spoof but it's a serious and straight-faced affair that stands as a good example of how Hammer films got better with each decade, not worse as many critics claim.

Of the "mini-Hitchcocks" that Hammer made to cash in on the success of *Psycho* (1960), most are unremarkable and two of them (*The Nanny* [1965] and *Crescendo* [1970]) are downright rubbish but *Fear in the Night* (1972) is a little gem, and stars Ralph Bates again as a teacher who is planning to do away with his wife (Judy Geeson) with the help of his mistress (Joan Collins), but gets sorted out with the aid of Peter Cushing's creepy, retired headmaster.

Going back to the 1930s and *Island of Lost Souls* (1932) is a spine-chiller that ended up being banned in Britain for many years, to the full approval of H. G. Wells (on who's novel *The Island of Doctor Moreau* the film was based) who hated it. The film has a strange atmosphere, and tells of a sinister surgeon on his own private island, carrying out experiments on animals in his "house of pain" and finally ending up being torn apart by them, in their own version of vivisection. Charles Laughton gives a memorable performance, and Bela Lugosi's thick Hungarian accent roars out from behind the Wolf Man-ish make-up he wears as one of the many failed experiments who now lurk in the jungle. I can certainly see why the film caused a stir back then, as it is certainly quite frightening even today, and the gruesome – and even sexual – details are not spared from the viewer, as Moreau intends to mate one of his human prisoners with a "Panther Woman"! Despite all the stuff on screen, which can be viewed as being in very bad taste, the film ends with a sprightly score of the type that might be heard on the end credits of a Laurel and Hardy, or W.C. Fields comedy of the time.

King Kong from 1933 is certainly a landmark of fantastic cinema (I remember seeing this film at the cinema, when it was re-issued in 1976) but I'm not keen on the "giant monster" sub-genre, though this film – along with 1954's *Them!* and 1957's *The Black Scorpion* – is one of the stand-outs. And it looks even better when compared to the awful 1976 remake.

The iconic climax of King Kong *(1933)*

From the 1940s, Boris Karloff made some great films for Columbia, *Before I Hang* (1940) being one of the best. In this one, Karloff plays John Garth, a scientist who finds a way to rejuvenate people by using blood. Unfortunately, Garth uses the blood of a murderer on himself and you can guess the rest.

Circus of Horrors (1960) is a British film with Anton Diffring as a failed plastic surgeon who ends up on the run after making shredded wheat out of a woman's face. He ends up taking over a circus after the previous owner (Donald Pleasence) gets mauled by a bear, and this leads to several gory murders when several of the troupe threaten to expose him, as well as a quite catchy song, "Look For a Star", which is inserted into the action.

Night of the Eagle (1962) is another above-average British film, with Peter Wyngarde as a college professor who gets drawn into the world of the supernatural, culminating in his being attacked by the titular stone eagle brought to life by witchcraft! I always remember this one being shown on a Friday afternoon in late 1981 on my local ITV station Tyne Tees. *Premature Burial* (1962), *The Raven* (1963) and *The Tomb of Ligeia* (1964) are all excellent AIP films in the Roger Corman/Edgar Allan Poe series. Ray Milland plays a guy terrified of being buried alive, who ends up the victim of a cruel plot by his cheating wife; Karloff, Price and Peter Lorre play duelling magicians who use their spells against each other in a large cliff-top mansion; and Price plays a man whose dead wife returns as a cat respectively in these three films.

It! (1967) is a fairly slow-paced but enjoyable little film, with Roddy McDowall playing a creepy museum curator who gets his hands on the Golem, the clay monster from mythology. Finding a way to control the creature by slipping a parchment in it's mouth, McDowall soon has it performing murder, theft and destruction. The scene where the Golem tears down Tower Bridge is quite a hoot, and I still don't see what all the fuss is about regarding Jill Haworth but this is an underrated film, and definitely the best Golem movie ever made.

Talking of monsters and mass destruction, the various Godzilla films from Japan are quite entertaining, with the 1954 original having an oddly downbeat and disturbing quality to it. Of the rest, *King Kong vs. Godzilla* (1963) and *Godzilla vs the Smog Monster* (1971) are the best of the bunch. Incidentally, did you know that Marvel Comics did a Godzilla comic in the late-'70s? If this book is a success, then one of the other book projects I'd like to do is one looking at US comics of the '70s/'80s, so I'll say more about Marvel's stab at the big green G in that one.

The Amicus 1967 anthology *Torture Garden* is a gem, with four Robert Bloch-based tales linked by Dr. Diabolo (Burgess Meredith). The film has a great soundtrack and the four stories are all entertaining, the Hollywood segment being the weakest of the bunch. The final tale has the ubiquitous Peter Cushing playing an Edgar Allan Poe-obsessive, who has raised the long-dead author from the grave so that he can continue writing! The film is not as good as *The House That Dripped Blood* (1971) or *Tales from the Crypt* (1972), but it's still a notch or two above films like *The Deadly Bees* (1966) and *The Terrornauts* (1967) from the same company.

Burgess Meredith (right) as Dr. Diabolo in Torture Garden *(1967)*

Tigon's 1968 Vincent Price-starring *Witchfinder General* aka *The Conqueror Worm* is another cult British folk horror certainly worthy of an honourable mention.

Frightmare (1974) has the creepy Shiela Keith playing an old woman who likes to eat people, and Rupert Davies is her long-suffering husband who has to supply her with fresh corpses, in this excellent British chiller. *House of Mortal Sin* (1976) is another Pete Walker film, with Anthony Sharp playing a crazy priest who becomes obsessed with a young girl at the confessional, resorting to murder in order to get her into his clutches. A very enjoyable film, though probably not for priests. Sharp has a good face for horror films and should really have many more of this type of picture.

The Shout (1978) is yet another British film, and is a minor masterpiece. Anthony Bates plays a sinister character who inveigles his way into John Hurt's house and tries it on with Hurt's wife,

Susannah York. Bates has a magical ability, picked up while he lived with aborigines in the Outback, and he can kill with a single shout. Bates shouts once during the film, and the effect is very impressive, leading to birds dropping dead out of the sky! This is a strange film, and well worth a look. It has an ending in which it seems as if the whole thing has been made up, but there's one last twist...

Witchfinder General *artwork by Jim Pitts*

Zombie Flesh Eaters (1979) is my favourite of the Lucio Fulci flicks, and would definitely have been included in a "Top 110 horror films" book, if only for the notorious eyeball skewering scene.

I'm afraid I can't recommend *The Changeling* (1980) much, as I found this film to be an overrated, colossal bore and I can't understand it's reputation at all. *The Shining* (1980), on the other hand, is excellent. I'm not a huge fan of Stephen King but some of the films based on his books are well worth a viewing and this – along with *Carrie* (1976) and the TV movie *Salem's Lot* (1979) – is one of the best. Jack Nicholson (who I've always considered to be an actor famous just for being famous) actually delivers the goods here and the film contains some very creepy and disturbing moments, as well as a literally chilling ending.

Jack Nicholson in The Shining *(1980)*

1982's King-penned anthology *Creepshow* is one of the best horrors of the 1980s, with all of its five stories being engrossing. The final one, with E.G. Marshall playing a potty-mouthed millionaire racist recluse, who ends up being eaten by marauding cockroaches, is a stand-out and a good laugh, and actually funnier than the film's genuine comedy segment which stars Stephen King himself as a simple, hillbilly farmer who is contaminated by "meteor shit" and ends up being transformed into a walking plant. The film's success led to two sequels, each of which was worse than the other.

The various *Halloween* films all made their mark in the 1970s and 1980s but I can only recommend the influential 1978 original, though it's not a favourite. That also applies to the various *A Nightmare on Elm Street* films, of which I only really like *Wes Craven's New Nightmare* (1994)! Their success has to be acknowledged though.

Halloween *artwork by Allen Koszowski*

In more recent years, the excellent horrors come thick and fast. These haven't been so analysed and reviewed as much as the older films so deserve a bit more time here. *Hard Candy* (2005) is a masterpiece. Patrick Wilson plays Jeff, a sleazy photographer with paedophile tendencies who, after outrageously flirting with her in full view in a coffee shop, takes his new victim Hayley Stark (Ellen Page) back to his secluded house. Unfortunately for him, Hayley turns out to be a psychopath. The film is essentially a two-hander and both Patrick Wilson (who I recognised from *Insidious* [2010] and *The Conjuring* films) and Ellen Page (who I recognised from delightful comedy *Juno* [2007] and the recent Netflix hit SF series *The Umbrella Academy*) are brilliant in their roles, with Page making a convincing transition from a flirty and coquettish teen (she was seventeen when she made the film, but looks young enough to play the fourteen-year-old Hayley) to a spine-chilling tormentor and castrator! There are some great twists near the end, and though he seems to be in danger of losing his balls, Jeff ends up well hung – literally! Hayley meanwhile rolls down a hill and then scurries away. It's a pity they didn't do a sequel to this film, as it would have been interesting to find out more about the Hayley Stark character and why she turned out to be a cold-blooded (and rather prissy and preaching) killer.

REC (2007) is a Spanish film, and it proved to be a great hit which led to an American remake. I've never seen the original but 2008's *Quarantine* is another modern horror well worth your time. Jennifer Carpenter – no relation to John, I presume – plays an LA news reporter who tags along with a fire crew and gets involved in strange goings-on involving a man-made virus which has gotten out of control in an apartment building (which looks like the building Robert Culp was battling alien invaders in *The Outer Limits* ep "Demon with a Glass Hand"), and is turning the residents into grotesque zombies! *Quarantine* is a powerful and scary film, and the ending doesn't disappoint – watch out for *Star Trek: Discovery*'s Doug Jones as the most god-awful looking zombie ever!

2009's *Orphan* has an amazing performance from Isabelle Fuhrman as a sinister, murderous kid who is adopted by a family who soon wish they'd left her at the orphanage! There's plenty of fun to be had here, with the murderous little swine killing pigeons and people alike, leading to a nice twist ending in which it's revealed... oh, I'm out of space, better move on to the next film!

Let Me In (2010) is one of the new breed of Hammer films (which unfortunately seem to have died out now). It's based on a Swedish film about a bullied kid who becomes friends with a (child) female vampire. Again, I've not seen the original but the Hammer version contains everything you could want. Kodi-Smit McPhee plays the bullied kid and Chloë Grace Moretz is the vampire, and both are excellent in their roles. One interesting thing about the film is the way it answers questions about the undead that we've all had but never really asked or had answered before – like, what happens if a vampire tries to eat something, or goes into a house unbidden? The film has plenty of gore and atmosphere but works best as a slow-paced character piece, with the vampire trying to defend her new human friend against bullies and engaging in a charming blood pact (which has the effect of showing her in her true colours). The ending, in which Abby literally tears the bullies to pieces in the school swimming pool, is amazing and this is another film crying out for a sequel.

Let Me In *(2010)*

The Devil Inside (2012) is a scarifying masterpiece and for a while, I was unsure if I was watching a genuine film or not! This is a found footage horror, which doesn't outstay it's welcome and I find it bizarre and incredible that this film has such a rotten reputation. The scenes of possession are as creepy as hell, with a contortionist being hired to twist her arms and legs in a most teeth-grinding way. The scene where a possessed priest attempts to drown the baby he's supposed to be baptising is one that I found hilarious, but maybe that's a sign of a sick sense of humour! The film ends abruptly, for the characters as well as the audience, and some end title cards inform the viewer that the case is still unresolved and for enquiring minds wanting further information, they should check out a website. Fernanda Andrade, Simon Quarterman and Evan Helmuth are the principal players and do great jobs but the real star has to be Bonnie Morgan as the possessed Rosa.

Peacock is a bizarre 2010 film, revolving around a guy who called was abused by his mother as a kid, resulting in him thinking he's a woman called Emma, who does his chores and cooks his breakfast before he heads off to work in a bank. When "Emma" is seen by the neighbours by accident, John (Cillian Murphy) has to fabricate a story that he's been secretly married and "Emma" is his wife. Things get even more complex when a young woman called Maggie (*Hard Candy*'s Ellen Page, now a fully-grown woman) turns up, wanting money for herself and her young son, and John defers to his "wife" here! This is more of a thriller than a horror but it's certainly weird and deserves a watch.

Elfie Hopkins: Cannibal Hunter (2012) is a slow-burning horror and for a while I was wondering if I'd made a mistake and it wasn't a horror film after all. It's a quirky British comedy-horror (though it's not actually funny) involving the title character who is played by Ray Winstone's daughter Jamie. Elfie is a bone-idle, work-shy slacker and misfit in a small country village that she's desperate to get away from. She invents stories to make her dull life more interesting, but things get interesting quite soon when some well-to-do cannibals move into a large house! It takes a while for the horror to kick in, but it's quite effective when it does.

Green Room (2015) is worth watching, though it's also more of a thriller than a horror. It contains buckets of gore and revolves around a punk band (three lads, one lass) who accept a gig in an out-of-the-way club, and soon suss out that the place is a meeting place for neo-Nazis. Unwisely taking the piss out of the club's patrons straight away, with a lively piece entitled "Nazi Punks Fuck off", the band are about to depart when they witness a murder that has just taken place in the titular Green Room.

From this point on, it's all action and cussing, with people being graphically shot in the face, having their throats torn out by vicious dogs, and plenty of effing and blinding! Two *Star Trek* stars are the main cast members here, with the late Anton Yelchin as one of the band members who gets his arm graphically sliced open but manages to stay alive till the end. Patrick Stewart plays the club's owner, and it's an odd thing indeed to see the famous Captain Picard-playing Shakespearean Yorkshireman as a foul-mouthed hard-case!

Unfriended (2014) is another excellent modern film, with Shelley Hennig, Moses Storm and a bunch of other actors you've never heard of, as a group of Skype-surfing teens who end up being haunted by a sinister presence that is the unquiet spirit of a girl who was bullied into killing herself. The whole film takes place on a Skype screen, with the realistic reactions of the terrified teens leading to a memorable climax that will make you jump! And probably put you off using Skype, if you don't already.

Unfriended *(2014)*

Finally, *Itsy Bitsy* (2019) is a film that will have you quaking if you have a phobia of spiders (and who doesn't?). Bruce Davison, Elizabeth Roberts and Denise Crosby (Tasha Yar from *Star Trek*) star in this creepy tale of a woman and her two kids, pestered by a large prehistoric spider in their house. The anamatronic nature of the monster means the scenes involving it are tolerable – I'm a borderline arachnophobe and can cope with this and CGI Spiders in other films and TV, but not watching footage of the real thing! And there's a nice little twist at the end.

Unlike this chapter.

"FrankenHomer" by Johnny Mains

Jim Pitts Prints

Each print is on high quality A4 paper, approved and signed by the artist before being sealed for protection inside a plastic envelope.

Colour prints are £7.00 each incl p&p

Black & white prints £5.00 each incl p&p

Any orders for 5 or more prints qualify for a 20% discount.

To order please email paralleluniversepublications@gmx.co.uk, listing which prints you would like. You will then be emailed a Paypal invoice.

Jim Pitts is an award-winning artist (two-times winner of the prestigious British Fantasy Award, plus Science Fiction's Ken McIntyre Award), whose work has appeared in numerous magazines and books, both professional and small press.

Check our website: paralleluniversepublications.blogspot.com/

Coming soon from Bogus Pictures...

Artwork by Dave Carson

~~~~

BIOGRAPHIES

Adrian Baldwin is a Mancunian now living and working in Wales. Back in the Nineties, he wrote for various TV shows/personalities: Smith & Jones, Clive Anderson, Brian Conley, Paul McKenna, Hale & Pace, Rory Bremner (and a few others). Wooo, get him.

Since then, he has written three screenplays, one of which received generous financial backing from the Film Agency for Wales. Then along came the global recession to kick the UK Film industry in the nuts. What a bummer!

Not to be outdone, he turned to novel writing - which had always been his real dream - and, in particular, a genre he feels is often overlooked; a genre he has always been a fan of: Dark Comedy (sometimes referred to as Horror's weird cousin).

Barnacle Brat (a dark comedy for grown-ups), his first novel won Indie Novel of the Year 2016 award (see above) - his second novel *Stanley McCloud Must Die!* (more dark comedy for grown-ups) published in 2016, and his third novel: *The Snowman and the Scarecrow* (another dark comedy for grown-ups) published in 2018.

Adrian Baldwin has also written and published a number of dark comedy short stories. For more information on the award-winning author, check out: adrianbaldwin.info (*You can read the beginnings of all his works there.)

Adrian cites his major influences as Kurt Vonnegut, Monty Python, Stephen King, David Bowie, Christopher Moore, David Mitchell, Robert Rankin, Galton & Simpson, Colin Bateman, Bruce Robinson and Irvine Welsh.

David Brilliance was born in the Summer of Love, June 1967, and grew up in the town of Willington, County Durham. Leaving school with no set goal for a career or job, he has done a variety of different jobs over the years and in fact has lived his working life in reverse, with his retirement period coming first followed by many years of gainful employment! Permanently single, and very happy with it ("The women I wanted didn't want me and the women who wanted me, I didn't want and what is the point of going with someone you have no feelings for just to prove to the world you are straight?"), David currently resides in Weardale, where he is content to be the resident star of the nursing home he works in, and is actively involved in his personal bodily improvement programme which began in 1997 and will be completed soon!

Randy Broecker has been drawing the things he loves – "Ghoulies and ghosties and long-leggitie beasties and things that go bump in the night" – for well over forty years now.

His art has appeared in books and magazines worldwide, most recently in the Aidan Chambers' collection *Dead Trouble & Other Ghost Stories* and the anthology *Terrifying Tales to Tell at Night: 10 Scary Stories to Give You Nightmares!* edited by Stephen Jones.

He also wrote and compiled the World Fantasy Award -nominated art book, *Fantasy of the 20th Century: An Illustrated History*, which was included as part of the three-in-one omnibus, *Art of Imagination: 20th Century Visions of Science Fiction, Horror, and Fantasy*.

He lives in an old house in Chicago, along with a monster or three...

Dave Carson has been a horror literature and film fan since he can remember. The low dives of Belfast fleapit cinemas in the '60s where a great education for him, and when he was about eight or nine he began going to see double bills of horror movies several times a week.

Later in life he took up art, ending up a "Lovecraftian" illustrator, and that early exposure to all those "creature features" of his childhood certainly left a lasting impression – he is very grateful that he was around at that time to enjoy it all. He's a huge fan of Italian horror films of the '70s and '80s, a lot of the time for the unintentional laughs, he must admit, but they hold a special place in his heart.

Trevor Kennedy is a 44-year-old writer, editor and radio presenter based in Belfast, Northern Ireland. Previous employment includes as a lithographic colour proofer, composite operator for Bombardier Shorts aircraft manufacturers, the BBC Complaints department, call centre operative and brief stints as a security guard and industrial cleaner. He currently edits *Phantasmagoria Magazine*, its *Special Edition Series* spin-off and the *Gruesome Grotesques* anthology series. He can be contacted at tkboss@hotmail.com.

Some of Trevor's favourite horror films are *The Exorcist* (1973), *Alien* (1979), *Twin Peaks: Fire Walk With Me* (1992), *The Witch* (2015) and *Titanic* (1997) – truly terrifying!

Allen Koszowski is married with two grown children. His art has been appearing in various fan, small press and professional markets since 1973.

Publications and publishers that have used his work include *Isaac Asimov's Science Fiction Magazine*, *The Magazine of Fantasy*

& *Science Fiction, Analog, Midnight Marquee,* Arkham House, Midnight House, *Whispers, Weirdbook,* Centipede Press, *Eldritch Tales, Crypt of Cthulhu, Fantasy Tales,* Fedogan & Bremer, Cemetery Dance, Subterranean Press and many others.

He has won The World Fantasy Award, The SPWAO Best Artist Award, a Fanex award, and more. He has been the artist guest of honor at the World Horror Convention, the World Fantasy Convention, Albicon, EerieCon and other conventions. He has also edited and published *Inhuman Magazine.*

He is still going strong and hopes to continue for many years to come.

Johnny Mains lives in the South West of England with his wife, child and dog. His next book as editor and publisher is *In Death's Mouth* – an anthology about disease and illness.

Jim Pitts is one of the leading fantasy artists in the UK and beyond and has been for the last few decades. His artwork has appeared in many publications on both sides of the Atlantic and more. Jim is also a folk musician, playing with The Jim Pitts Folk Quartet on electric blues harmonica and electric bass. He lives in Blackburn in the North of England and is still working in the field.

TREVOR KENNEDY's
CROWN OF THORNS
OUT NOW
'May make you think twice about rushing to the ice cream van next time it trundles down your street!' - Morgan K. Tanner, via Amazon
Paperback & Kindle
'Written beautifully and with a real nostalgic feel for the 80s.' - Scotty Dotty, via Amazon
amazon
DEMAIN PUBLISHING
CROWN OF THORNS
CROWN OF THORNS
CROWN OF THORNS

ACKNOWLEDGEMENTS

THE PUBLISHER HAS made every effort to source and credit the copyright details of all the photographic material and artworks used in this book, adhering to the "fair use" policy of using film images for critiquing purposes. The publisher would be pleased to correct any errors or omissions, if contacted: tkboss@hotmail.com

Cover image: Production designer Albin Grau's cover illustration for the German production book for Prana-Films' *Nosferatu, eine Symphonie des Grauens* (Dir: F. W. Murnau, 1922), an unauthorized adaptation of Bram Stoker's *Dracula*.

Cover design and *Phantasmagoria* logo copyright © Adrian Baldwin 2021, www.adrianbaldwin.info

"Foreword" copyright © Trevor Kennedy 2021.

"David Brilliance's Midnight Treasury" copyright © David Brilliance 2021.

Artwork

Pages 99: "Night of the Demon", 153: "The Skull", 159: "The Reptile", 209: "Blood on Satan's Claw", 233: "Tales from the Crypt" and 321: "The Woman in Black" copyright © Randy Broecker 2021.

Front page border artwork, *Phantasmagoria* advertisement artwork, and pages 373 and 388: copyright © Dave Carson 2021.

Dedication page, "Frankenstein's Monster/Dracula", "Stephen Jones", pages 19, 23, 45, 53, 75, 105, 113, 117, 187, 215, 223, 225, 261, 266, 268 and 381: copyright © Allen Koszowski 2021.

Pages 2: "Nosferatu" and 386: "FrankenHomer" copyright © Johnny Mains 2021.

Pages 6, 26, 27, 39 and 379: copyright © Jim Pitts 2021.

Film posters, publicity material and movie stills copyright © of the following studios: Universal Pictures, Paramount Pictures, Metro-Goldwyn-Mayer (MGM), RKO Radio Pictures, Ealing Studios,

Universal International Pictures (UI), Danziger Productions Ltd, Rolling M. Productions, Hammer Films, Sabre Film Production, Associated Producers (API), Alta Vista Productions, American International Pictures (AIP), Alfred J. Hitchcock Productions, Indústria Cinematográfica Apolo, Ibérica Films, Amicus Productions, Seven Arts Productions, Toho Company, Associated British-Pathé, Image Ten, Tigon British Film Productions, The Rank Organisation, Brigitte, Fitzroy Films Ltd., Ronald J. Kahn Productions, Chilton Films, Abacus Productions, London-Cannon Films, Pittsburgh Films, Harbour Productions Limited, Cineman Productions, Lorimar Productions, British Lion Film Corporation, Warner Bros., Hoya Productions, Vortex, European Incorporation, Rewind Film, Saber Productions, Twentieth Century Fox, Seda Spettacoli, American Film Institute (AFI), Libra Films, Barquel Creations, Cinema 77, Professional Films, Chips Productions, Sword & Sorcery, CBS Films, Cross Creek Pictures, Hammer Films, Talisman Productions, Filmgate Films, Film I Väst, Alliance Films, British Film Institute (BFI), Vertigo Entertainment, Strong Heart, Demme Production, Orion Pictures, Haxan Films, Rollercoaster Films, Aramid Entertainment Fund, Ghost House Pictures, Buckaroo Entertainment, Curse Productions, Mandate Pictures, Wonderworks Films, Snoot Entertainment, HanWay Films, 8383 Productions, Bloody Disgusting, Studio71, The Collective Studios, New Line Cinema, The Safran Company, Evergreen Media Group, Intrepid Pictures, MICA Entertainment, WWE Studios, Blumhouse Productions, Lasser Productions, Northern Lights Films, Animal Kingdom, Two Flints, Parts and Labor, RT Features, Rooks Nest Entertainment, Code Red Productions, Scythia Films, A24, Maiden Voyage Pictures, Mott Street Pictures, Pulse Films, Very Special Projects, Studio: Sailor Bear, Zero Trans Fat Productions, Ideaman Studios, Columbia Pictures, Hawk Films, Peregrine, Producers Circle, Overture Films, Exclusive Media Group, EFTI and Bazelevs Production.

Film images sourced from Google Images.

Additional research source: Internet Movie Database (IMDb), https://www.imdb.com.

RETRO-STYLE BOOK COVER DESIGNS

Not a big fan of many 'modern' covers - "a lot look the same these days" - author/designer Adrian Baldwin draws his inspiration from pulp novels of the 50s, 60s, 70s & 80s.

If you're a writer or publisher and fancy a cover that *doesn't* look like everybody else's, drop him a line at Adrian@AdrianBaldwin.info

visit www.AdrianBaldwin.info for more details

Printed in Great Britain
by Amazon